Want to learn something well? Make media to advance knowledge and gain new ideas.

You don't have to be a communication professional to create to learn. Today, with free and low-cost digital tools, everyone can compose videos, blogs and websites, remixes, podcasts, screencasts, infographics, animation, remixes and more. By creating to learn, people internalize ideas and express information creatively in ways that may inspire others.

Create to Learn is a ground-breaking book that helps learners create multimedia texts as they develop both critical thinking and communication skills. Written by Renee Hobbs, one of the foremost experts in media literacy, this book introduces a wide range of conceptual principles at the heart of multimedia composition and digital pedagogy. Its approach is useful for anyone who sees the profound educational value of creating multimedia projects in an increasingly digital and connected world.

Students will become skilled multimedia communicators by learning how to gather information, generate ideas, and develop media projects using contemporary digital tools and platforms. Illustrative examples from a variety of student-produced multimedia projects along with helpful online materials offer support and boost confidence.

Create to Learn will help anyone make informed and strategic communication decisions as they create media for any academic, personal or professional project.

Learn more about this book at: www.createtolearn.online

Renee Hobbs is a Professor of Communication and Director of the Media Education Lab at the Harrington School of Communication and Media at the University of Rhode Island.

Create to Learn

Introduction to Digital Literacy

Renee Hobbs

University of Rhode Island
Media Education Lab

WILEY Blackwell

This edition first published 2017
© 2017 John Wiley & Sons, Inc.

The right of Renee Hobbs to be identified as the author of this work has been asserted in accordance with law.

Registered Office
John Wiley & Sons, Inc., 111 River Street, Hoboken, NJ 07030, USA

Editorial Office
350 Main Street, Malden, MA 02148-5020, USA

For details of our global editorial offices, customer services, and more information about Wiley products visit us at www.wiley.com.

Wiley also publishes its books in a variety of electronic formats and by print-on-demand. Some content that appears in standard print versions of this book may not be available in other formats.

Library of Congress Cataloging-in-Publication data applied for

9781118968345 (hardback)
9781118968352 (paperback)

Cover image: (Background) © Vectorig/Gettyimages; (Left Image) © Maridav/Shutterstock; (Right Image) © Massimo Merlini/Gettyimages
Cover design by Wiley

Set in 10/12pt Warnock by SPi Global, Pondicherry, India
Printed and bound in Malaysia by Vivar Printing Sdn Bhd

10   9   8   7   6   5   4   3   2   1

Contents

What to Expect in this Book

Today, every student needs to be able to create to learn.

Digital Literacy for Academic Success. If you want to learn something well, don't just listen, take notes, and sit for a test. Instead, create or make something where you must apply and use what you learn. Learning is an active process, and most people learn best through hands-on, minds-on experiences. When you have to express your knowledge using language, images, sound, and multimedia, you invest the effort needed to internalize what you are learning. Plus, the finished product may have value to others who may learn from it, too.

Critical Thinking about Media. All forms of information require careful interrogation of the author's claims, evidence, and assumptions. In this book, you will activate analysis skills by encouraging critical questions about the purpose, form, and content of all forms of communication and expression. Analyzing media involves understanding the text, context, and culture in which messages are produced and consumed.

Creativity and Collaboration. Express your developing understanding of any subject, idea, or topic by using podcasting, digital images, infographics and data visualization, remix, vlogs and screencasts, video production, animation, web sites and blogs, and social media to express and share ideas. In this book, you'll learn about the strategic process of creating with all nine of these media forms.

Life Skills for Career Success. Today, nearly every field and profession depends upon a workforce that has effective multimedia communication skills. Digital and media literacy competencies are essential for success in the workforce. After creating digital media projects to demonstrate the knowledge and skills you have acquired in college, you will be at a competitive advantage to others who have not learned to create media.

Interdisciplinary Connections. Digital literacy competencies are important for learners in all fields of study. This book introduces you to media literacy and digital literacy and provides compelling insights from the fields of communication and media, information science, education, and the arts and humanities.

Part I

Developing a Communication Strategy

Overview of Part I

When creating to learn, you gain knowledge and demonstrate competencies by working with a variety of symbolic systems and a variety of genres to inform, persuade, and entertain target audiences. In Part I, you develop the pre-production process by developing a *communication strategy* needed to be an effective communicator as you create media as a way to learn. Here's what you can expect:

Chapter 1   Create to Learn
            Consider your identity as a digital author

Chapter 2   Getting Creative
            Develop a creative brief

Chapter 3   Decisions, Decisions
            Build a communication strategy

Chapter 4   Accessing and Analyzing Ideas
            Critically analyze a mentor text

Chapter 5   Creating Ideas
            Create a scope of work plan and produce work

Chapter 6   Reflecting and Taking Action
            Use the power of information and expression to make a difference

Create to Learn: Introduction to Digital Literacy, First Edition. Renee Hobbs.
© 2017 John Wiley & Sons, Inc. Published 2017 by John Wiley & Sons, Inc.

1

Create to Learn

KEY IDEAS

People learn best when they create. Creating media is a powerful way to demonstrate your learning. But it's also a way to generate ideas and transform static information into dynamic understanding. Today, the availability of free and low-cost digital production tools are contributing to a participatory culture where people are not just consuming media but also sharing, remixing, and creating. Although a college course can still rely on the exclusive expertise of one faculty member and one textbook, it's better when a course becomes a type of learning community where everybody learns from everybody. A learning community more closely models the kind of learning that happens in the workplace and contemporary society. To participate in a learning community, you can't just be a passive receiver of information. By creating and sharing media as a way to represent what you are learning, you can activate your intellectual curiosity in ways that naturally make learning more engaging and relevant.

You've grown up using the Internet. You may be comfortable with a variety of social media platforms that you access through your mobile phone, tablet, or laptop. You probably have a favorite way of using YouTube to support your interests in music and entertainment and you may participate in interest groups using Snapchat, Instagram, Reddit, Tumblr, or other platforms. Perhaps you're a gamer and engage in online social play with people from around the world.

But how skilled are you at using digital tools, texts, and technologies in the workplace or to advance your career? Most Americans admit that they're not as skilled as they need to be. More than 200 million US workers use digital skills on the job, but researchers have found that fewer than 1 in 10 feel proficient in the use of the digital tools and technologies they're required to use.[1] That's because, on average, the digital tools that we use change every two to three years. As digital products and platforms are rapidly proliferating, many people are challenged by the need to be lifelong learners when it comes to digital media and technology.

Create to Learn: Introduction to Digital Literacy, First Edition. Renee Hobbs.
© 2017 John Wiley & Sons, Inc. Published 2017 by John Wiley & Sons, Inc.

Today there is a *digital skills gap* as more and more people graduate from college without having had sufficient opportunity to develop competencies and habits of mind that are at the core of every job in a knowledge economy. According to management consultants, these core competencies include:

- **Attention management.** The ability to identify, prioritize, and manage in an increasingly dense information landscape involves strategic decision making about how and when to focus one's attention.
- **Communication.** The ability to use effective strategies for interacting and sharing information and ideas with others requires continual awareness of how, when, why, and what to communicate. This includes creating digital and multimedia documents, using language, image, sound, and interactive media effectively to express and share ideas.
- **Digital etiquette.** Awareness of privacy, legal, and security issues is essential to be effective in the workplace. The ability to use appropriate codes and conventions for communicating via e-mail, video conference, text message, and telephone also requires sensitivity to the ethical dimensions of social relationships in a networked age.
- **Search and research.** The ability to gather information and sift through it to identify what's relevant, trustworthy, and reliable demands a strong understanding of how information and authority is constructed in particular contexts. Tenacity and intellectual curiosity are a must in the search and research process.
- **Collaboration and leadership.** When people work together, they do many different things all working at the same time towards a shared and common goal. Skills of coordinating projects and organizing group activity are vital competencies for both workplace and citizenship in a democratic society.[2]

Knowledge Matters

Today, knowledge is not fixed and static. Knowledge is widely networked and distributed. As David Weinberger notes in his book, *Too Big to Know*, the smartest person in the room is the room. That is, in an era where anyone can access information, entertainment, and propaganda all at the touch of a fingertip, knowledge is less and less tied to expertise, authority, credentials, or public reputation. Indeed, anyone can start a cooking blog, not only someone trained at Le Cordon Bleu. Weinberger reminds us that before the Enlightenment, knowledge was understood as coming from God. Later, we placed our trust in the scientific method.[3] Today, we've grown up experts who disagree with each other about every topic imaginable. The explosion of new knowledge made possible by the Internet, with the disappearance of gatekeepers and filters, has contributed to the rise of niche communities or *echo chambers*, where a small group of people find comfort in their shared beliefs and attitudes. Indeed, it seems that the growing ease of access to information and entertainment is leading to both increased levels of apathy and political polarization.

Literacy Matters

When you hear the word literacy, you may think of the practice of reading and writing. But for a growing number of scholars and researchers, the concept of literacy is expanding as a result of changes in media, technology and the nature of knowledge. Today we define *literacy* as the sharing of meaning through symbols.[4] Everyone – from all walks of life – needs to be able to create and share meaning through language, images, sounds, and other media forms.

The concept of literacy has been expanding for over 2,000 years. In Ancient Greece, a literate man was skilled in the art of rhetoric, possessing the ability to use public speaking to move the hearts and minds of other men in the Forum. All over the world, in medieval times, to be literate meant to be able to read from the holy books, and only a very few scholars and scribes were specially trained to be writers. Then the printing press changed the definition of writing as more and more people were able to read – and then write – as publishers found there to be a marketplace for romantic and adventure novels, personal essays, and scientific books. During the twentieth century, literacy expanded again with the rise of popular photography and people began using photographs for self-expression and communication. The terms visual literacy, information literacy, and media literacy developed as educators, scholars, artists, and librarians all recognized the need for new skills that mapped onto the changes in society that are reshaping the business, communication, and information landscape.

It's obvious how much images, sound, and interactivity combine with language as essential dimensions of the way people share and communicate ideas. It's simply not fair to put written language at the top of the pyramid and consider multimedia forms to be lesser than or inferior. As the National Council of Teachers of English stated in 2005, "All modes of communication are codependent. Each affects the nature of the content of the other and the overall rhetorical impact of the communication event itself."[5] As a result, today the practice of acquiring, organizing, evaluating, and creatively using multimodal information is a fundamental competence for people in all fields of study and professions. Television programming, movies, and online videos are major sources of information and entertainment for people of all ages. Today, we see the integration of multiple modes of communication and expression in every part of life. Our social relationships with family and friends, leisure time, the workplace, and civic and cultural spaces all depend on the use of messages that skillfully combine image, language, sound, and interactivity.

What is Digital Literacy?

Digital literacy is the constellation of knowledge, skills, and competencies necessary for thriving in a technology-saturated culture. As information, entertainment, and persuasion are now shared digitally and personal, social and professional relationships are developed through interaction with social media as well as mass media and popular culture, people of all ages need the ability to *access, analyze, create, reflect,* and *take action* using a wide variety of digital tools, forms of expression and communication strategies.

Learning Matters

Learning is generally defined as the acquisition of skills and knowledge through experience, study, or teaching. When you think of learning, you may conjure up the routine practices of sitting in class, taking tests, and doing homework. If you were lucky, there was a teacher or two who recognized and appreciated your unique interests and talents. Perhaps you got to make a speech in class or compose essays on topics of your choice. If you were even more lucky, you got to create things – in art class, as a member of a robotics team, in the drama club, or even as a regular part of your coursework.

Learning happens through formal and informal means. During childhood and throughout life, *play* is a form of learning. Children learn by exploring their world, by using their imaginations, and by creating and building – using words, clay, paper and crayons, old blankets, and much more. During adolescence, we continue to play, learning by experimenting and taking risks as we discover ourselves (and the world around us) by doing things we have never done before. As we move into adulthood, we continue to learn on the job, by gaining experience through informal forms of *apprenticeship*. Throughout life, at every age, informal mentors and coaches help us learn as part of work and social life.

Today, people learn how to use digital technologies as an essential part of life. Digital media technologies are so much a part of our lives – for connecting to friends and family, for entertainment, and for learning. Just as the air, water, earth, nature, and architecture of the city are part of our physical environments, television, the Internet, music, celebrities, video games, and social media are part of our *cultural environment*. This term, developed by George Gerbner, refers to the set of beliefs, practices, customs, traditions, and behaviors that are common to everyone living in a certain population.[6] Today, forms of digital and mass media are so much a part of our lives that many people would find it difficult to go a day without YouTube. As Mimi Ito and her colleagues write, "The media and communication system underpins the spheres of work, education and commerce in ways that we increasingly take for granted."[7] If we think about digital media as a whole system, not as individual pieces of technology, then we see how vital they are to the lifelong learning process.

In higher education, there is a 1,000-year-old tradition of learning by lecture and memorization. Thus, educators have long relied on an approach to learning that depends on transmitting content knowledge verbally. Lectures and textbooks are primary tools in the college classroom. To be successful in many fields of study, students must gain knowledge through listening and reading.

But more and more, creating to learn is becoming an important part of higher education. At the University of Rhode Island first-year writing composition students worked in groups to brainstorm and create a public service announcement about the H1N1 virus.[8] At the University of Massachusetts-Boston, in the Gateway Seminar Video Project, environmental science students worked in pairs to develop 16 videos that highlighted aspects of their learning, demonstrating how the issues impact their home city of Boston. Students developed videos with topics ranging from bleaching of coral reefs to shipwrecks to climate change and erosion.[9]

At Dartmouth College, teams of students taking a geography class created short video *mash-ups*, remixing bits of video and audio material from a range of sources, to introduce and explain a key concept related to a case study of ecology and development in Africa. In a course on political communication, students created ads to demonstrate their understanding of political communication strategy. Although few students in the class had previously worked with video equipment or editing prior to this class, they were able to produce effective work that helped them build real-world communication competencies while learning to apply key theoretical concepts.[10]

Every discipline or field of study involves creative work of one kind or another. When we think about the word "create," we may think about concocting mixtures in chemistry lab or working in an art studio. In this book, you will be *creating to learn* by demonstrating knowledge and skills through creating a variety of forms of media – including web sites, infographics and data visualizations, vlogs animations, podcasts, memes, and more. But the idea of creating to learn goes deeper.

When we create media, we internalize knowledge deeply – we own it. *Internalization* is the process of consolidating and accepting ideas, behaviors, and attitudes into our own particular worldview. After all, if we can represent knowledge, information, and ideas in a format that makes sense to others, that's a form of mastery. Actually, the time-honored practice of writing academic research papers is rooted in this idea. When students write a report or term paper or research paper, it's based on the premise that you move through a complex process of identifying a question, gathering information and ideas, and evaluating them from the light of your own experience and values. You find a way to summarize and analyze information, organizing it into a linear sequence within the confines of specific rules and conventions for how to express your ideas. As you communicate ideas to a reader, your writing can be used to assess your understanding of the subject matter. Truly, this is a great way to learn.

Creating Media as a Way to Learn

Writing is an important way to represent knowledge – but it is not the only way. In fact, for most of human history, we used *oral language* to share ideas and information through the spoken word. You have grown up in a world surrounded with images, sound, music, and memes from mass media, popular culture, and digital media, which offer an endless array of new forms of expression and communication. While formal academic language is the dominant form of expression and communication among scholars, in the workplace, you need to be an effective communicator using *all* the tools at your disposal.

Too many people graduate from college without having had experience composing memos, building a web site, writing a blog post, or creating a compelling photo. They stumble when asked to create an infographic, deliver a speech, create a podcast, share a compelling story, or create a YouTube video. They have not had sufficient experience in creating to learn.

Fortunately, multimedia production is not just for specialists who work in the fields of journalism, television, the Internet, and social media. We live in a *participatory culture* where all of us are increasingly expected to share and contribute our knowledge with others.[11] And the results of this sharing have been tremendous! Type the phrase "how to" into the YouTube search engine and you'll see many examples of people from all walks of life who are sharing what they know with the world, whether that be how to cook Indian cuisine, analyze a poem, create an architectural masterpiece in Minecraft, or solve a complex quadratic equation. In a world of global interconnection and rapid change, you can expect to be a learner for the rest of your life. In participatory culture, we share what we learn through creative expression as part of leisure, work, and citizenship.

Many students like yourself are creating media as a direct and central part of your learning. Perhaps you will create a video about the causes of the French Revolution or post multimedia content about urban gardening to a class blog. Perhaps you will develop a short documentary about a contemporary author, or write original song lyrics to express the unique mathematical characteristics of pi (sung to the melody "Bye, Bye Miss American Pie"). You may interview a local politician and create a podcast about his vision for improving the community. Having a variety of different experiences in expressing ideas in different formats will strengthen your overall skills as a communicator and lifelong learner.

Perhaps you think of yourself as an author or creative person already. Review the Authorship Checklist below to reflect on your own identity as an author. You may be eager to express what you have learned in class by using video or digital media. You may have already collaborated with peers and shared your work online via Facebook, YouTube, or Blogger.

As you demonstrate your learning by creating media, others may learn from you. This is a key point because for millennia, learning and teaching were understood in relationship to strict hierarchies of control, power, and knowledge. Only certain elders were permitted to mentor youth. Later, advanced training and formal education was a requirement to become a teacher or professor. But today, the hierarchies have flattened as *networked learning* makes it possible to create a situation in which everybody learns from everybody. In this book, you'll learn how to create to learn using images, language, sound, music, multimedia, and interactivity with the goal of deepening your learning experience and contributing to the learning of others by composing messages using many different forms of media to represent your developing knowledge and skills. Creating to learn has many benefits: in addition to the learning experience itself, your completed work may have value to others.

Learning in College and Beyond

In college, the learning communities you participate in are often defined by the courses you enroll in. Classes are simply organized groups of learners, guided by someone who helps structure activities that promote learning.

But learning communities can't be defined merely by what happens in school. They happen outside of formal education all the time. Perhaps you have at times wondered how to use a wok to make Chinese food, fix some plumbing, change a tire on a car, or install a shelf on a wall. When you Google these terms, you find lots of people who have shared their insights on these topics. If you are highly resourceful, the Internet is a treasure trove – for both play and learning.

Perhaps you have created media with your friends just for fun, especially when you were growing up. Students often tend to underestimate the skills and knowledge they have learned through their playful use of video, graphic design, and multimedia. But researchers have demonstrated that many of the digital skills learned informally through play or exploration of personal interests – especially in a social context – represent a significant contribution to one's personal, social, and intellectual development.[12]

When you learn something just for school, to pass a test, or because it's expected of us, that knowledge is often flat and one-dimensional. What makes learning fun is the feeling of being connected to other learners, being part of a community or group. When you are part of learning community, you are motivated to ask questions, find out information and ideas, debate issues of concern, and contribute your own ideas and opinions. Learning becomes both fun and relevant when we see ourselves, not as individual learners, but as part of a group or team. In the context of the workplace, lifelong learning occurs as we stay connected to social networks, develop relationships with colleagues, make institutional linkages, engage in shared activities, and participate in communication infrastructures.

Because lifelong learning involves sharing information and ideas, *multimedia composition* occurs everywhere. Accounting professionals create videos to demonstrate and share new practices. Young nurses document the delights, trials, and tribulations of the first year on the job and older and more experienced nurses offer advice on building a career using Google Hangouts On Air. The process of creating media embodies the learning process. There's simply no end to the creativity of students who are creating to learn:

- At Temple University, student journalists created video news segments about a living statue standing in a makeshift fountain in the middle of Broad Street, documenting an event from the Philadelphia International Festival of the Arts.
- At the University of Southern California, students in Professor Anne McKnight's course, Fantasy and Travel Across the Pacific, explored the literature on travel and fantasy by creating alternative book covers for classic works.
- In Professor Carolyn Cartier's course, China and the World, students worked with a partner to create digital essays that investigated China's relationships both within and beyond its traditional boundaries.
- At West Kentucky Community and Technical College, students in Professor Beverly Quimby's Visual Communication class created a historical documentary about the history of uranium enrichment at the Paducah Gaseous Diffusion Plant.
- At the University of Rhode Island, students in Professor Tom Mather's Infectious Diseases course created video public service announcements about diseases that are transmitted from animals to humans, including cat scratch fever and Lyme disease.

These projects enabled college students to demonstrate their learning of rich content while the developed communication, critical thinking, creativity, and collaboration skills.

You may think to yourself, "But I am not a creative media person." Not every student comes to college with the knowledge and skills of a young Tina Brown, George Lucas, Shepard Fairey, or Ken Burns. Expert media makers have spent upwards of 10,000 hours of creative work to acquire real knowledge and skills that enable them to produce works of art using media.

In fact, while you have probably created a PowerPoint slide deck, you may not have created a YouTube video, a podcast, or an animation. Certainly you have shared content with your friends using social media like Tumblr, Facebook, Twitter, or Instagram. Most young adults have uploaded photos to a social media web site or uploaded video from their cell phone to YouTube. Have you created an infographic, a documentary video, or a podcast? Have you built a simple web site? Perhaps you have not yet done these things.

Researchers who look at the use of digital media for learning distinguish between *friendship-driven* digital activities where students use online social media to maintain social relationships and *interest-driven* activities where they "find information, connect to people who share specialized and niche interests, including online gaming, creative writing, video editing or other artistic endeavors."[13] Part of the problem today is that even though many educators may believe their students to be so-called "digital natives," most students have not yet acquired the full range of knowledge and skills they need to be effective multimedia communicators.

Even though the digital tools are literally at our fingertips, most people are not routinely creating media as part of daily life. For example, while most young adults have grown up sending text messages, only about 30 percent have created a blog. And while the use of social media is ubiquitous, fewer than 5 percent create media as part of their leisure activities. We really don't know how many young people have created and uploaded videos today. Back in 2006, the Pew Research Center's Internet and American Life Project conducted a study of young content creators – students who have created or worked on a web page or a blog, shared original content or remixed content they found online. What they learned is that young content creators generally developed their multimedia composition skills *only when they had support and guidance from a learning community* – either formally (in school) or informally (through play and social interaction with peers).[14]

This book and the web site that accompanies it will support your work as you engage in the process of creating to learn. You will benefit from the structure, advice, and strategic guidance that can help you to express yourself using digital media to create slideshows, videos, web sites, podcasts, screencasts, video games, and more. This book offers a guide to the entire process of multimedia composition, with an emphasis on developing the critical thinking and communication skills that are foundational to creating informative, persuasive, and entertaining messages in a wide variety of genres and forms. If you are reading this book, you are part of a community of people who see digital and media literacy as a critical competence for college graduates in every discipline and field of study. Everyone needs to be able to access, analyze, evaluate, compose, reflect, and use multimedia tools and technologies to take action in the social world.

The Ethics of Digital Authorship

Today people live with a continual flood of information, news and entertainment literally at our fingertips. You may encounter only a little of the staggering diversity of content that's available each day from the people in your social media networks who share it with you. But you also contribute to the pool of content that circulates online every time you share a photo, text a friend, post a comment or "like" something. Indeed, it's highly possible that you have accidentally shared misinformation or poor-quality content to people in your network. Researchers have found that 59% percent of Facebook users share news without actually reading it. According to Arnaud Legout, "This is typical of modern information consumption. People form an opinion based on a summary, or a summary of summaries, without making the effort to go deeper."[15] These communication practices are warping our shared political and cultural agenda and they contribute to ignorance and misinformation that works against the practice of democratic citizenship.

When someone is an irresponsible communicator, they can wreak havoc. When the term "fake news" started circulating in late 2016, it got people's attention and was used to describe political hoaxes, like the one claiming Pope Francis endorsed Donald Trump in the U.S. Presidential election. On Election Day, there was a flood of these hoaxes. For example, a website called the Denver Guardian claimed that an FBI agent connected to Hillary Clinton's hacked email had murdered himself and shot his wife. Another website stated that she promised amnesty to undocumented immigrants. On the campus of Bates College, fliers were posted to discourage college students from voting. The fliers falsely stated that if students wanted to vote in the college town, they would have to pay to change their driver's licenses and re-register any vehicle in the city.

The mayor of Mansfield, Georgia even posted a message on his Facebook page: "Remember the voting days: Republicans vote on Tuesday, 11/8 and Democrats vote on Wednesday, 11/9."[16] Although such fake news hoaxes can seem funny, they can have devastating consequences.

Almost immediately after President Donald Trump took office, and after questions began arising about Russia's disinformation campaign to influence the U.S. election, he began to use the term "fake news" in a way that shifted its meaning. Trump asserted that "any negative polls are fake news," blasting those who pointed out his inaccurate statements and calling the media "an enemy of the people." Some wondered if this were just a ploy to capture attention or a strategic campaign by an authoritarian leader to cultivate a sense of apathy and alienation towards the press and its efforts to report the truth.[17]

Intentional deception is abhorrent to a responsible communicator. As a digital author, you'll act in goodwill towards your audiences because you expect that others will behave accordingly. Societies advance on the basis of trust. In any case, the term "fake news" should not be used to describe reporting errors. Of course, you'll make mistakes as part of the learning process. Such errors happen every day: reporters are only human and plus, they work under intense deadline pressure. For example, consider the *Time Magazine* reporter who, after the election, reported that a statue of Martin Luther King, Jr. had been removed from the Oval Office – when really it was just obscured behind a door.[18] Mistakes happen, but when they do, a responsible digital author makes corrections and informs audiences about the error.

The book is based on a simple premise: with the right kind of strategic guidance, learners can gain the power of digital authorship, working individually or collaboratively, and in the process, begin to engage deeply with disciplinary knowledge while developing communication competencies through creating real-world media messages for authentic audiences.

Digital Authorship: A Checklist

Which of these activities have you done? Check all that apply to you.

_____I regularly search online for information on a topic of personal interest.
_____I use my cell phone to search for information.
_____I maintain a diary or journal to express my ideas.
_____I select and share images, music, or other content nearly every day.
_____I do creative writing – poetry, music lyrics, fiction, or short stories.
_____I have interviewed a person to gather information from them.
_____I have given a speech using PowerPoint slides I created.
_____I have performed a spoken word poetry or storytelling presentation.
_____I have performed in a play or helped behind the scenes with a dramatic production.
_____I have participated in a video chat.
_____I have live streamed video for people on the Internet to watch.
_____I have performed in a music video, dance video, lipsync or lip dub video.
_____I have taken photos that I intentionally design to be beautiful.
_____I have composed a song or written song lyrics.
_____I have produced a video.
_____I have produced a video and uploaded it to YouTube, Vimeo, or other site.

Add up the numbers and see where you stand in relation to your peers:

1–5	Emerging Digital Author
6–10	Developing Digital Author
11–16	Experienced Digital Author

Activity: Reflect on Your Identity as a Digital Author

After you complete the Digital Authorship Checklist, reflect on your own identity as a digital author. In informal writing, describe some of your experiences in creating media, recalling experiences from your childhood and adolescence. Consider these questions in composing:

1) When were you a leader in creating a project? When were you a contributor or a collaborator in the creative productions of others?
2) Describe the product you created and the process you used to create it. What do you remember liking and disliking about the experience?
3) If you could create any kind of media product at all (with no limitations), what would you want to create? Why would you want to create it?
4) What scares you most about the idea of becoming a digital author?
5) Name three aspects of your personality and character that will be helpful as you engage in the process of creating to learn.
6) What's the best thing that could result for you personally in becoming a digital author?

2

Getting Creative

KEY IDEAS

When you create to learn, you make important strategic decisions that are essential for an effective and high-impact project. Digital and media literacy is a process that involves accessing, analyzing, creating, reflecting, and taking action. The creative process starts with discovery. It's a process that can be best supported by providing creative constraints. Educators and employers may structure goals and expectations for your creative work. To develop a plan of action, there's real power in composing a creative brief, a document that helps you prepare what you expect you will be learning when working on a creative multimedia project. Visualize how to begin the creative journey by assembling ideas, information, and evidence that you will eventually synthesize into one of nine different media formats.

When Ginae, Krista, and Ebony decided to create a video about their first semester of college, at Mizzou, the University of Missouri, they wanted to talk about the transition from high school to college. The three girls shot the video in December, right before they went away for winter break, using Ginae's camera in their dorm room. They address the camera directly, offering insight from their experience. It's like they were speaking to their younger selves, or perhaps their younger friends and siblings still in high school. Ginae said, "For me, the time management, roommate issues, studying, and learning to live independently " were the issues that mattered most.

Ebony talked about what to expect from the classes, explaining, "In some classes, one test will determine your grade." Krista shared the positive overall thrill of being independent, noting "You learn more in your first semester of college than you do in all of high school."

At first glance, this video is deceptive: it looks like a trio of girls clowning for the camera. The video opens with Ginae looking at the camera, saying, "Is this recording?" But a more careful look reveals a polished and strategic video production. Within 10 seconds, an opening title sequence with jazzy music begins. The girls interact with each other, using a mixture of serious and playful talk,

Create to Learn: Introduction to Digital Literacy, First Edition. Renee Hobbs.
© 2017 John Wiley & Sons, Inc. Published 2017 by John Wiley & Sons, Inc.

like you might hear on a morning talk radio show, mixing informal stories along with more substantial advice and insight on the trials and tribulations of their first semester of college. The girls clearly had a purpose and strategic goal: they knew that they were communicating to a real audience of girls about to head off to college or in their first year like them. Krista noted, "By talking about our experience, we hope others will find it useful and entertaining."[1] Ginae is 18 years old and already an experienced digital author, and her video about freshman year has received 45,000 views as of November 2016. But so far, at least, she has not created any videos for her college coursework.

Play and Learning in Coursework

College and universities generally frame play and learning in the context of *co-curricular activities*, which are generally defined as activities that extend or complement what students are learning in school. Co-curricular activities may be organized and social, as in the clubs, fraternities and sororities, or other kinds of voluntary student activities. There are plenty of opportunities for these groups to create media that helps them increase visibility for their organization, promote an upcoming service project, or fundraise for a special event. Make no mistake about it: some of the most powerful learning experiences you ever have in college come from co-curricular experiences.

Fortunately, students also sometimes are able to combine play and learning when they create media as part of their coursework. Another college student, Derrick Davis, an undergraduate biology major at Stanford University, created a parody video of Jay Z's "Money Ain't a Thang" when he created "Regulatin' Genes" with his instructor, Tom McFadden, a graduate student instructor. The rap song explains in pretty technical scientific language about the process of cell specialization. How does a cell know to become a neuron or a skin cell? Transcription factors, or proteins which bind to DNA, interact with the cellular machinery to control gene expression, a biological process that explains how a single fertilized egg can turn into a full-fledged organism.[2]

And lest you think that college students making videos as a way to learn complex scientific concepts is a new thing, know that in 1971, Professor Robert Alan Weiss in the Chemistry department at Stanford University created "Protein Synthesis: An Epic on a Cellular Level," a free-love style outdoor dance video (that really is the best way to describe it!) to illustrate the process of protein synthesis.[3] It's still shown in biology classes today because it illustrates the scientific concept in a playful and highly memorable way.

Another YouTuber, YouArentBenjamin, worked with a small group to create a video for his college statistics class, called "Pivot Tables Make Everything Just Right." In it, the singer bemoans having too much data until his friend tells him about the pivot table, which "sounds too good to be true, sounds more like a fable." The rappers explain then how to condense information with a pivot table in Excel.[4]

When a student in England got the opportunity to create a video as part of a college assignment, his task was to come up with the premise of a movie, based on a book, and create a trailer for it. A *trailer* is a short promotional video that generally advertises key features of a movie plot to inspire viewer interest. Working with a creative team, he created "The Very Hungry Caterpillar – The Trailer," a hilarious no-budget *spoof* that remixes a children's picture book with the action adventure and the horror film genre. A father is reading the famous Eric Carle storybook to his son. Cut to a group of military officers talking, and one says, "Gentlemen, we've got ourselves a problem." A series of short shots follows, all communicating the severe danger of the very hungry caterpillar, who (as you may remember from the storybook) eats and eats and eats but is still hungry. From there, it's an escalating series of action shots remixed from Hollywood movies as the military goes all out after the killing of that bug.[5] It's quite silly but very entertaining – and it accomplished the goals of the assignment.

At this point, you are probably wondering: where did these people get their creative ideas? This chapter addresses the process of concept development where authors identify the purpose and aims of their multimedia production and engage in the first stage of the creative process: brainstorming and idea development.

College Students as Digital Media Entrepreneurs

When students create YouTube videos as a way to learn, they can also learn about the economics of the Internet. YouTube video makers can make real money from their creative work. After Ginae uploaded her video to her YouTube site, the video had reached over 27 000 views by the summer of 2015, only eight months after publication. By using the Social Blade web site, we can see that Ginae has uploaded 38 videos and has 8,900 subscribers. Ginae makes between $100–$250 each month from the advertising shown on her YouTube videos. And as of August 2015, the pivot table rap has had 27,000 views. So the work of YouTube video producers has some financial benefit to creative entrepreneurs.

Create to Learn: A Five-Step Process

Create to learn is an approach to education that is rooted in an expanded conceptualization of literacy. Sometimes called *digital and media literacy*, this approach owes its inspiration to a variety of scholars and writers whose ideas on learning and creativity were influential in the twentieth century.

They include John Dewey, a philosopher who taught at the University of Chicago. Dewey believed that communication, education, and democracy were fundamentally intertwined and that could not be understood independently from each other. Marshall McLuhan, a Canadian communication scholar, noticed how rapid changes in media and technology affected patterns of thought, learning, and action for individuals and society. He recognized that media and technologies are not neutral but each has a bias that encourages people to think and act in certain ways. Paulo Freire was a Brazilian philosopher, educator, scholar, and activist. Freire motivated Brazilian peasants to read by showing them how literacy enacts and reproduces power relationships between elites and working-class people. Reading is not just a cognitive skill – it's a form of cultural power. He observed that when people are learning to read and write, they can heighten their awareness of the social and political world around them and inspire them to take action to improve their conditions of life.

Digital and media literacy can be defined as the lifelong learning process that involves accessing, analyzing, creating, reflecting, and taking action, using the power of communication and information to make a difference in the world.[6] It includes five learning processes (AACRA) that work together in a spiral (see Figure 2.1):

- **Access.** During this stage, you gather resources that are relevant to the task at hand. This will require a strategic process of search, exploration, and discovery. You may do this through a process of formal and informal information gathering. You're also engaging in listening and deep reading comprehension, organizing information, and taking notes. In this stage, you will be drinking in as much as you can by reading, listening, viewing, and interacting with others.
- **Analyze.** During this stage, you are invested in the process of meaning-making, not just by understanding the content but by examining the motives, assumptions, and worldviews of the authors you encounter. Asking critical

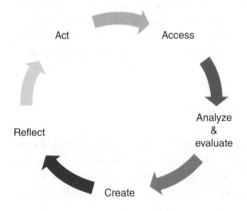

Act   Access

Reflect

Analyze & evaluate

Create

Figure 2.1 The AACRA model of digital and media literacy.

questions about what you watch, see, and read is the essence of this phase of the process.

- **Create.** Maybe it's a flash of insight. Or maybe it's just deadline pressure telling you it's time to move forward. Or maybe it's a vague sense that Idea X and Idea Q are related somehow. In this phase, it's an optimistic spark of possibility that motivates you to work towards a solution. Often, when you begin, the full-fledged ideas are not yet there – but stepping into the process of creation and getting started actually helps you discover them. This is the phase where you organize ideas, take a photograph, or start typing.
- **Reflect.** Reflection is a form of external and internal evaluation. Not all ideas are great ideas. In the external phase, you test the validity and quality of your work by giving it a critique. If necessary, in this phase, you modify, revise, or tinker. Sometimes you even throw out the work and start fresh. When the work is completed, then comes the internal phase of reflection, where you consider the implications of your work. How are you adding value to the world with your creation? How will audiences react? What are the consequences of your creative work as it may affect the attitudes and behaviors of others? What have you learned about yourself through the creative process? Great philosophers have noted that human creativity enables us to come to know ourselves better and that self-discovery is a natural outcome of creative work.
- **Act.** When your creative work reaches an authentic audience, what happens? Does the work accomplish its goals? In this phase, we look for evidence that the work had impact and value. Noticing, documenting, and accounting for the impact of a message is a part of using the power of information and communication to make a difference in the world.

Where Creativity Comes From

People believe that creativity comes from inside the human brain. When someone is creative, we think they find ways of translating their life experiences in a novel way. Creative people come up with an idea and act upon it. But this idea can be misleading if it leads you to think that creative people are special, different, unusual, or one of a kind. The truth is: everyone is creative.

People get creative ideas from a rich variety of experiences in the world around them. Let's start with your media experience. We are all swimming in a complex stream – a river of sorts – of cultural products: consider your own daily diet of media and technology use, including the games, movies, television shows, apps, and web sites you used in the last few days. Now some of that stuff is quality and some of that stuff is junk, right? But our choices of what we read, watch, play, and listen to matters because these become the building blocks for what we create.

Then there are your day-to-day experiences. They support the creative process, too. Your interactions with family, friends, and co-workers provide all sorts of fodder for creative thinking. Your sport and leisure activities fertilize your creative mind. Writers, poets, and scientists have long recognized the value of sleep to creative problem solving. Dreaming helps you with the creation of connections between things that didn't seem connected before. And that is the essence of creativity. Researchers have found that generating new insights requires time – and that sleep helps in linking ideas together.[7]

So let's define *lifestyle creativity*, where you take in experiences and think about them, and later, you re-arrange that stuff into ideas that are novel, beautiful, or useful for solving problems. When you're ready (or when you must), you then make something that expresses your understanding. Cognitive psychologists Thomas Ward and colleagues insist that "the capacity for creative thought is the rule rather than the exception of human cognitive functioning."[7] Every normal person is born ready to be creative.[8]

So now you see why the creative process is so very personal. As W. Glenn Griffin and Deborah Morrison write in *The Creative Process Illustrated*, it's not easy to describe how people come up with new ideas because the attempt to study the creative process changes it. That's why they developed an intriguing way to research the creative process among advertising professionals, who are people who are paid to be creative. They mailed a large 17 × 22 inch blank poster and a black Sharpie pen to participants and asked them to think about the creative process and illustrate the process in a way that creates a visualization that shares an understanding of the process. They then analyzed 75 drawings and interviewed the advertising professionals and their colleagues.[9] Some of the key insights include advice on the creative process:

- **Fill Your Head with Stuff.** Researchers and theorists call this the development of your *cultural capital*, a concept first articulated by Pierre Bourdieu that refers to nonfinancial assets that help you be successful in society, including your appearance, speech, education, intellect, and world knowledge.[10] According to Chris Adams, creative director at TBWA\Chiat\Day in Los Angeles, being creative is all about "devouring media – soaking up the world around me – words and images and music and life."[11] Being a cultural sponge gives you funds of creative material to recombine and manipulate to create something new. Creative people are voracious readers, viewers, and do-ers. But it's worth thinking about the quality of choices you make. If you want to learn by creating great stuff, seek out and find great stuff. According to Griffin and Morrison, "The world around us offers context. Everything we experience informs and influences creative thinking."[12]
- **Spend Some Time with the Mess.** The process of creativity is disorganized, chaotic, and messy. When it happens in the classroom, David Cooper Moore

and I have called it *messy engagement*, which is when learners struggle work through the first set of decisions about what and how to create.[13] For some, this is exhilarating but for others this can be terrifying. For this reason, sometimes people want to jump to the first solution they find. But actually, play and informal conversation – and even talk that drifts off course – can help people generate many ideas. Andy Azula, a creative director at the Martin Agency, says it's important to resist the impulse to solve a creative problem too fast. "Spend some time with the problem," he says.[14] Experts agree that out of the chaos of ordinary life, creative ideas appear.

- **Collaborate in Nonjudgmental Brainstorming.** Many creative people generate ideas in conversation with others, working as a member of a team. Some of these ideas will be good, others great, and some will be really mediocre – it's normal. *Brainstorming* is the process of idea generation and it works best as a social and collaborative process. It's a myth that people develop good ideas all by themselves. Whenever a group of people generate a lot of ideas, most of them will be crappy. If someone starts pointing out the flaws in an idea, people stop generating ideas. But when judgment is withheld, a whole pile of ideas will get generated. This inspires people to loosen up. Sometimes an idea that starts out crappy can polish up nice with time, effort, and hard work. It's often in the interplay or the association between ideas where novelty can be found. Ideas evolve through dialogue. According to Griffin and Morrison, "Sometimes the slightest change of perspective offers a new set of conceptual opportunities."[15]

- **Don't Fear Fear.** The poet Sylvia Plath is credited with this quote: "The worst enemy of creativity is self-doubt." *Self-doubt* is a lack of confidence in yourself and your abilities; it is a story you tell yourself that undermines the important process of risk taking. The things we create may be seen as extensions of our self: that's why most of us personally identify with the things we create, from the selfies we take to the doodles we scribble. Because of this, many people experience fear and anxiety about what people will think about their work. They worry about whether the work will be good enough. This is actually part of the creative process: "fear of failure helps you work harder to make an idea better," says Mike Heid, an advertising professional from New Orleans. Creative people all struggle with self-doubt.[16] Once you become aware that these feelings are part of the process, you gradually learn to believe in yourself and the ideas flow like water. Reducing self-doubt enables to you engage in *creative risk taking*, which can be defined as doing something that you have not done before. One example is the artist Pablo Picasso, who was asked to create a mural for the 1937 World's Fair in Paris. Angry and shocked by Nazi bombing of the Basque town of Guernica in 1937, Picasso created a giant mural explicitly making a political statement about the horrors of war. At 11 feet tall and

26 feet wide, the painting's mass is overwhelming. It was a significant act of risk taking to create and when it was first exhibited, the response was critical: people didn't like it. Only later was it recognized as modern art's most powerful antiwar statement.[17] It takes courage to be creative. And you have to be confident even when it's not working. Sometimes you need to start over. There are multiple paths to a solution. Discovering these paths is part of the process of creating to learn.

Creative Constraints and Creative Control

It's long been recognized that boundaries or limitations promote creativity. Genres like the short story and the haiku impose very strict limits on the length and the form of the writing. In business, product development teams have to create new products working within very precise cost constraints.

It may be counterintuitive to think that *creative constraint* promotes the imagination, but it's a powerful idea whose value is well established in virtually every art form. I love the work of Austin Kleon, a poet whose book, *Newspaper Blackout*, consists of poems created by selectively blacking out words in a newspaper article (see Figure 2.2). Working from the constraints of the words in a newspaper article, Austin uses a black magic marker to black out words, subtracting from the original content until only his own poetic form remains.[18]

Damien Correll, a graphic artist who serves as the art director at Tumblr, explains, "I think if you're given a clean, fresh palette, and you do whatever you want, it's almost too much freedom, at least for me." For Correll, one constraint he imposes on himself is short *deadlines*.[19] Many creative people use the Pomodoro Technique, which involves setting a timer for 25 minutes of focused work. The artificial constraint of time unleashes creativity and productivity.

If you're reading this book, it's probably because your instructor wants you to create multimedia as part of the learning process. Multimedia projects and assignments are assigned differently depending on the learning outcomes, content and discipline, and learning environment. Some educators may give students a lot of creative control, allowing students to select the format, genre, or medium. Other educators may be very specific, with precise directions about the creative process and product to be produced. In any case, the idea is that you will demonstrate your learning and creativity through application.

Why Creative Constraints Promote Learning

Assignments and deadlines impose creative constraint upon learners in order to structure and focus students' own creative control. When instructors design assignments, they consider both the learning *process* and the work *product*.

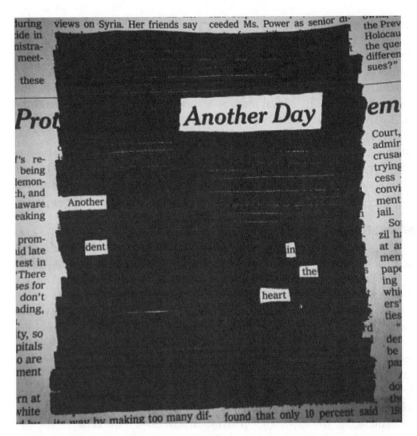

Figure 2.2 *Newspaper Blackout* by Austin Kleon.

For example, one instructor may value creative collaboration by requiring students to work with a partner or in a small group while another instructor may put emphasis on the construction of an argument. Some teachers may give very specific directions on how to create media (for example, even by specifying what digital tool o use) while the other instructors barely mention the process of creating with digital media. This parallels the kinds of experience you are likely to have later in life, outside of college or university, when as part of your work you receive work assignments that are structured differently depending on the situation and context.

Sometimes, students suffer because of the lack of creative constraint, when an assignment is too vague or general. If that happens, then you may need to artificially impose some constraints yourself to stimulate your thinking and creativity. If you are lucky, you will get a wide variety of different types of assignments while you are in college to prepare you well for the many different challenges you will experience in the world outside the classroom.

When you create to learn, the instructor's learning goals will serve as key elements of creative constraint for the work that you create. But although the instructor (and later on in life, the employer) sets up the parameters of the problem, it's your creativity that must be activated in the process of creating to learn. Instructors may deliberately or inadvertently intensify the creative potential of their students, as Patricia Stokes notes in her book, *Creativity from Constraints*.[20] Some constraints promote creativity, while others promote conformity. For example, deadline pressures and due dates generally help creativity while a step-by-step "to do" list may stifle creativity.

The Creative Practice in Action

Creative work actually inspires deep happiness in human beings. In his book, *Flow: The Psychology of Optimal Experience*, Mihály Csíkszentmihályi reports on research that demonstrates that people are happiest when they are in a state of *flow* – a state of attention where people are completely absorbed in what they are doing.[21] Everyone has experienced a flow state: it occurs when people are so involved in an activity that nothing else seems to matter. People may experience flow when they are sewing, running, ironing, or when playing a video game. They may experience it when editing video, building a bookshelf, or doing hobbies. You enter into a flow state when there is a careful balance between the level of challenge the task requires and your own skills. If the task is too challenging, you experience frustration, not flow. If the task is not challenging enough, you experience boredom.

As you get started with creating to learn, it's good to know what you can expect. When Graham Wallas wrote *The Art of Thought* in 1926, he was trying to understand how new ideas emerged. By interviewing creative people from many different fields, he synthesized their creative process into four stages: preparation, incubation, illumination, and verification.[22] The first stage of the creative process begins by establishing the brief or the scope of the task. By defining the task with precision, you focus your goals and pinpoint the problem that requires solving. This helps you generate potential paths that may lead to a solution. During the *preparation* phase, you are feeding your head with information and ideas from others and critically analyzing those ideas.

In the *incubation* phase, you "push the task out of your immediate attention" as graphic designer David Gill puts it. "Quite simply – forget about it," he says.[23] During the 1920s, when Wallas was writing about creativity, the field of psychology was embracing the work of Sigmund Freud, who was trying to understand human behavior by exploring the concept of the unconscious. As the dominant psychological theory of the time, psychoanalysis was appealing to creative people because it helped explain how new ideas emerge. Researchers have discovered that multitasking, may contribute to learning and creativity because "adapting to a high input level of varying distractions can increase situational awareness that is beneficial to creativity."[24] In the beginning of the twentieth century, psychologists explored people's dreams, believing that they were connected to the unconscious or intuitive dimensions of cognition. The idea is that when you disengage your conscious attention – by walking on the beach, driving to Connecticut, or working out at the gym – this allows the unconscious to efficiently process a mass of data. Sounds like magic? People who have tried it say, "It works!"

In the *illumination* phase of the creative process, inspiration comes through some kind of "aha" insight. This phase is where the actual creative product gets built. The way this happens is unique and situational, depending on what form or medium you are working in.

In *verification,* the final phase of the creative process, you analyze your creative produce in relation to your original goals and objectives. You return to your creative brief and see if your work "solved" the problems you identified at the beginning. It's hard to be impartial about your own creative work; feedback from other people helps us see our own ideas more clearly. Time away from the work also helps us return with fresh eyes, where the revision process bring out true creativity as we transform through perfecting and polishing.

Creativity is an Act of Intellectual Freedom

When people compose stories, write essays, take pictures, make videos, build web sites, or use symbols to solve problems, they are really shaping the world. For example, when you see a photo of a place you have not visited, you take it for granted that the place looks like what's in the photo. But authors make choices of how to depict places, things, events, and people. Media consumers depend on media creators to be fair and accurate in how they represent the world. This form of power is tremendous. And of course not all media creators are fair or accurate – and our Bill of Rights makes this legal. That's why the concept of *intellectual freedom,* which is at the heart of the First Amendment, is so important to the practice of creating to learn. In the United States, freedom of expression is the cornerstone of democracy. While all people – including children and teens – are free to speak and write freely, with this freedom comes responsibility. Responsible authors value fairness and accuracy, knowing that they are ethically accountable to their audiences. They make sure that what they create and share is true, has value to others, and that it doesn't do harm.

We should be grateful to be alive at a time when the Internet has contributed to a blossoming of human creativity because there are no editors, no censors or gatekeepers. But undoubtedly, there's plenty of "awful" in the variety of creative products that people create. Because of intellectual freedom, people are free to create anything. It may be sublime, inane, or simply evil, or anywhere in between. Today the burden of responsibility is on the consumer to sort out and evaluate the quality of human creativity in all its many forms. But if everyone tries hard to create and share what is true, what is beautiful, and what has value to others, and if we all avoided creating content that harms people, the world really would be a better place. Human creative expression has the potential to transform the world, by enabling people to construct and share work that has meaning and value.

The Creative Process in Stages

Preparation. The problem to be solved is carefully considered and resources are gathered in order to confront the task. The conscious mind is focused on the problem.

Incubation. Drawing upon these resources, consideration of the problem is internalized and becomes a largely subconscious activity. The mind makes connections more freely and abundantly.

Illumination. Possible solutions to the problem transition from subconscious to conscious thought. This is a moment of insight and optimism.

Verification. Solutions are tested and may be modified if shown to be viable.

Source: Wallas, Graham (2014/1926). *The Art of Thought*. Kent, England: Solis Press.

Students and Teachers Create to Learn

In the create to learn process, obviously, teachers may provide some (but not all) of the guidance for your multimedia project. For that reason, your multimedia project may depend upon the guidance and specifications set out by your instructor. It's likely that you will face constraints and limitations that will shape what you create. Before your creative process can truly begin, you must have a firm idea of what you need to do to be successful. It's also important to practice experimenting with digital texts, tools, and technologies in the spirit of creating to learn.

You may want to develop your own creative brief by using a digital bulletin board, where you can post your creative brief online. In the example shown in Figure 2.3, students enrolled in a class on library and information services wanted to demonstrate what they were learning by creating a short video depicting a special workshop on animation that was offered to children in a local library.

Library Programs for Youth - Our Creative Brief

What is the problem or opportunity?
Librarians and filmmakers are working together to create a learning experience for kids in the library .

Who is it really for? And why should they care?
The target audience for this is librarians who do not yet have many programs for teens. They probably don't realize that it's relatively easy to develop this kinds of program and that it's very appealing and valuable for teens to have this kind of experience.

What needs to be done? By whom? By when?
We have already observed the program and taken photos and videos to document it. Now we need to interview the organizers, write a script, sequence the images and videos, select music, perform the voiceover, and put it together using iMovie.

Where and how will it be used?
We'll submit it to our professor and send a copy to the library for them to use on their website.

Who will become engaged with it directly and indirectly?
The kids, parents and teachers who participated might enjoy seeing themselves in this video. The librarians and filmmakers who organized it will certainly watch it carefully.

How will it be remembered?
The cute kids having fun and learning are the part of the story most likely to be remembered.

Figure 2.3 Students compose a creative brief on Padlet.

Activity: Build a Creative Brief

A *creative brief* is a kind of mind map that serves as the framework or foundation for your work. Here you put together your evolving understanding of the project by identifying the target audience, message purpose, key ideas, tone/voice, and point of view. A creative brief is used at the beginning of the creative process to jumpstart your thinking: it's not the complete plan.

A creative brief can be constructed by reflecting on the specifications of the assignment as your instructor has offered specifications and criteria for evaluation. Synthesize and capture your ideas about your work by answering the questions below:

1) What is this project? What form will it take? What's the task at hand?
2) Why are we doing it? What is the problem or opportunity?
3) Who is it really for? And why should they care?
4) Where and how will it be used? When?
5) Who will become engaged with it directly and indirectly?
6) How will it be remembered and retold?
7) What needs to be done? By whom? By when?

3

Decisions, Decisions

KEY IDEAS

Many decisions are made as part of the creative multimedia production process. Learn how the rhetorical modes of exposition, argument, and narration shape the choices that authors make in the multimedia composition process. In making strategic decisions about how to inform, entertain, and persuade, nine types of media can be used for creating to learn: blogs and web sites, digital audio and podcasting, images, infographics and data visualization, vlogs and screencasts, video production, animation, remix production, and social media. Recognize the affordances and limitations of each media type that need to be considered in light of your purpose, target audience, point of view, timetable, experience, and access to resources. It's important to be aware of the generic features that shape the tone and sensibility of diverse works. By making strategic decisions in selecting the appropriate type of production based on a careful consideration of specific factors, people advance their deep learning of academic content while creating to learn.

One girl "hates her freckles." Another is "afraid of being fat." This powerful 30-second ad was released during the Super Bowl XL in 2006 and it featured pre-teen girls who are apparently dissatisfied with their appearance. The purpose of the advertisement was to promote Dove's Self Esteem Fund, which is linked to Dove's Campaign for Real Beauty and was "created to act as an agent of change to inspire and educate girls and women about a wider definition of beauty." One of the videos in the Dove campaign, entitled "Onslaught," introduces us to a young white girl with red hair, followed by a fast montage of depictions of female beauty set to rock music. It's a blur of billboards, television shows, magazine imagery, and even early-morning infomercials selling weight loss pills and facial creams. Then the tone of the music and the images shift to feature graphically detailed images of cosmetic surgery, including images of the surgical process used for tummy tucks and nose jobs. The mood is creepy and dark. In the closing seconds of the ad, we return to the little girl, and on screen we see the words, "Talk to your daughter before the beauty industry does." Then the logo of Dove's Campaign for Real Beauty appears.[1]

Create to Learn: Introduction to Digital Literacy, First Edition. Renee Hobbs.
© 2017 John Wiley & Sons, Inc. Published 2017 by John Wiley & Sons, Inc.

The emotional power of this ad is undeniable: indeed, the ad's shock value helped Dove accomplish several goals in relation to brand and product messaging. The overall message of this ad served to differentiate Dove from other sectors of the beauty industry. Dove clearly wants to send the message that it cares about the future of girls and women and is dedicated to social good. The advertisement, aimed specifically at mothers and fathers, takes aim at the social norms and values of beauty culture. The video critiques commercials that suggest that buying a specific product will make women better in some way. By distinguishing itself as different from beauty companies that tell women they are not good enough, Dove is claiming the moral high ground and establishing the beauty industry as the "problem" that can be solved by Dove's Campaign for Real Beauty. Working with organizations including the Girl Scouts USA, Dove has reached over 15 million girls with educational programs about self-esteem since 2015.

But Dove's campaign was interpreted differently by others, who imitated the format and structure of this ad to communicate a completely different message. When Greenpeace, the global environmental organization, wanted to get the attention of American consumers about the problem of global deforestation, they decided to capitalize on the popularity of this particular Dove campaign. Greenpeace knew that the Dove campaign had been successful in reaching a large audience. So it created a video parody of Dove's "Onslaught" ad with its own "Onslaught(er)" commercial, in which it criticizes Dove's parent company Unilever and its use of Indonesian palm oil. In the Greenpeace campaign, we see a young Indonesian girl, with dark skin and eyes, who looks directly at the camera. This is followed by a fast montage of depictions of deforestation set to rock music that sounds very similar to the music of the original Dove ad. It's a blur of trees being felled, animals dying, smoke, and forest clearing efforts. Then the images shift to feature graphically detailed images of deforestation and loss of forest animals and natural habitat. In the closing seconds of the ad, we return to see the little girl again, and on screen we see the words, "By the time Azizah is 25, 98% of Indonesian rain forests will be destroyed. Talk to Dove before it's too late."[2] Then the logo of the Greenpeace company appears. Because palm oil has long been the base ingredient in modern soaps, countries like Indonesia have experienced economic stability and growth by clearing tropical forests to create palm plantations. But deforestation and clear-cutting threatens wildlife such as orangutans and has other impacts on global climate. In this advocacy campaign, Greenpeace positions Dove as the villain whose reliance on palm oil makes it directly implicated in the loss of global wildlife. By closely imitating the format of the Dove campaign, Greenpeace was effectively able to link the issue of clear-cutting tropical forests to Dove's marketing effort to define itself as the "white hat" in the beauty industry. Figure 3.1 displays a still frame from both videos.

As a result of this highly effective communication campaign, public support for Greenpeace surged, and in April 2008, Unilever agreed to play its part in

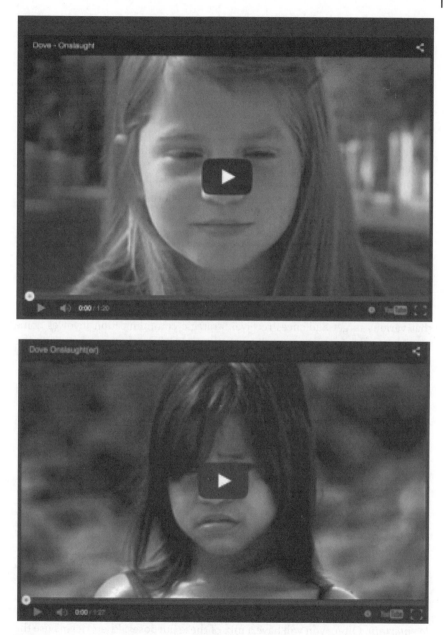

Figure 3.1 Dove "Onslaught" and Greenpeace "Onslaught(er)" videos.

saving the forests of South East Asia. The parody video helped get the attention of Unilever executives.[3] Greenpeace's forests campaigners were invited to meet with senior executives at Unilever headquarters because in just two weeks, the company had received tens of thousands of protest e-mails from people around the world. In dialogue with Greenpeace, Unilever agreed to support an immediate moratorium on deforestation for palm oil in South East Asia. It agreed to use its leadership role within the industry to aggressively build a coalition of companies to support the moratorium. Unilever also agreed that it would lobby the Indonesian government to support the immediate moratorium.[4] Using the power of communication and information for advocacy, this organization was successful in offering a critique of a beauty company in a creative way that increased awareness of the impact of deforestation.

Strategic Communication Decisions

The term *strategic communication* is used to describe how people make the "right" decisions when creating media messages. Some refer to it as good alignment between the goals of the organization or individual and the interpretations that various target audiences receive. Strategic communication involves communicating the best message, through the right channels, and measuring the impact in relation to specific organizational goals. As one public relations expert has put it, "It's the difference between doing communications stuff, and doing the *right* communications stuff."[5] Strategic decisions about mode, medium, and genre reflect how digital authors conceptualize their purpose, their target audience, and their specific goals. Creative risk taking, as we have seen with the case of both Dove and Greenpeace, can have real political, social, and cultural impact.

Rhetorical Modes: Purpose and Target Audience

The most important decisions a digital author must make concern the strategic communication objectives of intent to communicate a message. Who is your target audience? What do you want your audience to think, feel, or do as a result of your actions? Although you might think you can create messages for a wide target audience – "everybody" – in reality, messages are most effective when they are designed for a particular, targeted group. When you create to learn, you may have one or more of these purposes: *to inform, to persuade,* or *to entertain.* Often, you will have a mix of these purposes. Rhetoricians use the term *exposition* to mean works that inform; they use the term *argumentation* to refer to works that persuade. *Narration* is the mode associated with works that entertain. These modes blur in so many creative ways because, in real life, creative people have a mix of purposes and goals.

When you examine creative work carefully, you can generally identify the purpose and the target audience by looking at the *choices* made in how the message was constructed. Increasing your awareness of the constructed nature of media messages is a fundamental skill of digital and media literacy. It can be activated any time you use media. For example, when I watched the 2015 film *Suffragette*, it was obvious to me that Sarah Gavron, the director, wanted to create a story inspired by historical events in the early twentieth century as women in Britain fought for the right to vote. She wanted to portray the experience of an individual who becomes radicalized to the point of using violent actions to accomplish political goals. The director chose to use a *narrative* mode, but the authorial intent is also informative and persuasive. The film visually depicts the harsh working conditions that women experienced in the early twentieth century. Just before the closing credits, a list of the years in which women in different countries achieved the right to vote helps the author be transparent about her many goals in informing, persuading, and entertaining audiences, all at the same time. As I watched, I could see how all the many different choices of the filmmaker helped her construct a film that enabled her to express her goals of engaging audiences to care more about the importance of protecting and extending women's legal and political rights around the world.

Creative teams make decisions early on about whether and how their work will inform, entertain, or persuade and what they want the audience to know, feel, and do. Among communications scholars and media professionals, the *knowledge–attitude–behavior (KAB) model* is useful for strategic planning and decision making.[6] As you gain knowledge, you form attitudes that shape your behavior. Many forms of expression and communication aim to increase knowledge, reinforce or change attitudes, and motivate behavior. In the public health community, this approach has also been modified and is known as the *theory of reasoned action*, which includes an examination of how people's knowledge interacts with their perception of their own self-efficacy and the social norms of the people around them to affect their attitudes and their behavior.[7] If I see a public service announcement about texting and driving, for example, it may be effective in informing me about the risk of getting in an accident. But if I feel unable to control my compulsive use of the cell phone or if the people in my life also text and drive, it will be hard for me to change my behavior. So an effective public service announcement will have to consider the emotional and social dimensions of texting while driving in order to influence attitudes and behavior.

In Professor Tom Mather's classroom, a group of students were learning about tick-transmitted diseases. Students were encouraged to create some digital media to demonstrate their learning. They discussed some specific goals that reflected their understanding of their audience and purpose. The students had a mix of informational and persuasive goals, as they want their target audience of dog owners to gain knowledge about the risk of contracting Lyme disease from

Table 3.1 Communication strategy: science students identify their goals.

Communication strategy	Our plan
Who are we?	We are science students learning about tick transmitted diseases
Who is our target audience?	We want to reach dog owners
How will they encounter our message?	Through messages shared by people on their Facebook and Twitter social network
KNOWLEDGE	
What do we want them to know?	People are at risk of contracting dangerous Lyme disease if their dogs bring an infected tick into the house; dogs need to get special treatment to reduce their risk of getting ticks
ATTITUDES	
What do we want them to feel?	We want them to feel fear as they realize that their loveable dogs can cause them health problems
BEHAVIOR	
What do we want them to do?	We want dog owners to buy and give tick treatments to their dogs

ticks on their dogs, but they also want to persuade people to buy and use pet tick treatments. To capture the attention of dog owners, they knew they needed to provide some entertainment value, perhaps using a narrative story, a playful parody, or some other creative approach. Table 3.1 shows how they defined their communication strategy.

Critically Analyzing Media to Understand Principles of Effective Design

When you talk directly with creators, like the science students who created the tick treatment video, they can tell you their purpose, goals, and target audience. But can you infer the author's purpose from the clues provided in the creative work they produce?

Consider a screencast video created by a college student, Jordanna Packtor, from the University of Rhode Island. Entitled, "Fantasy in the Classroom," it's a 5-minute video with a selection of 20 images and a script that summarizes the main ideas of her academic research paper.[8] Figure 3.2 depicts a screenshot of this creative work. Her overall argument is that negative attitudes about fantasy are misguided and that classroom teachers should make greater use of fantasy genres in teaching in high school.

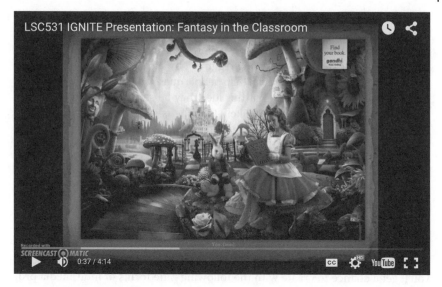

LSC531 IGNITE Presentation: Fantasy in the Classroom

SCREENCAST O MATIC ▶ 🔊 0:37 / 4:14   CC ⚙ You Tube ⬚

Figure 3.2 Student screencast.

Who is the target audience? When I critically analyze this screencast, I pay attention to the overall main idea, the use of evidence, and the tone and structure of the piece. From the verbal content and image choices, I recognize that she is aiming to reach an audience of English teachers and school librarians and that she is simultaneously informing and persuading them. Of course, I recognize that, as the instructor giving the grade, I am the ultimate target audience. But it's clear that Jordanna is addressing a wider audience. By using a mix of classical and contemporary references to fantasy literature, I can see that she is aiming to persuade people that *Harry Potter* is just as legitimate and important a book as *Gulliver's Travels*. Because Packtor is a skillful persuader, she directly identifies the arguments of those who think that fantasy is a lesser genre because of its childishness and lack of realism. She takes critics of fantasy seriously, which lends credibility to her message because she acknowledges there are many points of view on this topic.

How will the audience encounter the message? Jordanna has created a screencast that has been uploaded to her YouTube site. Everyone who has a Gmail account has a YouTube site that can be activated with just a few clicks. She has also embedded the video on her blog and used metatags including the words "fantasy," "literature," "media," and "subversion" to reach those who are searching for content related to these themes.

What does the creator want the audience to know, feel, and do? This student offers examples to provide information to her audience, noting, for example, how *The Lord of the Rings* addresses the harms of war. She seems to want to inspire some sympathy for those people who are fans of the genre, as she explains that young adults who read fantasy encounter ideas about isolation, prejudice and injustice, which can be explored from the safe distance that fantasy provides. Packtor makes a strong argument by explaining that fantasy genres can be subversive because they can help people question their everyday realities. I expect that Jordanna knows that this idea may be surprising or new to some members of her audience. So it's likely that she is aiming to get teachers and librarians to change their behavior. She is providing arguments that could help a high school teacher or librarian feel comfortable assigning students to read fantasy as a supplement to (or instead of) literature from the classical canon.

Choosing the Medium

After you have thought deeply about your target audience and purpose, you have a big set of decisions to make about what type of media to use to create and share your ideas. Many factors will shape your decisions. In this book, you'll get a chance to create with the following nine forms of multimedia production that are essential for creating to learn.

Nine Media for Creating to Learn*
1) Blogs and web sites
2) Podcasts
3) Images
4) Infographics and data visualization
5) Vlogs and screencasts
6) Video
7) Animation
8) Remix
9) Social media
*Learn more about free and low-cost digital tools for creating videos at www.createtolearn.online

Often these forms work best when combined, as when an image slideshow and a blog entry are combined on an informational web site and then promoted using social media. As you learn more about these types of media by reading below, consider which ones are most relevant to your life, work and career interests.

Blogs and web sites

For many years, to create a web site meant learning HTML, CSS, and JavaScript, the three core technologies of web content production. Today, many young people and college students have developed their own professional web sites and blogs by using simple drag-and-drop tools from easy-to-use digital web platforms like WordPress, Wix, and Blogger. Developing a professional web site while in college can be effective in helping get internships, part-time jobs, full-time jobs, and even to earn extra cash. A variety of simple free or low-cost platforms are available that enable a high degree of customization with no need for coding skills.

We have little data on how many students maintain web sites while they are in college, but Professor Larry Atkins was surprised to discover that only a small number of his students had developed their own professional web sites. He writes, "Everyone is on Facebook or MySpace, but only 10 or so of the approximately 500 students that I've taught over the last seven years had their own web site, which featured their writing samples, articles, or other work."[9]

Still, the skills and exposure gained from creating a web site can be useful in developing your career. One of Atkins' former students, Leah Kauffman, was a junior at Temple University in 2007 when she collaborated with others to create the popular music video "I Got a Crush on Obama" for the online magazine *BarelyPolitical.com*. Today the web site is a YouTube channel that the online magazine, *NewMediaRockstars*, rated as among the top 30.[10]

When you create a blog or web site, the first major issue to be addressed is establishing voice and tone. These terms are used to describe the style of writing and the personality of the writer. *Voice* is the distinct personality that your writing communicates. Consider the various adjectives we may use when reading different kinds of writing. Is it informal? Friendly? Accessible? Serious? Authoritative? *Tone* is the term used to describe the mood or feeling of a piece of writing. Word choice, sentence structure, and even punctuation all come into play in establishing your voice as a communicator. You will probably need to choose whether or how to use *jargon*, the specialized vocabulary of specific disciplines, professions, or fields. In the growing field of social media marketing, professional communicators pay a lot of attention to the voice and tone that is associated with certain products or brands.

Lest you think web site building is just for communication majors, consider the career of Matt Lane, the creator of the web site Math Goes Pop, a blog focused on the ways mathematics intersects with popular culture. After graduating from Princeton University with a degree in mathematics in 2005, he had a brief stint as an analyst for an Internet advertising company in San Francisco, but the pull of mathematics was too strong, and he received his Ph.D. in mathematics in 2012 from UCLA. His web site fosters mathematical dialogue among people who might not otherwise consider themselves mathematically inclined. He writes about the way statistics and probability are represented in newspapers, television news, and on entertainment programs like *CSI*.[11]

Podcasts

Storytelling is rooted in the long tradition of radio's power to entertain, inform, educate, and inspire and can be thought of as part of the digital evolution of radio broadcasting. The power of the human voice is at the heart of a good podcast. That's why good podcasting feels like a real relationship between the listener and the speaker. The spoken word conjures up mental images in the imagination of the listener. Perhaps that's why the average person listens to a podcast for 22 minutes. Marketers have discovered that podcasting is ideal for reaching a *niche audience*, which is defined as a group of people with similar interests and information needs. Although once podcasting was too technically complicated to be done by people without specialized tools, today, digital tools make it easy to create a podcast with a simple app on your cell phone. You can edit to combine spoken words and music in flexible ways and upload the podcast with one-touch ease.

Podcasters are evolving new genres and forms of expression. When NPR journalist Sarah Koenig created "Serial" as part of the *This American Life* radio program, the podcast focused on the 1999 murder of Hae Min Lee, she reported on the story of Adnan Syed, who may or may not have been wrongly convicted for the murder. It's a long-form narrative crime drama where tension builds as we engage with the characters involved in the murder and wonder who is telling the truth and who is lying. It has been downloaded 68 million times since 2014.[12]

Podcasts are also created by marketers, activists, educators, and storytellers and research shows that more than 32 million people listened to podcasts in the last month. One source of the appeal: people can listen to podcasts at the gym, in the car, or anywhere. Many popular podcasts use a serial or episodic format. A *serial* format offers a continuing storyline that people follow over time. Each episode continues the overall story arc so that audiences are encouraged to listen or view in sequence. An *episodic* format offers a self-contained story or plot where it is not expected that people have listened to or viewed previous episodes. If they like the theme, topic or content, listeners can use RSS feed syndication to be alerted when a new podcast is available.

Images

Images are a powerful form of communication because of their emotional power and ability to convey a sense of authenticity. You're probably already taking pictures and sharing them. And perhaps you're paying attention to the design, color, line, and balance of the images you create. Many people have an intuitive understanding of graphic design principles just from being attentive to good design. Social media tools like Instagram help people create and share images as a way to inform, persuade, and entertain. Journalists, scientists, and business professional use multimedia image slideshows to communicate complex ideas in a way that attracts and holds attention.

Today people also create and share meaning through the process of image *curation*, which is defined as a type of digital authorship that involves selecting a mix of images or graphic resources produced by others to accomplish a particular purpose. At the *National Geographic* web site, photo editors curate sets of images on a wide range of issues collected from the archives of the magazine, and they intersperse those images with headlines and short texts that provide context and add narrative structure.

At the Pulitzer Center for Crisis Reporting, editors curate and sponsor news coverage of systemic global issues, using powerful images and quality reporting to help maintain a spotlight on often ignored topics ranging from water and food insecurity to homophobia, prejudice, and stigma. Nathalie Applewhite, managing director of the Pulitzer Center, explains that her organization's photojournalists carefully choose a sequence of emotionally powerful images and combine it with narrative storytelling.[13] At the *New York Times* web site, image slideshows make use of a variety of multimedia. One production, entitled "Ten Years After Katrina," uses a combination of images, videos and infographics, along with headlines and written text to tell about the many changes that have occurred in New Orleans after the 2005 hurricane.[14] This form of journalism can have real impact to increase visibility of events, people, processes, and social, political and economic issues that might otherwise not get attention.

Infographics and data visualizations

Infographics and data visualizations capture an audience's attention by expressing data and information with *concision*, an important concept in the field of communication and media. When ideas are concise, they can be interpreted quickly. Because people are much more likely to remember what they see than what they hear or read, image slideshows and infographics can help express ideas clearly and with emotional impact.

Once you have an understanding of basic design principles, you can use a variety of infographic design web sites that make it easy to create memorable messages. Figure 3.3 shows an infographic about the power of infographics. Great infographics tell a story and develop a main idea using images and data. They can be useful for explaining a complex process, comparing and contrasting, presenting a timeline or sequence, or pulling something apart to see its constituent parts. Easy-to-use infographic web sites offer drag-and-drop templates to help you express your ideas.

Vlogs and screencasts

Vlogs are an informal form of video production that rely on the ability of the performer to communicate directly to an audience. Screencasts are another type of video production where the movement on a computer screen is recorded. Vlogs are ideal for communicating a distinct point of view or opinion, while screencasts are generally considered to be a good way to show someone how to do something with a computer. If you have ever watched a Khan Academy video to refresh your memory about a mathematical formula or

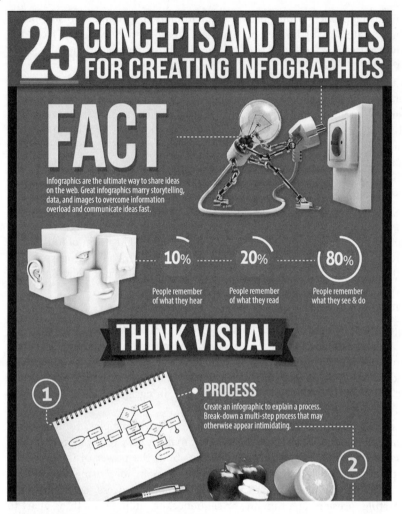

Figure 3.3 An infographic about infographics.

problem-solving process, you will have seen a screencast. Screencasting and vlogs can be sophisticated or simple. Uploading to YouTube is often simply a matter of linking an account to the platform and pressing "Publish."

Video

Video is becoming normative as a means of communication: for work, school, and leisure. Now that it's possible to create video with our cell phones and simple video editing tools, more and more people are creating videos themselves. Some have said that video's superiority comes from its ability to combine so many forms of expression – using language, image, and sound to engage the viewer and actively advance their knowledge, inspire deep feelings, and even alter their behaviors.

When producing a video, one important decision a digital author must make concerns the genre. What type of video you create depends on your goals, your intended target audience and the content of your work. You're probably familiar with the genres of literature that include short story, poetry, drama, and novel and you're likely familiar with the genres of commercial broadcast television, including news, talk show, reality, sports, and sitcoms. YouTube videos, for example, can also now be recognized by their genre, as people create how-to videos, comedy videos, review videos, cat videos, Vine videos, reaction videos, prank videos, clip compilation videos, lip dub videos and more.

Video genres are simultaneously stable and dynamic: media professionals rely on the familiarity and conventional features of a genre even while they modify, alter, and rework a genre as they create new work. Genres do important work for audiences: they help in the interpretive process. When you are watching a parody, for example, you sometimes can recognize the references that are being made to the original work. Viewers of the Greenpeace "Onslaught[er]" video, for example, which we explored at the beginning of this chapter, may have recognized the visual similarity of the video to the original Dove video. Those who did recognize the relationship between the two videos certainly would be expected to have a deeper understanding of the strategic purpose of the campaign.

Video can be produced with high-end professional equipment or with ordinary smartphones. Some colleges and universities have been building campus studios equipped with green screens, multiple cameras, and microphones. Gardner Campbell, former vice provost for learning innovation and student success at Virginia Commonwealth University, notes the growth in self-service production facilities, which are on-campus studios that require minimal setup and are easy for anyone to use.[15] The Dartmouth College Innovation Studio encourages students to use video for general academics. Penn State University has created a simple-to-use setup called the One Button Studio, which is available at more than 19 locations. It enables students and faculty members to simply plug a flash drive into the studio's computer and press a button, which automatically controls the green screen, the lighting, and the video recording. When they are done, users push the button again and retrieve their flash drive, with their new video saved.[16]

Thanks to the power of the mobile phone, most students can create a video even without a studio, a high-end camera or light kits. Today's smartphones can be used to create digital video and a variety of inexpensive apps enable students to edit video, adding titles, music and transitions to make a polished video. These tools enable you to publish your video online simply and easily.

Animation

Animated videos are among the most powerful ways to get people's attention. Our experience as children has shaped the way we make sense of cartoons. There are many types of animated videos. *Whiteboard animation videos* are a type of hand-drawn animation that have risen in popularity with the rise of YouTube. While we hear a voiceover, we may see a hand that is drawing pictures that correspond to the ideas we're learning about. *Paper animation* videos use cutouts of simple paper shapes to create animation. There's even a whole genre of LEGO animation created by both children and adults using the Danish toy blocks to create characters and stories.

The level of abstraction in cartoons may help us focus on the author's deeper message, says, Ilya Spitalnik, the creator of PowToon, a simple web tool for creating animated videos.[17] We may also be less critical of ideas that come in animated forms as they are seen as innocuous and harmless. That's because we naturally think of animation as a way to communicate innocent messages to children and young people. But animation can be a powerful form of persuasion. In the animation "Dumb Ways to Die," with more than 141 million hits as of November 2016, we see simple circle shapes come to life as characters singing a song that offers us silly ideas like "eat a tube of superglue," "disturb a nest of wasps for no good reason," and "stand on the edge of a train station platform." We see these characters getting playfully mutilated as they engage in these activities. It's a funny, silly little video. Only at the end, do we hear the sponsor's message: "Be safe around trains. A message from Metro."[18] A public service announcement, presented as animation, can manage to break through the clutter and draw our attention to the positive message that serves as the punch line.

Remix

People have always created by mixing together bits of other people's creative works. That's because, as Aristotle said, there are no new ideas. Human creativity is re-combinative, as people rework and manipulate older ideas and expressions into new forms. The origins of the term remix come from music as during the 1970s and 1980s DJs used loops and other types of aural manipulation to bring people to the dance floor.

Remixes are a good sign of changing conceptualizations of authorship. As more and more people become creators, we are moving away from the idea that authors are single individuals towards the idea of authorship as a social and collaborative process. Roland Barthes, a French literary critic, made this argument: it's wrong to think that text contains a single meaning. A text, he said, is a "tissue of citations" born of a multitude of sources from culture In remix media, the reader needs to be familiar with and aware of a reference to another form of media in order for meaning to circulate.[19] The concept of *intertextuality* refers to this interdependence. To make sense of one text, you must be familiar with the other texts that are referenced in it.

One of the most interesting online remix communities is called HitRecord, which is an open collaborative production company. It's an online studio where artists collaborate on projects and remix each other's work with the potential to contribute to money-making productions. Users upload original audio, video, text, or images to share with others in the community. A person may share a piece of writing that inspires an illustration, which could then be turned into a piece of video animation.

Social media

In social media, we create works using platforms that others have created, resulting in a kind of *second-generation creativity* where our own creative work is contingent upon the creativity embedded in the digital platform.

Social media requires that you engage with other users by creating, curating, and sharing media. For example, when you use Instagram or Snapchat, you create and share images with your friends. Using filters, you may manipulate those images to be serious or silly. These forms of media may invite us to position ourselves as *prosumers*, where we both use and produce media as part of our engagement. On social media platforms, your choices are shaped by the options available to you. In Instagram, you do not have an infinite number of choices of filters or stickers. Your expression is shaped and channeled by the platform in ways that make creation seem relatively effortless.

The rise of the "Code to Learn" movement is linked to the principles at the heart of this book. A growing number of educators believe that learning to create games is an important way to introduce students to the power of programming and coding. Many recognize that the skills of computer coding are increasingly valuable in all fields, including health care, manufacturing, and service industries. Douglas Rushkoff, in his book, *Program or Be Programmed*, worries that people are unaware of the constructed nature of the games and user-friendly platforms and programs that make our work with computers easy.[20] In order to avoid becoming further removed from the code that actually creates the applications we use, programming and coding can be a powerful form of learning about media and technology. Object-oriented coding tools enable us to see how computer programming works without having to invest thousands of hours into mastering a coding language. Rushkoff believes that familiarizing ourselves with how to program helps restore the power balance between people who create software and platforms and those who use them.

What Type of Media to Create?

So how do creative producers decide which of these different types of media to create? In making strategic decisions about how to inform, entertain, and persuade, you can't just make an easy list of the strengths and weaknesses of these nine different types of media. Each can be used well for creating to learn and each can be used to inspire, educate, inform, and persuade.

It all depends on your learning and communication goals. When you create to learn, you have to have a good understanding of your audience, your purpose, and, to some extent, the kinds of ideas, information, or content that you would like to share. An infographic is a great way to communicate facts and specific information. A web site/blog is ideal for complex information that may not be easily communicated as a story. An animation is great for grabbing attention and persuading. A podcast is optimal for information that appeals to a niche audience.

In the next chapter, we'll talk about how your formulations about the ideas you want to communicate (your content) shapes the choices you make about how to communicate (your form). During the process of developing the content, you are likely to get a lot more clarity about the form of your project. You will probably take into consideration your timetable, past experiences with media and technology, and access to information resources. Your motivation will matter, too. In the end, your decision making about which media type to create is likely to come down to your passion, interest, and intellectual curiosity.

Activity: Develop a Communication Strategy

To develop a communication strategy, use informal writing to answer these questions with as much clarity and concision as possible:

1) Who am I?
2) Who is the target audience?
3) How will they encounter this message?
4) What do I want them to know?
5) What do I want them to feel?
6) What do I want them to do?

4

Accessing and Analyzing Ideas

KEY IDEAS
Authors use a variety of strategies to find information, brainstorm ideas, evaluate sources, and organize material to create a coherent, high-impact multimedia message. When the power of Google and Wikipedia is combined with a sustained approach to library browsing, the results can stimulate the imagination. Finding ideas and information also comes from paying close attention to the world around you. Understanding how to make tacit knowledge explicit may involve using a variety of different types of knowledge management tools. When students analyze the print and multimedia works of others, they develop heightened awareness of the relationship between a message's form and its content. You can deepen your awareness of the many choices that authors make in controlling how audiences receive and interpret information. The key concepts and core principles of digital and media literacy help you develop critical thinking skills in responding to multimedia messages, which can be a catalyst to your own creative expression. By critically analyzing media, you can increase your knowledge by acquiring new ideas, and placing them in the context of your own life experience and career goals.

Caitlin was fascinated with makeup tutorials on YouTube, those popular videos that feature young women and girls reviewing cosmetic products and demonstrating novel techniques for face or hair care. This is a unique and very popular type of amateur media production that combines "how-to" functionality with entertainment. These *vlogs* – short for video blogs – are not difficult to produce and yet they are very popular. Four of the top 100 most subscribed-to channels on YouTube are beauty vlogs from around the world, including Michelle Phan, whose YouTube channel has over 8 million subscribers. Her 350 videos have been viewed more than 1 billion times. The talented Mariand "Yuya" Castrejon from Mexico makes over $50,000 per month in advertising revenue from her famous beauty vlog that receives more than 41 million views per month.[1]

Create to Learn: Introduction to Digital Literacy, First Edition. Renee Hobbs.
© 2017 John Wiley & Sons, Inc. Published 2017 by John Wiley & Sons, Inc.

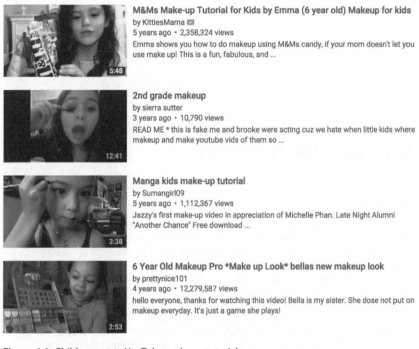

Figure 4.1 Children create YouTube makeup tutorials.

People who watch beauty vlogs are part of a robust online community. For example, Caitlin noticed that the onscreen vloggers interact directly with their viewers, asking questions or taking requests for new video content. Feeling part of an online community is a pleasurable feeling. But when she stumbled across examples of young children only 5–10 years old hosting beauty vlogs where they demonstrated beauty products (Figure 4.1), she was stunned and fascinated and curious. Would creating a beauty video at age five be considered a positive or a negative thing? Why did the parent help the child to create this? She had so many questions. She remembered that her mother had a "no makeup" rule until she was about 11. She had an "aha!" moment when she realized that this was potentially a topic she could explore for her final project in her Child Development class at the university.

Wondering about Makeup Tutorials

For many of us, Google is always the first step in the process of accessing information and ideas. Caitlin began with using Wikipedia, which had some information about the most famous beauty vloggers. This information also included citations for articles from popular magazines like *Vanity Fair* and *Forbes.* When Caitlin looked at some of these articles, she learned that the beauty industry is eager to support the most popular bloggers. But this angle on this topic – as interesting as it was – wouldn't enable her to incorporate any of the information she had been learning from her college class. Caitlin even explored Google Scholar to search for scholarly writing about beauty videos, but nothing came up.

Brainstorming with some friends, Caitlin considered her topic in relation to some larger themes, using the digital *mind mapping* tool Popplet to create a map of the connections between ideas. Figure 4.2 shows an example of a mind map, a visual representation of the relationship between ideas. Mind maps are often used as a tool for generating new ideas. As Caitlin started to brainstorm, the mind map quickly grew into a multi-pronged affair. After creating it, Caitlin was able to widen her search strategy in order to use a greater variety of keywords. This helped her to find a number of important sources. Using *keywords* including "online video," "online fame," "family videos," "children and fame," "children and gender identity," she was able to find a number of interesting sources to help her learn more.

Using these same keywords in the database of her university library, she was pleased to find a book entitled *Kids on YouTube* by Patricia Lange, a researcher who had interviewed dozens of children and teens about how they created and uploaded videos to YouTube.[2] This book turned out to be the rock upon which her whole project developed. "It was worth the trip to the library, that's for sure," she said. "These days we tend to rely on Google so much that we don't necessarily realize how much great information is in the library," she said in reflecting on her efforts to access information for this project. Her online searching led her to print media that helped her build a strong foundation for her own ideas.

The Power of Inquiry

The most interesting research questions come from the process of asking questions and paying attention to the world around us. The term of art for this process is *inquiry*. In an essay entitled, "The Pattern of Inquiry," John Dewey wrote about inquiry as a state of being confused, lost, or not knowing what to do. To address this ordinary state of being, you must ask questions about what you experience, watch, see, listen to, and read.[3] It turns out, as we will see in this chapter, that *the way you ask questions* can determine the insights and learning that result.

Sometimes it's simply a matter of framing problems by looking at them from different perspectives. For Caitlin, one effective strategy was to talk about her interest in kindergarten beauty vloggers with friends and family, who offered a

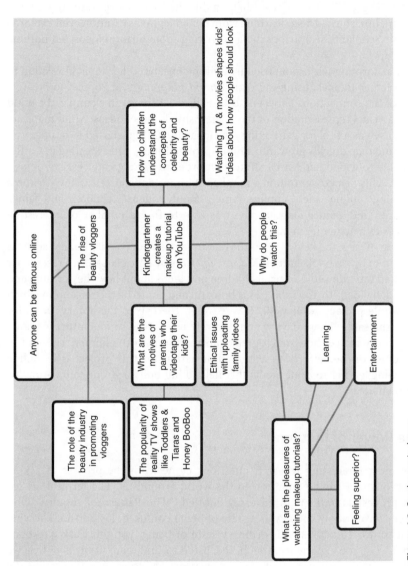

Figure 4.2 Student mind map.

variety of different information and opinions that helped her see her topic in new ways. Information literacy researcher Alison Head found that a large number of college graduates take advantage of their *personal learning networks* to learn more about a topic when they are beginning the research process.[4] A personal learning network (PLN) is an informal group of people that serve as resources to an individual for lifelong learning. For example, you may have family members or parents of your friends who have shared information and ideas with you that have shaped your knowledge. In fact, research shows that students are far more likely to rely on their friends and family than they are to reach out to their instructors or librarians. As you talk about what you are learning with the people around you, you may feel comfortable enough to acknowledge the limits of what you know, and they may ask you questions that inspire you to search for more information to answer their questions or satisfy your own curiosity.

College students get to learn about so many things as part of their course work: depending on your major, you might investigate the role of African American soldiers in the Civil War, learn about wave form mechanics, explore the state of working mothers in rural communities, gain a deeper understanding of population genetics, personality theories, or Hurricane Katrina's impact on New Orleans. For these topics, your instructor may provide resources to help you learn. But college students also conduct informal research as part of their everyday life, including what to buy, where to work, where to eat, and what kind of leisure activities to pursue. In these cases, you largely make your own decisions about the information sources you use.

The issue of how much time people spend finding information is a fascinating one. In the real world, there is always a *quality time trade-off* between the information quality you seek and the amount of time you have. Most people are willing to spend hours researching which computer or car to buy – after all, those are big-ticket items so making the right decision is important. People also tend to spend more time researching companies and potential jobs as they consider career possibilities for the future. And college students also spend time researching travel and trip planning before heading out on a vacation adventure. In fact, information literacy researchers Alison Head and Michael Eisenberg found that college students are more engaged in everyday life research than with course-related research.[5] That's because research on real-world problems has such obviously relevant consequences. But when done well, school research projects can also have important consequences for your life, work, career and citizenship.

Knowledge Management

Have you ever seen someone carrying around and writing in a little black notebook? It's a common sight on many college campuses. Some people keep track of the information in their daily life by jotting down notes from meetings, keeping "to do" lists, or just writing down things they see or hear. That's because they're aware of the creative process, since ideas come forth at any time. You may not be able to remember your best ideas if they strike you when you're having a cup of coffee, exercising at the gym, or hanging out with friends.

If you are the organized type, perhaps you have your own knowledge management system already – with binders and notebooks for each class, for example. Some people take notes on their cell phone or take photos of key documents to keep key information close at hand. Other people maintain bulletin boards near the space where they work, using sticky notes to capture key ideas. They may sometimes even color-code or organize them in clusters to see how ideas fit together. To access information and gain knowledge, it's obvious that a wide range of *access*, knowledge management skills and competencies are involved. Some dimensions of access include:

- Keyboarding
- Familiarity with hardware, storage, and file management practices
- Understanding of hyperlinking and digital space
- Competence with software applications
- The use social media, mobile, peripheral, and cloud computing tools.

Habits of mind and competencies also can be understood as access skills, including the following:

- Identifying information needs
- Using effective search and find strategies
- Troubleshooting and problem solving
- Learning how to learn
- Listening skills
- Reading comprehension.

Knowledge management is the concept used to describe all the different ways that individuals organize and manage knowledge, especially in the workplace and in the professions. Today, with the rise of so much information, researchers are discovering "best practices" in how people manage information to get things done. The simple practice of writing notes in a notebook works because when people write down their ideas, they are more likely to remember them, act on them, and manipulate them to see connections between ideas.

Researchers have discovered that there are a variety of attitudes and cultural norms that shape people's individual approaches to knowledge management, so there's no one right way to do it. People from different professions, communities, or fields may approach knowledge management in different ways.[6] In law school and medical school, for example, students develop and learn techniques for managing the large amount of information they are expected to learn, using some fantastically creative and elaborate approaches to knowledge management. Engineering students have approaches to their work that support both their critical thinking and their creativity.

There are individual and social components to knowledge management, too. You might not think about the lunchroom at your workplace as an important place of knowledge management, but the idea of *communities of practice* posits that wherever people who share a common interest in a particular domain or topic congregate, there will be a common interest in sharing information with each other. But communities of practices aren't confined to a physical location – they happen online, as in the thousands of people who share videogame cheat codes with others or the numerous Reddit communities on topics from the serious to the inane. Researchers also use online knowledge communities like Mendeley to share information and resources among peers. Sharing information helps us manage it.

Most of us are not really conscious or aware of how much knowledge we actually possess. We take it for granted. Most of the knowledge we use on a daily basis (especially in the home and in the workplace) is *tacit knowledge*: this is the knowledge that comes from personal experience and based on the stuff we do each day. For example, the world-famous linguist, Noam Chomsky, explained that although every speaker of a language has mastered and internalized the grammar of the language in order to speak fluently, most people cannot explain the rules of grammar that shape their language structure.[7]

When you have tacit knowledge of something, you are likely to be unable to provide a verbal statement of those rules or principles. It's not easy to explain to someone or to write down all that we have learned from life experience. This is why apprenticeships, mentoring, and internships are such a valuable part of learning. Some kinds of learning methods can help people reflect on experience and articulate ideas that formerly had been part of tacit knowledge.

Researchers have found that people learn most from apprenticeships when they are required to write and reflect about their experiences.[8] The concept of *reflection-on-action* can be an important tool in the workplace where people learn from their own professional experiences and make connections between theory and practice. By using evidence of past actions and events and emotions, along with experiences, actions, and responses, people who practice reflection-on-action experience dramatic advances in their professional development not just in college, but throughout their working lives.

We also learn a lot from films, television shows, news media, and social media, but we may not always be aware of what we have learned from these sources. For example, Media Education Lab researcher Elizaveta Friesem discovered that her college students did not think they knew very much about the topic of child sexual abuse. But when they gathered in small groups to discuss the films, television shows and news events about the topic, they discovered that, collectively, they possessed a significant amount of knowledge about the topic. The simple act of classroom discussion turned the tacit knowledge into *explicit knowledge.*[9]

Other strategies can be effective for making tacit knowledge explicit. For example, many business and computer science professionals use *project management software* that enable a team or group of people to collect documents, data files and other shared resources, establish "to do" lists and create deadlines, and engage in brainstorming and problem solving. When this happens, people need to explain to members of their team what they're thinking and how they're working. Since everyone on the team is aware of what each other is working on, this approach transforms tacit knowledge to explicit knowledge and increases people's ability to explain their work to others and benefit from knowing about the work of their colleagues. Online project management sites like Basecamp or Trello help teams work together; knowledge management platforms like Evernote or Mendeley enable people to gather and keep track of what they learn while reading, listening, and viewing. Knowledge management platforms are continually changing and developing, adding new features to meet the needs of people who create to learn.

Digital Knowledge Management Tools

Knowledge management software tools help you:

- Keep track of the web sites you visit
- Annotate and comment on PDF files and other documents that you read on a screen
- Share digital documents and files with members of a creative team
- Automatically create academic citations of the sources you use
- Tag documents and web pages to identify their key themes
- Create "to do" lists and assign deadlines for completing tasks
- Organize ideas and engage in online discussion about your work
- Ask questions or requests for information to other members of a global knowledge community
- Engage in collaborative writing with members of a team.

Analyzing and Evaluating Information

Knowledge is the toolbox of imagination, says Tina Seelig, Stanford business school professor and author of *inGenius: A Crash Course on Creativity.*[10] But how do people unlock that toolbox? As people gather information and make sense of it, they may consciously or unconsciously analyze and evaluate it, and this active stance towards analyzing information helps unleash the imagination. Humans have a tendency to engage in the practice of *comparison-contrast,* which is a simple but powerful way to analyze messages. You simply compare the new information to what you already know, making note of the similarities and the differences.

Most searches for information involve sizing up the information quality of a source once it is found. Is the source credible? Is the source up to date? Is the information accurate? Is the source useful? When analyzing a message, it's also important to identify the message genre or type. Messages use codes and conventions that signal how they should be interpreted or read. The form and structure of a message even communicate what kind of reading process should be used. For example, a poem has a structure of lines that are broken into phrases while a newspaper article has a headline, byline, and dateline. A scholarly article has an abstract and keywords while a blog post includes hyperlinks and tags. Learning to recognize these structural features helps you determine what kind of reading strategies to use to comprehend the work.

In some knowledge communities, some people – especially professors and librarians – have developed elaborate hierarchies about what types of knowledge are "best." You may have been told that a web site that uses a .gov or .edu extension is "better" than one that ends with .com, for example. You may have been told that a scholarly article in a library database is "better" than one that's available freely on Google Scholar. You may have been told that Wikipedia can never be used as a source of information.

But the old pyramids that created hierarchical relationships between data, information, knowledge, and wisdom are shifting as a result of the rise of *network culture,* which is characterized by the interplay between real and virtual space, shaping the way people live, work, and play.[11] While books once shaped the way we define expertise, today ideas are often generated by groups of people, working with high levels of social awareness and cooperation. Geographically dispersed, we exchange information in blogs, in threaded discussions like Reddit and The Well, and through other forms of online informal communication. Throughout human history, Weinberger notes, people have always felt there was "too much to know." We have relied on experts and authorities to guide us. But expertise and authority are themselves a type of construction, created by groups of people as a form of power. That's why we must critically analyze and evaluate information that circulates in the context of a networked community.

You can use the power of the Internet to evaluate and analyze information. New ideas about how to support student learners are reshaping the practice of information literacy. Today, no checklist that asks you to evaluate information sources with a simple yes-or-no answer will suffice. College professors may suffer from *the curse of knowledge,* having long forgotten what beginners don't know. That's why academic librarians can be so helpful in filling in the gaps in understanding between students and their professors. Researchers tell us that, whether they have been exposed to information literacy training or not, most students use self-taught criteria for assessing the quality of information they find online. It turns out that some of the practices that you tend to do automatically when you encounter information turn out to be smart and productive.

For example, people generally evaluate both the message *content* and the *form* of the message simultaneously when they encounter new information. We naturally judge a web site by both the visual design and the quality of information that's provided. For more than 2,000 years, people have been exploring the complex relationship between *what* is communicated and *how* it is communicated. For example, Aristotle first articulated the difference between *logos* (the logical content of a speech) and *lexis* (the style and delivery of a speech), while recognizing that form and content are inseparably linked and interdependent. After all, information content only can exist when it is expressed in one form or another.

For most people, when it comes to online sources, the *web site design*, more than any other factor, is most commonly used as a proxy for quality. For example, if I stumble onto a web site where the color is bright green, or where many hyperlinks are broken, or if looks like it was made in 1990, then I think it probably isn't worth my time. I quickly click away because the form doesn't match my expectations for what contemporary web sites should look like. At first glance, this may seem superficial, an example of judging a book by its cover. But actually, judging a web site by its design quality is a *heuristic*, a cognitive shortcut that is generally pretty effective in most situations. When people think of the concept of web design, they may be referring to the shape of the page layout, the colors and font styles used for the headlines, the quality of images used on the page. But often they also are describing how easy it is to navigate the page, to know where to click next, and how to find what they need.

When we evaluate a web site by the quality of the *user interface*, we consciously or unconsciously are assessing the look and feel of the web site. When a web site is well designed, it's intuitive to use and this shortens the learning curve attached with using the system. Colors, images, and symbols convey ideas about how to use the web site. Most people are unconsciously affected by the information architecture or overall structure of the web site. Simply put, it's *not* superficial to judge the quality of information by the usability of the web site. To build a web site that's intuitively easy to use takes time, money, and expertise, and a well-designed and easy-to-use web site can indicate the fiscal health of the organization or institution that is responsible for authoring it.

But the art and science of user interface is still in its infancy, and people have changing preferences for navigating through the use of menus, drop-down selections, and mouse-over actions. So you must be aware that while large corporations can afford to invest hundreds of thousands of dollars to make their web sites easy to use, independent organizations, non-profit and advocacy groups, libraries, and universities often do not have the resources to invest in usability studies or top-notch web designers to help them create the latest web designs. That doesn't mean the information they provide is low quality or useless. We must consider how differential access to economic resources may shape the design and usability of web sites we visit.

Still, for some kinds of decisions, the attractiveness and usability of a web site can be critical. For example, recognizing the different levels of investment in web design may help you judge whether it's safe to make an online purchase. It may also help you distinguish between an information source that's been created by one guy working out of his basement or a large organization with multiple employees.

Learning to Think Like a Researcher

As you start reading, viewing, and exploring ideas as part of the creative process, the following key concepts developed by the Association for College and Research Libraries offer insight on the way new knowledge is created through participation in knowledge communities.[12]

Search as Strategic Exploration. When you begin to search for information, you often don't know exactly what you are looking for. Sometimes it can be frustrating or feel like you're not making progress. It helps to have mental flexibility so that you can pursue alternate avenues or ideas that emerge as your new understanding develops. As you develop knowledge, you also develop the ability to engage in sustained searching because it becomes easier to understand what you're reading, viewing, or listening to. Sometimes browsing or accidents of serendipity also can lead to relevant sources. No two people will take exactly the same path in the process of strategic exploration or encounter the same information resources, which is partly what leads to new ideas and helps create new advances in the field.

Information Creation is a Process. As this book makes plain, when creating information, people use an iterative process of researching, creating, revising, and disseminating. Since the content and form of messages are interdependent, creators make choices about what content to include and what formats to use depending on their goals, as well as the target audiences they aim to reach. Information products are valued differently in different contexts, such as in higher education, the workplace, or in the home and community. Scholarly journal articles, for example, are considered valuable in part because there are many levels of editorial review before publication. But for some information needs, a first-person perspective that's presented on a blog post represents a highly appropriate form of valuable knowledge. Knowing how blog posts, YouTube videos, infographics, books, journals, and scholarly documents are created help people evaluate and assess the quality of the work.

Scholarship is a Conversation. When students first begin exploring a topic, they enter a type of "room" or space where communities of scholars, researchers, or professionals have been talking amongst themselves for years (and even decades and centuries). New insights and discoveries occur over time because new voices bring varied perspectives and fresh interpretations. On any topic, therefore, there may a number of different competing views and perspectives. When we access an information resource, we must ask: How might different people interpret this message? While some topics have established answers, many more are unresolved. That's why it's important to seek and examine points of view that go beyond – or even contradict – the ones that are already familiar to you. In any community, people have ideas about what sources of evidence, research methods, or ways of developing arguments matter. One of the reasons why your professors insist upon "citing your sources" is that providing attribution to relevant previous research demonstrates your awareness of being part of a knowledge community.

Research as Inquiry. It's all about asking questions. The more you know, the better your questions become. We create and share information in order to solve problems because intense and sustained collaborative effort is required to advance new knowledge in any field. Many times, this process includes points of disagreement where debate and dialogue work to deepen the conversations around knowledge. When we point out weaknesses in the information and ideas shared by others, we're not just "being critical." Asking questions is actually one of the fundamental ways we discover what new information, additional evidence, or other points of view may be needed. Experts respect peer review critique as a generous form of feedback that helps advance knowledge.

Information has Value. Today, there's so much information at our fingertips that many people think information is "free" which may affect how, when, and whether it's perceived as valuable or not. But information always circulates within an economic context where several dimensions of value may be operating all at the same time. When we access an information resource, we must ask: Who is making money or benefiting financially from this message? Obviously, the value of information isn't only in how much money it can be sold for: information may also have value that is non-monetary, helping advance civic, economic, social, cultural or personal goals. But intellectual property laws do influence how information is produced and consumed. People are responsible for making deliberate and informed choices about when to comply with and when to contest current legal and socioeconomic practices concerning how information is valued in the marketplace.

Authority is Constructed and Contextual. Authority is not an inherent property of an individual – it's a social construction in the sense that various communities recognize different types of authority. How we define the authority of a source depends on the context of our specific needs, as users.

For example, if you are looking to find a clinical psychologist to provide you with mental health counseling, their affiliation with a local hospital may be more important to establishing their authority than the number of scholarly articles they have published. When we access an information resource, we must ask: Who is the author and what is the purpose of this message? The expertise and credibility of a creator is a perception that is ultimately based on the user's information needs and the context in which the information will be used.

Unfortunately, some people in some fields may hold on to a simplistic, hierarchical view of expertise – a view that positions researchers at the top and practitioners at the bottom. According to this view, rules like "never quote from a blog post" have emerged. But that's a very misguided perception. It's better to approach the concept of expertise and authority with an attitude of informed skepticism; both novices and experts offer insights from which we can learn. Non-experts may be open to new perspectives, voices, and schools of thought that experts may overlook. Because there are many biases that privilege some sources of authority over others, it's important to critically examine all evidence – be it a short blog post or a peer-reviewed conference proceeding – and to ask relevant questions to analyze its suitability for your current situation and needs.

The Power of Representation to Shape the World

Messages are representations of the world. The term *representation* is rooted in the discipline of philosophy: it is the practice of using signs that stand in for and take the place of something else. The reason why media messages are so powerful is that viewers and readers depend on them so much. When you were little, you learned about the world through stories that may have offered moral lessons. As you have grown up, you have seen, viewed, and listened to messages that depict human relationships and behavior in certain ways. When playing videogames, you have inhabited a character and taken actions as if you were that person. Watching movies and television, you've encountered a wide range of teen heartthrobs, single dads, blonde bombshells, celebrity wanna-be's, and up-and-coming athletes. You have encountered hundreds and thousands of hours of stories about crime and law enforcement, dysfunctional families, and people striving to become famous. On your social media, you've seen people depict all manner of emotions, from deep compassion and generosity to jealousy, ambition and blind rage, using text, images gifs, animations, and more. All of these experiences have been structured as mediated representations.

The ability to create symbols to represent lived experience is a distinctive feature of humanity: for many philosophers, humans are representational animals as we create things that stand for or take the place of something else. The logical and conceptual relationship between the symbol and the thing symbolized has been studied in detail for more than 2,000 years. One of the classic tensions in both the fields of philosophy and communication concerns the question of the power of representation. In ancient Greece, Aristotle viewed representations as mostly unproblematic. After all, learning and being requires the use of language where we express how we understand the world – we create verbal representations as part of being alive.

But Plato was more skeptical, concerned at how easily language and images can be used construct *worlds of illusion* that may lead people away from reality. Plato believed that representation could foster antisocial emotions, misinform people, or encourage the imitation of evil. Under what conditions can people get confused about the distinction between representation and reality? One reason why children are thought to be more vulnerable to negative influence from viewing media violence, racism, or sexism is because they have less direct real-world experience to compare with the representations provided by mass media. Are soldiers as aggressive as the ones we represent when playing videogames? Are American dads really as clueless and bumbling as they appear on sitcoms? Is our community really as dangerous and violent as it appears from watching local news? Undoubtedly, media representations shape our understanding of the world and our sense of ourselves in it.

There's more to the power of representation. Doublespeak is a term used for political language that deliberately obscures, disguises or reverses the meaning of words. In 2017, the term "fake news" became used in ways that altered its meaning, which originally referred to the rise of political hoaxes used in the U.S. Presidential campaign. President Donald Trump started to use the term to refer to inaccuracies in mainstream news media coverage. This reversal of meaning is a classic example of doublespeak – and it can be very confusing. Some would say that the meaning of "fake news" is closer to terms like "lies" or "propaganda."[13] Euphemisms are words that are intended to "soften" ideas that make us uncomfortable or are taboo topics. When people do not know enough about a subject, they may not recognize how language can be used to conceal, distort, and mislead. That's why people must read widely and intentionally select information from a large array of sources. To detect the point of view of a representation, it can be helpful to notice how language and images can be used to intensify and downplay ideas. You do it yourself all the time: you intensify ideas through *repetition*, for example. Saying something over and over makes the idea more memorable. You downplay ideas when you omit them from your communication. You indicate a distinct point of view about an event or a group of people when you make a joke about it. Everyone does this – it's a natural part of the choices we make as we communicate with language, images, and multimedia.

Media critics like Jean Baudrillard claim that today, it's futile to even try to parse out the relationship between the symbol and the thing symbolized. He believes that media symbols have replaced all reality and that most of human experience is enacted as a *simulation*. Humans are so disconnected from the natural world that Baudrillard believes that media messages construct our reality and that reality cannot be conceptualized apart from media representations. Writing at a time when "reality TV" was in its infancy, Baudrillard observed how media messages may pretend to represent "what happens in the real world," but actually no authentic representation is taking place.[14] It's all a simulation. Reality TV shows have little relationship to any reality whatsoever and as a result, we simply don't expect representations to be accurate or connected to something in the world "out there." In this view, which is sometimes identified as a *postmodern perspective*, we are so reliant on language and media symbols to structure our perceptions that any representation of reality (whether that be a TV news report, a scholarly article, a blog post, a research report, or a video) is always already ideological, constructed by simulations.

The Practice of Critical Reading

The importance of being a critical reader, viewer, and thinker is now obvious. If we are trapped in a world of illusions, we are not likely to make good decisions about our personal and collective futures. The only way forward is to internalize the practice of critical analysis. When we first learn to read, we use texts to gain facts and information. But the critical reader is aware that any single text provides just one representation of the facts. Reading researchers have studied the behavior of skilled readers and have found that many engage in practices that advance their learning. Some simple and rather obvious things actually matter a lot: researchers have found that people read better in the morning when the lighting is good and the location is not distracting.[15] They know that reading for short periods of time is often better than long-haul reading. When people have to create notes or summaries of what they read, they always have higher levels of understanding. That's one of the fundamental reasons for the premise of this book: creating media is a good way to learn a variety of literacy competencies, especially the practice of critical reading. Here are some strategies that will help you improve your critical reading.

Approach #1: Survey the whole text

When I demonstrated my own reading technique to a group of graduate students, one remarked, "You start by skimming over the whole thing? I thought that was cheating!" Sadly, many people don't preview and scan texts before reading, as expert readers usually do. Understanding the overall structure of a text is important. Skimming, browsing, looking at the pictures, charts or tables, and flipping through the pages is the first stage in the reading process. As you do this, ask yourself, "What is the purpose of this work? How has it been designed and structured?" When you have a clear understanding of the work as a whole, you can be more strategic in how to read it.

Approach #2: Vary your reading rate

Good readers are flexible. They know that you don't always have to read every word to comprehend a written document. They strategically adjust their reading speed depending on the text and the nature of the task. They may use different reading speeds for different types of articles; they may slow down their reading speed for specific passages. Depending on your goals, the nature and difficulty of the material, and your own familiarity with the content, your reading speed must vary. Skimming and scanning are reading skills that are well developed in good readers. You can skip over examples and illustrations if you don't need them. But when you encounter an unfamiliar word, slow down and re-read to see if you can guess the meaning. Pay attention to the clues the author provides about the main arguments and ideas. Take the time to untangle long sentences and complex paragraphs. Like driving a car, knowing when to speed up and when to slow down takes practice. Fortunately, new software tools make it easier to learn to be a better, faster reader (or listener) while in college. Speed reading software can help you avoid subvocalizing words and help you read phrases and whole lines of text.

Approach #3: Use social reading practices

Most people are familiar with highlighting, underlining, and annotating text as a reading strategy that helps in identifying key content and maintains the position of being an active reader for longer periods of time. For example, a sociology professor makes highlighting into a collaborative and social activity. She asks students to refer to their assigned readings and share with the class passages they underlined and reasons for their selection. When students have to explain their choices, they demonstrate purposeful, active reading.

Of course, students underline passages in the reading for a variety of reasons. You may use highlighting to *mark main ideas* and build content knowledge by identifying the essence of the author's claims and arguments. You make *text-to-self* connections, when underlining a passage that relates to a personal experience or something you already believe. You make *text-to-text* connections, when something you have read or viewed reminds you of other things that you have read, viewed, or listened to. You may highlight ideas that address larger philosophical, sociological, scientific, practical or political questions and connections, making *text-to-world* connections.[16]

Today, digital annotation tools make it possible for small groups of readers to collaboratively annotate a document. With digital annotation tools, close reading becomes a social practice. Students can comment on a text by adding words, images, video, or other content. When they comment, others can "like" or comment on their comments, so that users are notified when other users have interacted in some way with their annotations.

What's most fascinating about digital annotation tools is that they have been adapted to work with many different kinds of texts, including videos and still images. Annotating an image, in particular, is a powerful way to develop *meta-cognitive thinking* where you sharpen your awareness of your own perceptual and cognitive processes. In Chapter 5, we'll learn how digital annotation tools may support the creative process by helping people think strategically about the relationships between ideas.

Once we start thinking of close reading as the practice of comprehending, commenting on and marking up texts (including print, visual, sound, and multimedia resources), the concept of critical reading becomes obviously relevant not just for school success but for lifelong learning. When people analyze information and ideas, they engage in practices like the following:

- Understand how symbols work
- Identify the author, genre, purpose, and point of view of a message
- Compare and contrast sources
- Evaluate credibility and quality
- Understand one's own biases and worldview.

At the same time, knowledge about the economic and political structure of information, technology, and media industries helps you:

- Recognize power relationships that shape how information and ideas circulate in culture
- Understand the economic context of information and entertainment production
- Examine the political and social ramifications of inequalities in information flows.

Five Critical Questions

As perhaps the oldest pedagogy in existence, asking questions is a great way to learn. But questioning and dialogue inevitably concern the complex relationship between teacher and student.

Media literacy educators have relied on a set of core concepts borrowed from theoretical work and scholarship in literary theory, media studies, and other fields. British scholar Len Masterman pinpointed the first key idea – the concept of *constructedness*.[17] He noted that the media are symbolic (or sign) systems which need to be actively read, and are not unproblematic, self-explanatory reflections of external reality. The media are actively involved in processes of constructing or representing "reality" rather than simply transmitting or reflecting it. In different fields, this term may have different names. For example, media studies scholar Henry Jenkins has named it the *transparency problem* and people in other fields have used still other terms for this idea.

The *core concepts of media literacy* help people gain critical distance from messages in order to deepen their ability to analyze and reflect upon them. They include the following ideas:

1) Media messages are constructed.
2) Messages are produced within economic, social, political, historical, and aesthetic contexts.
3) The process of interpretation consists of an interaction between the reader, the text, and the culture.
4) Media use language and other symbol systems with codes and conventions associated with different forms and genres of communication.
5) Media representations shape people's understanding of and participation in social reality.

Because most people use mass media, digital media, and popular culture as entertainment, we tend to engage with these texts at a very superficial level. The core concepts of media literacy invite us to think more deeply about how and why advertising, news, movies, videogames, and web sites are constructed.

Asking questions can activate and deepen critical thinking and the practice of close reading or close analysis can be a powerful tool to understand how media are constructed and how media texts construct reality. However, research shows that when teachers use questions in the classroom, they often use *closed questions*, which have only one right answer. Such questions do not advance media literacy competencies. Teachers often "go fishing" by asking questions that can only be answered in one way – with the right answer. Pay attention to the questions your professors ask and notice how many of them are open-ended, usually beginning with "how" or "why." In contrast to closed questions, *critical questions* are fundamentally interpretive – there are multiple answers possible. Your professor should be asking questions and *requesting elaboration*, asking, "Tell me more," "Why do you think that?" or "What's your reasoning?" to get more explicit information.

Media literacy is relevant to all subjects and disciplines as it is a metacognitive practice. In many fields in the humanities and social sciences, close reading is a time-honored practice of creating new knowledge. The analyst or reader engages in multiple readings or viewings of the text, looking at its social and historical contexts. For some readers, it may be useful to deconstruct the text using a variety of theoretical lenses including Marxism, feminism, poststructuralism, postmodernism, and so on. These theoretical perspectives advance insight on some ideas but they may also bring their own baggage and may be misused if people find it easier to reproduce or "parrot" the teacher's views and ideologies instead of engaging fully in the critical analysis process at a personal level.

Authors and Audiences

When students create to learn, they take on the power of authorship. When they read, view, listen, or play, they stand in the position of an active audience member. Many of the media texts we encounter are created by a collaborative team, working in highly capitalized industries including those in Silicon Valley, Hollywood, or on Madison Avenue. Other times, authors are people we know, our friends and family who send us text messages, pictures or e-mails. Rather than seeing authorship as only restricted to the industry of book publishing, we consider the full range of creative practices and norms used to compose messages – formally or informally, using language, magazines, academic writing, photography, graphic design, videogame production, narrative storytelling, journalism, web sites, and many other forms.

Just as authorship can be defined broadly, the concept of audiences is also broadly defined. Communication doesn't exist without an audience (a receiver, a reader, a viewer, a listener, or a user). When we read a work of classic literature, contemporary audiences make a connection across time and space with authors. Audiences never know for certain about the author's intended purposes and goals; people make *inferences* from clues provided in the text and our understanding of the message context. Thinking about the relationship between authors and their audiences involves consideration of ethical and social responsibilities. As a member of a particular audience, I'm aware that my attention has economic value in the marketplace and that media industries buy and sell my attention. Mass media authors sometimes make (sometimes stereotypical) assumptions about my demographic characteristics as an older, affluent, white female, just as other authors make assumptions about what teens ages 12–17 or young adults 18–25 value.

Messages and Meanings

When people compose, they create messages; when they interpret messages, they construct *meaning*. The work that authors do is reflected in their choices – authors create messages through construction, carefully considering many elements in putting together a message. The work that audiences do is reflected in their interpretations – audiences create meanings. Production and reception are linked together because each is a type of creative construction process, as authors *encode* by creating messages and audiences *decode* through making interpretations and creating meanings.

Messages in every genre and form use a set of *codes and conventions* that create expectations for audiences in their process of interpreting messages. Good readers adjust their *expectations* based on the genre and form of the expression. The meaning-making process I use in reading poetry is different than the approach I use in reading a newspaper, watching a reality TV show, reading a novel, playing a videogame, reading a text message, or listening to an audiobook. Because meaning is variable and media messages can affect our head, heart and spirit, it's important to assess the *potential effects* of media messages as they impact individuals, groups, and society. Media messages can have variable and unexpected effects as a result of differences in meaning and interpretation. Some messages that are innocuous to some people can be destructive to others. People are affected by media messages in different ways.

Representation and Realities

When students compose, they depict aspects of both their life experience and their media experience. The power of communication comes from the way that messages represent reality in some way. Since we can only experience the world through our senses, I use the plural form "realities" to reflect this idea. We can judge or evaluate the quality of a message by examining how faithfully it represents some aspect of our life experience. For example, I might compare a film that features a graduation ceremony to my own experience of graduation as a student, a parent, and a faculty member. When I lack personal experience, I still try to evaluate the realism of a message, often by comparing one message to another. For example, I've never been on a space ship. But I may judge the realism of the film, *The Martian*, by comparing and contrasting its representation of living in outer space to other representations I have encountered in science fiction movies, in science courses and at the Air and Space Museum in Washington DC. Because media representations stand in for my lack of direct experience, they can truly be said to "create the world." The ability to shape people's understanding of reality is the major source of media's political, economic, and cultural power.

Over time, representations that become familiar through constant reuse come to feel "natural" and unmediated. But media messages are always *selective and incomplete*. That's why noticing *omissions* can help people recognize the way messages selectively represent the world, which becomes a process for recognizing how social, political, and economic power are maintained through media and communication technologies.

Critically Analyzing a Mentor Text

As part of her research inquiry on children who create YouTube videos, Caitlin identified a mentor text that was created by a kindergarten child. A mentor text is a work of communication that is used to inspire or generate creative work. In this case, Caitlin found a powerful example that illustrated the broader issue she was interested in: young girls and beauty culture. She critically analyzed a YouTube video using the five critical questions of media literacy. Caitlin was able to make some good connections to ideas she encountered in her reading and life experience as she analyzed this video. To make this video, she first watched the YouTube video and made detailed notes of her key ideas. Then she practiced her talk while stopping and starting the YouTube video displayed on her computer. Using screencasting software, she created her video in a single take, as shown in Figure 4.3.

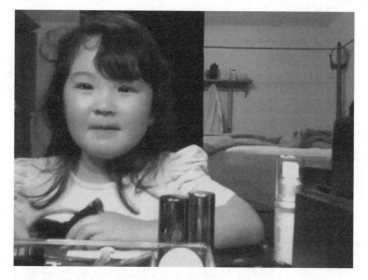

Figure 4.3 Critically analyzing a kindergarten makeup tutorial.

Kindergartener makeup tutorial: a critical analysis script – five critical questions

MADISON: I'm doing a tutorial. Hi, my name is Madison.

1 Who is the author and what is the purpose?

CAITLIN: Okay, so right off the bat, we know who the author of the video is. She just told us her name is Madison, and we know from the title of the video that she is five years old. Additionally, we saw an adult walk by in the background, and the tagline for the video refers to "my daughter," so we know that her mother was involved in publishing the video online.

MADISON: I'm using some brushes and some makeup, so this one and this – it's like a very soft brush. I like it to blend the makeup out on my eye, and I use it most of the time and this is, like, the same.

2 *What techniques are used to attract and hold your attention?*

CAITLIN: Things that are grabbing my attention in this video: She's obviously familiar with the conventions of a makeup tutorial, and because of her age, there's a novelty factor to it by having her introduce the brushes, show them to the camera, talk about the brand of the brush, talk about why she loves the brushes because they're soft and they're good at blending her nonexistent makeup onto her five-year-old face. These are all things that grab my attention about the video.

MADISON: Brushes like this, I really love for to blend the eyes and this brush is really good for blending the makeup and put blush on.

CAITLIN: Okay, so as the video goes on, Madison continues to explain what she likes about the different brushes. She never actually applies makeup to her face, but she goes through a nice tutorial of all the different brushes that she has.

3 *How might different people interpret this message?*

CAITLIN: Different ways that people could perceive this video: Obviously, it could be pure entertainment value, just the novelty factor of having someone so young speak as if they're knowledgeable about a subject like makeup. That's humorous. There's a novelty factor to it. Other people could really not like this video. It's a young person who is talking about makeup. A lot of people have really strong feelings about how old you should be when you start applying makeup and may see her as being too young or without parental supervision or parental guidance that would keep her away from adult things like makeup. Other people could actually see it as part of a *Toddlers and Tiaras* culture and maybe see it as a beneficial tutorial for young people putting on makeup, despite the fact that she never actually applies anything to her face. And still others would see it as a sign of the times and evidence of how much media consumption affects children's mentalities towards subjects such as beauty.

4 *What lifestyles, values, and points of view are represented?*

CAITLIN: This is obviously an influence of her mother, how much her mother watches beauty tutorials, and she's mimicking the attitudes of her mother in this video. As far as lifestyles and values expressed in the video, Madison has clearly been exposed to a lot of makeup tutorials. Her mom even comments in the video notes that "my daughter has watched too many makeup videos with me." The video, all at once, expresses some "do it yourself" values. She's doing things herself, putting on her own makeup. It also expresses an Internet savvy culture. She's only five, but she is able to speak with confidence. She knows how to record things. She knows where the camera is and how she can show things to the camera, and it also expresses a beauty obsessed culture that trickles down into younger age groups. The fact that she knows about brushes, she knows that brands are important, she knows what is valuable in makeup. That's apparent.

5 *What is omitted?*

CAITLIN: As far as things that are missing in the video, what's omitted? Interaction with her mom. This is clearly a video that is influenced by her mother and her mother's relationship with makeup, so it would have been a really excellent opportunity to interact, not only with media for Madison, but also with her mother, and see how you learn from older age groups. In the end, Madison never actually puts on her makeup, but she does walk us through all the steps and all the soft brushes. It's a very entertaining video. It says a lot about children and how they experience media and how they not just consume but are now able to create – and she's so funny and cute!"

Generating Ideas through Critical Analysis

When Caitlin recalled this assignment, she noticed how the discovery of the mentor text helped her get more clarity about her interest in learning more about the attitudes of parents (especially mothers) towards the practice of watching and creating YouTube beauty tutorials. "By focusing on this one example, it made it easier to generate specific ideas and it stimulated my thinking and wondering about how parents were supporting and enabling this creative practice," she wrote. "All of a sudden I realized some connections to what we were reading about parents and how their beliefs and attitudes support or discourage some forms of media use in the home." Caitlin began reflecting on beauty culture as a dynamic relationship between parents, children, the media industry, and the beauty industry. For Caitlin, critically analyzing this YouTube video and creating a screencast was a first step in her process of creating to learn. The process opened up intellectual curiosity, leading Caitlin towards more sophisticated questions than when she first began. Mentor texts, whether the take the form of a book, a web site, a video, podcast, or infographic, can help inspire our own creativity. By critically analyzing a mentor text, you can generate ideas that may develop and deepen your thinking, leading your work to become more substantive and important.

Activity: Critically Analyze a Mentor Text

Using keyword search strategies, find a mentor text that inspires your interest. This might be a work that is rich in content, or one that illustrates a phenomenon of interest, or an example of a work that is similar to what you intend to create. You may choose to work with a partner or in a small group. In informal writing or in an oral performance, describe and analyze the mentor text by responding to the following questions:

1) Who is the author and what is the purpose of this message?
2) What creative techniques are used to attract and hold audience attention?
3) How might different people interpret this message differently?
4) What lifestyles, values, and points of view are presented?
5) What is omitted?

5

Creating Ideas

KEY IDEAS
Immersing yourself in other people's ideas, it's time to create. Creating ideas starts with play and tinkering. By understanding the concept of transformative use, creative expression seems like a natural extension of the processes of reading, listening and being open, alert and attentive to your own lived experience. Once you begin, good practices for creating ideas involve keeping track of information sources, avoiding cut-and-paste plagiarism, and using medium-specific forms of citation. A deep understanding of the rights and responsibilities of authors and users in relation to intellectual property, copyright, and fair use helps you create ideas that have value. Attention to structure, design, and sequence enables your message to attract and hold your viewers, readers, listeners, and users.

When I was a freshman in college, a book changed my life. It was a slender little book, as I recall. The book freaked me out because it was like no book I had ever read before. The book itself was unusual: filled with images, the short essays were designed to be read in close interplay with the pictures. Typically, in other books I had read, the pictures were mostly decorative, not central to the argument. Weirdly, the book's main font was boldface, with emphasized words and phrases in non-bolded type, which is the opposite of how bold font is typically used in traditional written prose.

In *Ways of Seeing*, John Berger introduced me to how changes in the camera have changed our ways of understanding the world.[1] He helped me notice how the camera's "mechanical eye" could offer a multiperspectival view, showing me things that my human eyes could not see: what things looked like from far away or from both above and below a subject. The invention of the camera fundamentally changed both what we see and how we see it, Berger explained. Developing an idea from the scholar Walter Benjamin, he showed how classical artworks, once rare, precious and one of a kind, have been transformed by media technologies, where we see these works reproduced in endless variety, as postcards, in books, magazines, and in movies, web sites and television shows.

Create to Learn: Introduction to Digital Literacy, First Edition. Renee Hobbs.
© 2017 John Wiley & Sons, Inc. Published 2017 by John Wiley & Sons, Inc.

Today, we can barely grasp the more ancient ways that people once encountered images – as sacred and sublime. But in a way, by reading and looking at Berger's book, I began to imagine how works of art could be understood as forms of magic. In many ways, the author offered me my first real exposure to the idea that authors can *violate the codes and conventions* regarding how things are "supposed" to be created. I became fascinated with how de-familiarization serves as a catalyst for creativity. At the time I read *Ways of Seeing*, I didn't even realize that the book was itself a type of *transmedia*: it was an adaptation of ideas that Berger had previously presented in a British documentary television series of the same name.

Learning to see the world from a different point of view turns out to be surprisingly productive. Over time, as I got to work with creative people in film, television and video, journalism, web design, and multimedia, I noticed that many of them were comfortable with contrariness and nonconformity, willing to go against the grain. I watched with delight when screenwriter Graham Moore received the Oscar for his work on *The Imitation Game* in 2014. In his acceptance speech, he described how he felt so weird and different as a teen that he tried to kill himself. As he clutched the film industry's highest award for screenwriting, he said, "For the kid out there who feels like she's weird or she's different or she doesn't fit in anywhere, yes, you do. I promise you do. Stay weird. Stay different."[2]

Creative people take risks: they are confident in their own *creative nonconformity*. It happens when people expand their capacity for ambiguity and uncertainty, when they are willing to be open to new directions and new ways of thinking and feeling. For example, Branda Miller is now an internationally recognized media artist and professor of media arts at Rensselaer Polytechnic Institute. An Emmy award-winning editor, Branda's media artworks have been screened at festivals, museums and exhibitions, broadcast nationally and internationally, and used in community organizing and education. By combining media literacy with community education projects, she co-creates media with the people she teaches. But long ago, when I worked with her in Boston at the Taft Middle School, we spent time together teaching middle-school kids how to create videos as a way to learn about English and social studies.

Branda taught me that play was the foundation of creativity. Secure in her identity as an artist/educator, Branda created playful learning environments. She had worked with urban teens in settlement houses and juvenile detention centers to create videos as part of her "Empowerment Video Workshops." She helped young people see that they didn't have to just copy or imitate the television shows and movies they enjoyed; through play, they could comment on, critique, and respond to media and popular culture while telling their own weird little stories – in ways that sometimes disrupted viewers' expectations and sometimes shocked or surprised them. Miller was a pioneer in what is now called *youth media*, showing young people how to create, not just consume media.

In the video "Birth of a Candy Bar," the young people who created the video came together as part of a pregnancy prevention and parenting program at Henry Street Settlement in New York City. The title of the video comes from a raunchy poem and song, popular in the 1980s, that comments on sex and birth by way of names of candy bars ("nine months later, out popped a Baby Ruth"). Poetry, fast-action music, dancing, interviews, statistics, street scenes, and docudramas are combined in segments written, taped, and produced by each participant – personalizing the problems of teenage pregnancy and assessing its causes.

For Branda, the practice of unleashing creativity involved tapping into people's willingness to play around with ideas and expression, to challenge conventions, and respond to the real issues people are experiencing in life period. But the creative process also involves challenges, wrong turns, blind alleys, and disappointments. Things you try don't always work out. Ideas that you first think are exciting can come to be seen as mundane and superficial. Author Julie Burstein notes that there is a "spiral of excitement and despair" built into the creative process.[3] There is failure in the creative process. But many people report that despair and failure, as heartbreaking as they can be, are productive. These complex negative feelings actually stimulate the development of new ideas. Handling the ups and downs of the creative process are *emotional competencies* that are useful in all fields and careers and indeed they are relevant to all aspects of life.

When we think about creating and composing media, the following skills and competencies come to mind:

- Recognize the need for communication and self-expression
- Identify your own purpose, target audience, medium, and genre
- Brainstorm and generate ideas
- Compose creatively
- Play and interact
- Edit and revise your work
- Use appropriate distribution, promotion, and marketing channels
- Receive audience feedback
- Work collaboratively
- Comment, curate, and remix.

Collaboration as Play

By the time you're in college, you probably think of play and playfulness as something that happens on the margins, on the weekends and evenings, but not that much in classes. As children, we start out playing in pre-school and kindergarten, but play gradually becomes less and less a part of learning as we advance through school. But play is, as Jean Piaget has put it, the foundational work of childhood. It's how people learn best.[4] And play is often (but not always) social: we generally only like to play with people we trust and respect.

That's why, in creating to learn, there is much to be gained from working in a creative team. Having a partner can propel your own creativity to new heights. In his book, *Powers of Two: Finding the Essence of Innovation in Creative Pairs*, Joshua Wolf Shenk offers a close examination of how dyadic communication unleashes human creativity. Using a multitude of examples from across history, the sciences, and the arts, Shenk describes the stages of a creative partnership, beginning with the initial meeting that establishes the partners' mutual interests and inspires their need to create or build something together.[5] The similarities and differences between people contribute to the spark that ignites their creativity.

Unfortunately, academic culture often prizes the ideal of the lone creator, a figure that is deeply rooted in the Enlightenment mythos of the self-contained individual, working solo, perhaps even by candlelight, to create works of art. As a way to counter this stereotypical set of beliefs, filmmaker Tiffany Shlain has explored the importance of networked creativity. She examines the shift in cultural values from independence to interdependence in the short film, *Declaration of Interdependence*. In the film, which was created using an approach she calls *cloud filmmaking*, Shlain edits video contributed by people from around the world as they recite a manifesto. We see and hear people of all ages, races, and nationalities sharing ideas like: "What will be propel us forward as special is our curiosity, our ability to forgive, our ability to appreciate, our course, and our desire to connect."[6] With roots in the concept of remix culture, this film directly connects to ideas from Steven Johnson's book, *Where Good Ideas Come From*, where creativity is seen as emerging from people dipping into the cultural resources of the whole community ecology, remixing and connecting ideas.[7]

We can think of play as having cognitive, emotional, and social dimensions. Henry Jenkins and his colleagues explicitly define play as a form of learning, seeing it as the capacity to experiment with one's surroundings as a form of problem solving.[8] Play has a lot of emotional depth and complexity as well. Play has been called the "royal road" to understanding people's inner emotional life. Through play, we express our loves and hates, our hopes, ambitions, and anxieties.

To engage in play with digital media, it's important to be able to understand the web's participatory nature. Erin Reilly and her colleagues point out that teachers themselves need to participate in new digital networks, using digital media tools to "experiment with these new practices, and thus come to see the world through different eyes."[9] Becoming comfortable with *tinkering* is critical for creating to learn. In the context of this book, we can think of tinkering as *trial-and-error* experimentation with the intention of getting

something to work. Sometimes in the process of tinkering, you may accidentally stumble onto a brilliant solution. In the *do-it-yourself* or *maker movement,* people interact with digital fabrication tools, 3D printers, digital
textiles, and advanced robotics. Creating media and creating material objects
have a lot in common: both can help people learn how to learn. Education
theorists like Jerome Bruner have long described *authentic learning* as based
in the practice of constructing ideas through the process of hands-on manipulation and experimentation. Whatever the focus, learning happens when
people manipulate ideas and materials, using their hands, hearts and minds
to create.[10]

Standing on the Shoulders of Giants

You can't be a writer without being a reader, and you can't be a filmmaker
without being a film viewer. Kirby Ferguson says, "There is no creating without
being influenced by other work."[11] As you create, you will inevitably copy,
transform, and remix the ideas and experiences you have encountered. One
important way that people generate ideas and create new knowledge is by
building upon, refining, critiquing, and commenting on the work of others.

It's so easy to gather information and facts by typing a few keywords. But it
takes time and tenacity to really build knowledge that you can put to use. When
handling print materials, we use the practices of summarizing, paraphrasing,
and direct quotation. When you *summarize,* you take the author's overall main
message and express it in a concise way. When you *paraphrase,* you restate
specific facts and details that an author includes in their work. When you use a
direct quotation, you pull out a bit of prose that is directly expressed, insightful
or beautifully written, enclose it in quotation marks and incorporate it into
your paper, generally with framing commentary of your own in response to the
quote. Summarizing, analyzing, and direct quotation are a part of the creative
production process for academic work and generally for the professional workplace, too.

When handling images and multimedia, we might also use these three
techniques, but we also use copying. *Copying* is an important part of creating.
Beginning in the Middle Ages and continuing on to the twenty-first century,
copying has been essential to training in the arts. How did people learn to be
artists? You study a great masterpiece, then you copy or imitate it. Imitation
is a profoundly human response based in the psychology of how people learn.
Copying occurs as part of learning how to be creative. At film schools,
students may be assigned to reproduce a scene from *Citizen Kane, Gone with
the Wind,* or *Star Wars.* They study each shot of a particular sequence and
reproduce it exactly, paying attention to camera placement, lighting, sound,
and acting.

Attribution

As you create to learn, you will inevitably be standing of the shoulders of giants, using and building upon the ideas and creative work of others. Whether and how we identify the source of the information we use in our own creative work depends on what we're creating. The term *attribution* is used to describe the way that authors identify the source of the information they use. You might have heard the message, "Always cite your sources!" It's true: in academic discourse, much of the writing you do will require you to master norms established by various professional knowledge communities. In social science fields, it may be the norms as laid down by the American Psychological Association (APA). In fields such as history, literature, and the humanities, the community norms are defined by the Modern Language Association (MLA) or the Chicago Manual of Style formatting rules. Because these are social norms, they represent a consensus and they change slowly over time. But it's useful to know that the norms of including a *reference list,* for example, have been around for only about 100 years. The use of internal *author-date citation,* where embedded in the writing is a parenthesis at the end of the sentence that points to the source (author, date), is even more recent.

Attribution is situational and contextual. It is important to note how different forms of expression and communication use different systems of attribution. In many forms of professional communication and expression outside of higher education, attribution is not used. You have noticed already that in this book, references are presented as endnotes at the back of the book. This enables you to review what sources I used in writing this book but without the distraction that author-date citation may cause.

Attribution norms vary across genres. In professional communication like memos, for example, the source is usually described within the context of the sentence. For example, an author will write: "As Kurt Kimple from the *New York Times* explains, U.S. Muslim teens suffer from prejudice at an early age." In news reporting, there may be a photo or video credit when video footage has been received rather than directly gathered. When you use images or multimedia, your approach to attribution will vary based on the genre or form of communication you use. In infographics, for example, viewers expect that you identify the source of the data you use, but they don't expect you to identify the source of the images you select. In video public service announcements, no form of citation is generally expected, except when a fact is presented that is so startling and unusual that the audience may discount it without "proof" of validity. When you are writing a blog post or other online communication, the *hyperlink* has largely replaced the "Works Cited" list. But since hyperlinks can distract readers and actually interfere with reading comprehension, when writing online, authors have to think carefully about where, when, and how to use hyperlinks as citation. Sometimes, even in an informal piece of writing like a blog post, a Works Cited list is an ideal strategy to show your readers where you got the information you present in your work.

Remix Creativity

The term *remix* can be defined as to combine or edit existing materials to produce something new. And while the term originally applied to hip-hop music, today we are recognizing remix as the essence of creativity itself. Aristotle said it well: "There is nothing new under the sun." Human creativity is combinatorial: we take old ideas and mash them together to create new ideas. That's why, in Chapter 2, we talked about the importance of being intellectually curious and even voracious: what you read, view, and listen to becomes the "stuff" that helps you create. As NPR journalist Ann Powers explained, "This is the essence of the popular arts in America: Be a magpie, take from everywhere, but assemble the scraps and shiny things you've lifted in ways that not only seem inventive, but really do make new meanings." Through this process, Powers says, the creative individual presents her own vision in ways that "channel and transform the vast and complicated past."[12]

To understand remix creativity in context of creating to learn, it's important to have a good understanding of intellectual property, copyright, and fair use. *Intellectual property* is the term used for the bundle of legal protections that are afforded to people who create messages in fixed and tangible form. American copyright law is among the strongest in the world, and that makes sense because intellectual property is our nation's second largest export product (after military hardware).[13]

Whether you create a song, a photograph or a video on your cell phone, compose a script, or write an essay (and even your typed up lecture notes or a cartoon you scribble on a napkin), you can count on a bundle of strong legal protections that enable you to control how your work is copied, distributed, performed, or displayed. You don't need to fill in any forms, consult with an attorney, or pay any fees – the minute you complete your work, the full legal force of copyright is automatically granted to your work. You can choose to sell or give away your work, as you see fit. You can put it up on the Internet or not – in any case, your work is always protected by copyright, which means that others cannot distribute or share it without your permission, except in some circumstances.[14]

Those circumstances include the situations when a user of your creative work can claim fair use. *Fair use* is the part of copyright law that offers the balance to the strong protections offered by copyright law. After all, if an author had 100 percent control over their work at all times, true freedom of expression, which is constitutionally protected by the First Amendment, would be impossible.

Transformative Use

The concept of transformative use is at the heart of the creative process. It's a very powerful concept that can help you create to learn. The concept emerged in the 1990s as changes in society brought about by the rise of the Internet led to debates about copyright and fair use. As computing and copying technologies advanced to make it easer and easier to make copies, copyright owners began to assert their copyright with more intensity. During the 1980s, copyright legal cases became more and more unpredictable. Everyone it seemed, including creative producers of books, movies, and music, their lawyers and even judges was confused about the scope of fair use, which allows people, under some circumstances, to copy or use copyrighted materials without payment or permission. It got so confusing that even publishers became reluctant to publish certain works because they were worried about the legal risks of copyright infringement.

In 1990, Judge Pierre Leval published an influential article in the *Harvard Law Review* called "Toward a Fair Use Standard," which helped clear away much copyright confusion. He emphasized that *the purpose of copyright law* is clearly stated in the U.S. Constitution: copyright law is designed to promote new knowledge, creativity and innovation. It does that by balancing the rights of the copyright holder with the rights of the user. Leval's concept of transformative use may help you as you create to learn, since you are likely to be using bits of other people's writing, images, information and ideas in your own creative work.

Transformative use occurs when an author, filmmaker, or creative individual uses quotes, clips, or samples from copyrighted material productively to create something new. Leval explains that, to be lawful, the quoted matter must be used in a different manner or for a different purpose than the original. If you merely repackage or republish the original work, your use of the copyrighted material is not transformative. If your new creative work can be a *substitute* for the original content, then your work is not transformative. But if, on the other hand, your use of copyrighted content adds value to the original – "if the quoted matter is used as raw material, transformed in the creation of new information, new aesthetics, new insights and understandings – this is the very type of activity that the fair use doctrine intends to protect for the enrichment of society."[15]

For example, if you create a music video, using a song from Justin Bieber but adding new video footage you shot yourself, is that an example of transformative use? Depending on the particulars of the content and format, it might be argued that your new video footage creates a new insight on the song. But it also might be argued that your music video could be a substitute for the original Justin Bieber music video. If your work borrows too much from the work of others, if you are "free riding" on the creativity of others by merely repackaging what they created or exploiting their popularity or fame, then you may violate copyright. So in such a circumstance, if you want to use a large portion of the song, it would be a good idea for you to ask permission and pay a license fee.

In another case, let's say you want to make a documentary about music and politics. In your documentary, you explore the case of John Lennon's antiwar activism. You use small portions of a number of different Beatles songs combined with photojournalistic images from the protests against the Vietnam War along with interview footage you created yourself of local historians and music experts. In this case, it might be argued that your documentary creates new insights and advances new knowledge. It would be hard to claim that your documentary could ever substitute for the original songs and photojournalism that you used. So in this case, it is not necessary to ask permission or pay a license fee to use song clips or image files. You simply use the material and claim fair use. Copyright law authorizes you to create new content that includes bits of other people's ideas as you repurpose or transform those ideas. Once created, your new work also gains the full legal protection of copyright law.

Copyright and fair use cases are always handled on the particulars of the specific context and situation. As you create to learn, it's wise to ask yourself the three key questions shown in Figure 5.1 whenever you use copyrighted material in your own creative work.

CREATIVE AUTHORS MUST ASK CRITICAL QUESTIONS TO MAKE A FAIR USE DETERMINATION

1. Did my use of the work re-purpose or transform the copyrighted material? Did I add value?

2. Did I merely re-transmit the original work? Could my work serve as a substitute or replacement for the original?

Exercising fair use reasoning involves critical thinking

3. Did I use just the amount I needed in order to accomplish my purpose?

Figure 5.1 Critical questions for making a fair use determination.

There are no simple formulas to determine whether a work makes transformative use of copyrighted content. Thank goodness for that. There is important nuance in ensuring that copyright law fulfills its obligation, under the Constitution, to increase creativity and innovation. Sometimes artists can create work that is transformative even if they don't seem to add much value to the original. The concept is called *appropriation* and it is the practice of artists who take existing objects or artworks and use them, with little alteration, in their own works. They could be everyday objects or elements of other art pieces. They could be commercial advertising material, newspaper cuttings, or street debris.

Consider the work of the early twentieth-century modern artist Marcel Duchamp. In 1919, he created L.H.O.O.Q., a work of art which depicts the famous image of the Mona Lisa, created by Leonardo da Vinci. He reproduced the image and added a tiny moustache on the lady's face. The phrase L.H.O.O.Q. is a crude French phrase about a woman's sexuality. But these small changes made a major difference in the way you look at the work. Something totally new resulted from very small changes to the original.

Creativity takes so many fascinating forms. When Davy Rothbart found a note mistakenly left on his windshield, he and his friends started collecting the little notes people make as part of everyday life. He organized and curated these notes into a magazine entitled *Found*. A powerful message about humanity was expressed through Rothbart's skillful organizing of these little bits of everyday expression. His important creative contribution was in the selection and sequencing of other people's (thrown away) intellectual property.

More recently, the painter and photographer Richard Prince created an art exhibit called "New Portraits," using people's Instagram photos. He enlarged them and installed them in a gallery, selling them for as much as $90,000 each. Prince added "bizarre, esoteric, lewd, emoji-annotated comments" beneath the pictures. But these comments and the presentation of the photos as art in a gallery transformed their original purpose into something new.[16]

Even memes help illustrate the transformative power of media. Figure 5.2 shows the crying Michael Jordan meme, a Photoshop meme featuring a cutout image of former professional basketball player Michael Jordan crying during his 2009 Basketball Hall of Fame induction speech. The juxtaposition of this image over a scene from the 2016 Superbowl shows how new meaning is created from old media to offer a satirical commentary on the New England Patriots.

Figure 5.2 Crying Michael Jordan meme at the 2016 Superbowl.

Unleashing the Power of Structure

Creative people working in all forms of communication and expression think carefully about structure. Structural features include beginnings and endings, concision, and internal segmentation. Good structure can make the difference between good creative work and great creative work. In the business world, people use a *scope of work* to present the design and development of creative projects to a client or team. It's a formal written agreement that identifies "who does what" to produce creative work. A scope of work helps people communicate their intentions and goals when it comes to producing and creating anything new.

A Student's Scope of Work

This Scope of Work was developed by Tracey Dann as part of her work for Renee Hobbs in the course, "Digital Authorship."

Creative Brief. The assignment requires that we select a subset of ideas from the course readings and use still or moving images with some language to explain the ideas in a video of no more than 2 minutes in length. My thesis statement focuses on the power of digital authorship to transform student learning. Using key ideas from the Howard Rheingold book, *Net Smart*, I will be persuading people who see my video on YouTube or via my blog that learners become more self-directed and engaged when they create to learn.

Working Title. "Digital Literacy: Why it Matters"

Executive Summary. This 2-minute video introduces viewers to Anne, who hates school until her teachers activate her intellectual curiosity by using project-based learning and inquiry approaches that enable her to use the power of the Internet to create to learn. The video will be an animation that features a child and takes the form of a children's nursery rhyme. The intended target audience is elementary and middle-school teachers and the parents of school-aged children who may have outdated ideas about the uses of educational technology. It will be posted to YouTube and embedded on my blog.

Communication Strategy

Who am I? This project gives me a chance to experiment with creating a simple animated video using the Moovly platform.

What are my goals? I want to develop a concise way to explain the meaning of the term, "digital literacy" in a way that will be memorable and enjoyable to watch.

Who is my intended target audience? I'm aiming to reach elementary school teachers and parents of school age children. They may remember educational technology as incidental play after schoolwork has been completed (a la "Oregon Trail") and not be aware of new ways that digital media is used in elementary and secondary education.

What knowledge will they gain? Viewers will learn about the key features of project-based learning, which includes concepts like exploration, choice, and perceived relevance to real-world contexts. Concepts of authentic audience and analyzing messages by asking critical questions will also be referenced.

How will their emotions be activated? The viewer will feel sentimental and inspired as they see Anne change from disengaged student to real learner by finding her true voice. They will feel like they can help develop digital literacy competencies to open up possibilities for every child.

What attitudes will be reinforced or changed? This video acknowledges that traditional school assignments that are teacher-directed and competitive do not meet the needs of many learners. Those who think that technology in education is just kids working at computers on drill-and-practice math software will be surprised to see that digital literacy is focused on student choice.

What behaviors you are aiming to change? This video is informative and persuasive but there is no call to action. If viewers are able to define digital literacy as involving the concepts of choice and intellectual curiosity, that is a big enough behavior goal for a 2-minute video.

Deliverables. A 2-minute video uploaded to YouTube and posted on my blog.

Treatment. Imagine a storybook that begins: "Once upon a time, there was a girl named Anne. She had a problem. School was boring. But when Anne used the Internet to create media, she learned about many things. She was engaged in the learning process because she had choice and control over what she was learning." Using simple animation, we see the girl transform into a self-directed learner as she gains knowledge about science, geography, nature, history and much more.

Timetable/Schedule

Week 1 Milestones
- Submit this written scope of work to the instructor.

Week 2 Milestones
- Experiment with several animation platforms and decide whether to use Moovly or PowToon.

- Create a folder of images and select images to use in the video.
- Draft voiceover script.

Week 3 Milestones
- Rehearse and perform voiceover script and revise as needed.
- Select image objects and place them on pages.
- Experiment with how much movement is best for each object.

Week 4 Milestones
- Make final audio recording of voiceover and align with completed animation.
- Upload to YouTube and embed on blog.

Resources Needed. I think this project will take at least 8 hours of my time over 4 weeks. I intend to use the free version of either PowToon or Moovly animation software. I may ask a child to read the script if I can find a kid with suitable reading ability.

Constraints. The 4-week deadline is tight. I have not used Moovly before so I'm not sure what the learning curve involves.

Figure 5.3 A 2-minute animation about digital literacy by Tracey Dann. *Source*: Tracey Dann.

Structuring Time

You probably already know the importance of *beginnings and endings*. The average YouTube viewer will watch for only 3–5 seconds before deciding whether to click away. In advertising, the first 5 seconds need to break through the clutter by capturing and holding our attention, perhaps by using startling sounds, introducing an emotionally rich problem, presenting a visually stunning image, or using dramatic ambiguity. Endings satisfy us when they reveal a hidden surprise, wrap things together in a tidy way, validate our feelings, or leave us wanting more.

Concision is another a key feature of good writing, and it's also at the very center of time-based media, like film, video, and sound media. The average YouTube video is only 2 minutes long. The average length of a news segment on local television news is only 41 seconds as compared to the average length of a national television news segment, which is 2 minutes and 23 seconds.[17]

You may think concision is a twenty-first century concept, born of the past-based world of multitaskers. But as far back as 1918, William Strunk recognized the power of concision. Author of the legendary book, *The Elements of Style*, he explained, "Vigorous writing is concise. A sentence should contain no unnecessary words, a paragraph no unnecessary sentences, for the same reason that a drawing should have no unnecessary lines and a machine no unnecessary parts. This requires not that the writer make all his sentences short, or that he avoid all detail and treat his subjects only in outline, but that every word tell."[18] Unnecessary words include empty adjectives, bloated phrases, and words that make you sound pompous and self-important. You may find that you improve dramatically as a writer when you simply remove, "in my opinion" and "I believe that" from your work. Good writing helps you create concision in video and other media.

Another important component of structuring time is the use of *signaling devices* that help readers see the shape and flow of ideas. Internal structure takes different forms in different media. In writing, it takes the form of *subheads*, those bolded or italicized phrases make it easier for writers to scan an article and see the overall architecture of your argument. In infographics, internal structure is evident in the position, layout, and juxtaposition of your content elements. In time-based media like videos or podcasts, internal structure is evident in the sequence of content and the skillful use of *transitions*. For example an interview between the host and an interview subject may be followed by a first-person direct-to-camera address along with a transitional device like music or sound effects. Without the effective use of internal structure, authors make the work of interpretation more difficult for the reader, viewer, or listener.

To Create is to be Seen

In traditional classes, when you take a test to demonstrate your learning, you take a quiz or hand in your paper and eventually you get back a grade. Perhaps there is a grading rubric that offers feedback by giving you a score on some kind of scale. The typical norm for most college students is to file away the work, tell no one, and perhaps later, you look at the feedback or corrections privately.

But when you use digital media to create, your work becomes generally much more visible to others. To create is to be seen (by yourself and others) and this involves risks. There is the distinct possibility of being judged, criticized, and analyzed by others for the creative work that you produce. Your work may even be misunderstood. That's because you can't control the interpretations people will make of your work. You may intend it to be serious, and they may see it silly or superficial. You may create the work for one context (for example, a class assignment) but it may be viewed and interpreted by people in a different context.

Fear of rejection and failure can lead you to play it safe by putting constraints and self-imposed limitations on your creative work. However, this generally is an unproductive strategy. That's because your creative project (whatever that is) may indirectly reflect whatever you are trying to hide. There is always going to be a gap between your imagination and the execution of your ideas. This can be disconcerting sometimes. Psychologist Diana Pitaru says that the end product of our creative endeavor is almost always less than what we imagined. "There's always a great gap between what we thought it will be (look like, sound like) and what is," she explains. But this point is crucial:

> Every single choice you make when you create something, will take you further away from the image you had originally while at the same time leaving you with an enormous number of possibilities for what's to come. It may feel like you are at a loss when in reality it's an unrecognized gain.[19]

Deadlines and Prototyping

A fundamental component of *design thinking* involves the important role of deadlines and rapid prototyping in the creative process. As you create to learn, it's wise to take advantage of the power of deadline pressure. As one reporter told me, "Deadlines are your friend." Many creative people have discovered that creativity is like a muscle that strengthens when pushed to its limits. When Valeri Potchekailov, a Belgian graphic designer, was exploring "the grace of the deadline," she challenged herself to create one project every day for a year, posting her lab work at "One Project a Day Challenge." Her daily deadline was an artificial constraint on time that motivated her to complete projects.[20] Some people believe that the reason deadlines motivate creativity is that the time pressure prevents you from second-guessing yourself. Ironically, under deadline pressure, many people wind up creating something they would have never created if they had more time.

A *prototype* is a visual and sometimes experiential manifestation of an intangible concept. You make something that is just good enough to be understood by others. Often crude and unfinished in appearance, prototypes are sketchy, incomplete, and not polished. They are works in progress, taking the form of outlines, storyboards, drawings, user scenarios, illustrations, or even working models. Rapid prototyping is an iterative set of activities that happen very quickly as the concepts are generated brought to life.

One of the biggest mistakes that inexperienced creators make is to *overplan* their project. Overplanning can destroy creativity because when students attempt their first media production, they often develop grandiose ideas that lead them astray if they don't recognize how time, money, and access to resources naturally limit what can be accomplished. When students spend too long on planning, research and scriptwriting, they may run out of steam when it comes to the inevitable process of revision that's so essential to a production's success.

That's why most professionals suggest that students adopt an approach based on the principle of *rapid prototyping*, where creative projects move through a design-evaluation cycle that continues throughout the life of the project. This cycle is considered to be *iterative*, meaning that creative projects are continually improved as the cycle continues. In the business community, this approach enables ideas to be tested as they are developed. Flaws and problems are addressed by changes that are made during the creative production process.

Tenacity and Persistence

As you create to learn, the creative process requires *tenacity*, which is the best possible word for the habits of mind that contribute to excellence in expression and communication. When someone is tenacious, they have a firm grip on something: they don't let go. It takes stamina and persistence to create to learn. Some people give 70 percent effort but fail to achieve excellence. They are too easily satisfied with "good enough." Many authors, advertising designers, filmmakers, and engineers have described a form of *artistic discontent* when they have a terrific idea that really excites them, but in the development process, they recognize that it's just not right. Some may even start a project and then, after a little while, they abandon it. When it's too easy to give up or too easy to be mediocre, this can kill creativity. Tenacious creators celebrate artistic discontent and use it to go the extra mile to achieve excellence. As President Calvin Coolidge wrote:

> Nothing in this world can take the place of persistence. Talent will not; nothing is more common than unsuccessful people with talent. Genius will not; unrewarded genius is almost a proverb. Education will not; the world is full of educated derelicts. Persistence and determination alone are omnipotent. The slogan "press on" has solved and always will solve the problems of the human race.[21]

Activity: Create a Scope of Work Plan

If you have reflected on your identity as a digital author (Chapter 1), developed a creative brief (Chapter 2), built a communication strategy (Chapter 3), and critically analyzed a mentor text (Chapter 4), then you are ready for this culminating activity before you begin production.

The final pre-production stage is the creation of a *scope of work plan.* A scope of work document is used to communicate your vision for your project to collaborators, funders, and associates. It conceptualizes the creative project and defines the specific tasks undertaken by you (and potentially a team of people working with you). A scope of work serves as a contract between a media producer and the individual, organization, or institution that supplies funding. In the business world, the scope of work document serves as reference point for both the producer and the client. In the education world, the scope of work signals to your instructor exactly what you will be creating and how you will complete the project. The scope of work plan describes what you will create and how you will create it.

A scope of work generally includes a treatment, a detailed timetable, list of resources needed, and (sometimes) a budget. The usual structure of a scope of work plan is a document with distinct components. It often has brief sentences and makes use of tables, charts, and bullet-pointed lists. Some elements include:

Working Title. The project name should be concise and attention-getting. The working title may not necessarily be the final name of the project.

Executive Summary. This is a 3–5 sentence summary of the project that describes the concept, genre, format, and purpose along with the intended target audience and strategy for disseminating your message.

Creative Brief. This provides the background and context of your work, including the specifications of the assignment.

Project Objectives. This is a brief summary of your creative brief and communication strategy, where you identify your purpose and goals and how you expect your audience to respond to your message. What knowledge will they gain? How will their emotions be activated? What attitudes will be reinforced or changed? What behaviors you are aiming to change?

Deliverables. This is a description of what the final product will consist of, with specific details about length and format. If it is series of photographs uploaded to Instagram, the number of photographs and the types of captions provided is specified. If you're creating a podcast, describe the expected length of the program in minutes, the format (if it's an interview program or uses another format), and where the podcast will be available online. If you are creating an infographic or data visualization embedded on a web page, include information about the data sources, the variables or concepts you'll be showcasing, and details about whether the content will be a static picture or dynamic web content.

Treatment. This is a 1-page narrative description of the project. Some call it an elevator speech or a pitch. Here you capture the spirit, energy, tone, and structure of the project to communicate your artistic vision. The treatment visualizes for the reader what the user, viewer, listener, or reader will experience.

Timetable/Schedule. This is a list of tasks that need to be done, presented in rough sequence, with specific dates when you expect this step will be completed. Key events are called *milestones.* By tracking your progress of accomplishing milestones, you can move through the production process smoothly.

Resources Needed. In this section, you make a list of what resources you need to complete the project. Most create to learn projects require access to a computer and the Internet, for example. Creative projects always involve *playbor*, which is the term used to describe a combination of play and labor. Your resources should include a list of all the people who will participate in the creation of the project. These people (including yourself) are donating their time, and you can estimate the amount of time that you (and others) may spend to complete the project. You may also have other expenses, including for hardware and software, transportation expenses, or other costs. If your project includes an interview with a source, you may also need to arrange transportation to meet with the interview subject. If your project involves a voiceover, you identify your need for a voice talent and describe some ideas about how to recruit or hire this person.

Constraints. This is a description of the limitations you are aware of. For example, you may be producing your project under deadline pressure. You may have limited access to people, resources, and equipment. Good producers are aware of and candid about the limitations of the project before they begin.

6

Reflecting and Taking Action

KEY IDEAS

Communication and information have the power to change the world. How? By breaking down barriers and connecting people and ideas, we become inspired to imagine new possibilities. Through collaboration, we can work together to promote change. Communication is simultaneously personal and political. It involves the practices of metacognition, critical reflection, and "talking back" to media. In these ways, ideas can turn into actions. Through the process of creating to learn, you experience personal growth and change. And as your ideas spread, they may influence the thinking and feeling of others, helping to reshape social norms and cultural values.

Throughout history, people have used the power of communication and information to make a difference in the world. Sometimes these actions get a lot of attention and other times only a few take notice, but often such initiatives produce results. In 2012, a college student, Jake Glass, created *en Plein Air*, a documentary film designed to raise awareness about the need to protect the 88,000-acre Scotchman Peaks in Montana. By featuring the works of watercolor artists who paint in one of the largest remaining wild areas in the region, the film combines a focus on the relationship between artists and the environment. As Jake explains it, digital media storytelling helped to raise awareness of the importance of protecting this particular wild place. He is proud that the surge of public support for the wilderness designation led to endorsements from Montana Governor Brian Schweitzer.[1]

Patrick Bennett and Amanda Bennett are students at the University of Alabama, where in 2016 they created a powerful video, *How Does It Feel to be a Problem?* This short film describes the complex experience that students of color face at the university. Amanda explains, "It would be a lie to say I've never been fearful for my safety. I've been called the 'n' word by fraternity men. I've had Muslim friends called the 'n' word. Because of how Alabama is, black kids don't have the political connections to make their voices count, so they're

Create to Learn: Introduction to Digital Literacy, First Edition. Renee Hobbs.
© 2017 John Wiley & Sons, Inc. Published 2017 by John Wiley & Sons, Inc.

even more vulnerable."[2] Her filmmaking is a part of her developing identity as a young black activist.

Rameel is a North Philadelphia teenager involved with a nonprofit media arts program called POPPYN, which was developed as a university–community outreach project by Professor Barbara Ferman and media educator Nuala Cabral at Temple University. In creating a video about housing insecurity, Rameel visited the Red Cross Family Residence on North Broad Street, where he learned about the services provided to families who are in need of temporary housing, counseling, and other services. Each night, more than 800 Philadelphia children and teens sleep in temporary housing. In a city where over one-third of students don't graduate from high school and the unemployment rate is double the national average, civic media programs like POPPYN aim to inspire youth to become agents of change. This half-hour news-magazine show is produced by a team of young adults in Philadelphia. The show fills a gap in the media landscape, providing positive news about local initiatives that affect young people.

To create an episode, young people first study previous episodes, take on roles as reporters and videographers, and collaborate with peers and program staff. They conduct research about programs and services in the community that help young people, exploring topics like LGBTQ teens, the school to prison pipeline, police brutality, and urban farming. The program is distributed to over 350,000 viewers on the local public access channel. It's screened in high school and college classrooms, in community spaces, and it is spread via social media outlets.

In their episode on housing insecurity, the POPPYN team documented their visit to the Mural Arts program, Journey2Home, which uses poetry and visual arts to address the relationship between housing insecurity and domestic violence. In another segment, a student named Karee conducted man-in-the-street interviews to discover the misinformation that people have about homelessness. He asked, "What can the city do to prevent homelessness?" Another youth, Terence, visited the School District to learn about afterschool enrichment programs for school students who are experiencing homelessness.[3] By collaborating in media making, students learn camera skills, interviewing, and editing.

But even more important is that through their work, these students magnify the visibility of important community initiatives and help people learn about programs and services that help people solve the problems caused by poverty and unemployment. People who watch these shows gain information about local programs and become inspired to see their city in a new light.

Henry Jenkins and his colleagues describe how personal relationships actually help us embrace the practice of civic engagement, noting that shared media experiences often build a sense of community and activate a wish to help.[4] But it's not easy to use communication and information to make a difference in the world. How does it get done?

Metacognition and Critical Reflection

Metacognition and critical reflection are two types of reflective thinking that have the potential to transform people's ideas into actions that improve society. The philosopher John Dewey observed that people do not learn from experience. They learn from reflecting on experience.[5] In the context of digital and media literacy education, one type of reflection includes the practice of *metacognition*, which is defined as the practice of thinking about your thinking. Metacognition improves learning because it helps people transfer or adapt their learning to new contexts and tasks.

Metacognition also helps you become aware of your particular style as a learner and the choices you make about information and ideas, including how you use news media, mass media, popular culture, and digital media as resources for learning. Research has shown that people who are more aware of their strengths and weaknesses are more likely to "actively monitor their learning strategies and resources and assess their readiness for particular tasks and performances."[6] Critical reflection about the media helps us recognize how we select messages and how they circulate in culture. As a result of a combination of knowledge, skills and habits of mind, a reflective person can:

- Recognize how entertainment media communicate values and ideology
- Understand how differences in values and life experience shape people's media use and message interpretation
- Appreciate risks and potential harms of digital media
- Apply ethical judgment and social responsibility to communication situations
- Understand how concepts of "private" and "public" are reshaped by digital media
- Appreciate and respect legal rights and responsibilities (copyright, intellectual freedom, and so on)

To be a lifelong learner in a culture saturated with media and technology, it is important to gain some *critical distance* from the culture. The Canadian media theorist Marshall McLuhan famously described critical distance as the necessary but difficult process of learning to recognize the embedded values of one's cultural environment. Because mass media, digital technologies, and popular culture are immersive, it can be difficult to notice the many ways they shape consciousness. McLuhan said, "We don't know who discovered water but we are pretty sure it wasn't a fish!"[7] Think about it this way: when something in your life is as all-encompassing as water is to fish, the tendency is to not notice that it exists at all.

Because media simultaneously reflect and shape cultural values, we often don't notice how entertainment values shape our own priorities, beliefs, attitudes, and behaviors. Yet this practice is at work in our daily lives. You have probably watched hundreds of films that frequently depict violence and aggression as justified and justifiable, where little attention is paid to the consequences, pain, and suffering that results. But because justified violence is portrayed as normal, we hardly notice it. Similarly, you've watched thousands of television commercials, and each one promises happiness, power, sexual attractiveness or love, all available to us simply by making a purchase. Because in advertising, buying things is linked to personal identity, happiness, and social relationships, we rarely question the assumptions underlying these messages.

This practice of looking for how cultural values and ideologies are embedded in media messages is called *critical media pedagogy* and it enables scrutiny of the cultural impact of commercial media in maintaining dominant cultural values and ideologies. When people engage in reflection and ethical thinking, they recognize personal, corporate, and political agendas and are empowered to speak out on behalf of the missing voices and omitted perspectives in our culture.

Thick and Thin Engagement

When people use the power of communication to tackle important social issues like climate change, poverty, racism, drug abuse, or crime, the term *communication for social change* is sometimes used. Defined as a process of public and private dialogue through which people define who they are, what they want and how they can get it, communication for social change offers voice to previously unheard members of the community, where people become agents of their own change. Instead of focusing on transmitting information from outside technical experts, communication as social change emphasizes the value of dialogue, debate, and negotiation on issues that resonate with all members of the community.

Young people have always been key stakeholders in social change. Some teens and young adults engage in interactive, peer-based acts where they exert both voice and influence on issues of public concern. About half of all teens report starting, joining, or "liking" an online political group, blogging about a civic or political issue, or forwarding a politically slanted comic, video, or other content to friends or followers on a social media site.[8]

Today, many people get information about politics from humorous and satirical content that is shared through Facebook or other social media networks. Sometimes this content comes from online publications like *National Report* or television shows like *The Daily Show with Trevor Noah* or John Oliver's *This Week Tonight*. These shows feature political satire, which to be fully appreciated requires background knowledge of politics. But not everyone "gets" the joke, it seems. Researchers who investigated what happens when young people view satirical and humorous political videos that circulate online were troubled to find that many did not have a good understanding of the messages they viewed. In one study, a large sample of 15–25 year olds were randomly assigned to view one of two short, humorous YouTube videos relating to immigration policy and were then asked questions that tested their comprehension of what they had seen. Sadly, many youth were unable to demonstrate even a basic understanding of the messages conveyed in these videos.[9]

Media scholar and activist Ethan Zuckerman recognizes that a variety of civic media strategies are important to advancing social change. He uses the term *thin engagement* to describe communication and actions that take little thought and creativity. Clicking a "like" button, sharing a meme, or posting a message to your social network about issues like police brutality, racism, or a presidential campaign require little thought and creativity, but do contribute to raising awareness. By contrast, *thick engagement* is the more intense focused work of building allies, identifying solutions, and taking collective action to solve a civic problem.[10] As Eric Gordon and Paul Mihailidis explain, giving money to a homeless person on the street is thinner than figuring out which organizations do the best job of reducing hunger in your city. For social and political change to occur, thin and thick engagement are both important.[11]

Consider the case of those middle-school students in upstate New York, who videotaped themselves as they bullied a school bus monitor. When people saw the viral video of the young bullies, they were infuriated. The boys appeared on the film, calling Karen Klein, the school bus monitor, a "bitch" and a "fat ass," mocking her appearance and age, threatening her, and making her cry. The video has had more than nine million views since it was published in 2012. Clearly, many people watched the YouTube video of the harassment as a form of entertainment. But some responded with feelings of empathy towards the bus monitor. As Morgan Jaffe explained, many people were inspired to "talk back" to the bullies online. Some people just posted a comment on Facebook. Others created response videos on YouTube and engaged in discussion threads about the incident on Reddit, an online community that (based on points and voting) shares web content such as text posts, videos, and other links. Reddit and 4chan users were watching the video that the bullies had posted as well as producing discussion that incited curiosity. These factors helped the video to reach a large audience.[12]

But in reflecting on this situation, some users moved from relatively thin engagement into somewhat thicker engagement by mounting a campaign to give Karen Klein, the bus monitor, the "vacation of a lifetime" using *crowdsourced fundraising*. People were asked to chip in a little money to a web site that accepted donations. People were attracted to this idea because it represented a positive way to provide assistance to a person in need.

Thick engagement can be wonderfully unpredictable. Although the plan was to raise a modest amount of money for a vacation, because the online campaign attracted the attention of the local and national news media, the crowdsourcing web site ultimately raised more than $700,000. This enabled Karen Klein herself, who had been a victim of bullying, to move towards even thicker engagement when she decided to use the money to establish a charitable foundation to address the problem of bullying.

Risks of Civic Participation

Some scholars have argued that casual, purposeful, and strategic approaches are all markers of the *digital civic imagination*. This concept has been defined as the capacity to "imagine alternatives to current social, political or economic institutions or problems."[13] Civically engaged youth envision and take action in relation to the opportunities, challenges, and implications that new media provides. Howard Rheingold has emphasized the power of new opportunities to express one's opinion through blogging or online commenting as a robust form of public participation.[14]

But participating in online discourse comes with some very real risks. Online harassment is more likely to happen to women than men. One study found that when the gender of a username appears to be female, the user is 25 times more likely to experience harassment. Consider the work of Anita Sarkeesian, who offers her critique of the gaming industry by creating video commentaries on depictions of women in video games. She began making videos to critically analyze pop culture and in 2012, she developed a series of videos on the topic of computer games. Called *Tropes vs. Women in Video Games*, the series got attention, including from a large number of people who vandalized her Wikipedia page with gender-based slurs, tried to hack into her online accounts and reveal private information about where she lived. Some detractors have even manipulated images of Sarkeesian to make them appear pornographic, or depicted images of her being raped by video game characters. And when she was scheduled to give a speech at Utah State University in 2014, the university's administration received an e-mail threatening a mass shooting. But despite the abusive behavior she has encountered from critics, Sarkeesian's work has begun an important conversation among video game executives about the lack of female developers.[15] By building awareness of the stereotypes embedded in video games, Sarkeesian is helping the industry to change.

Feminist Frequency

Founded in 2009, Feminist Frequency is a not-for-profit, educational organization that believes media has the power to change the world. Founded by Anita Sarkeesian, the organization provides comprehensive analyses of modern media from a critical perspective on societal issues such as race, gender, and sexuality. Creating publicly available and ad-free videos, Feminist Frequency encourages viewers to critically engage with mass media and provides resources for media makers to improve their works of fiction. They advocate for the just treatment of all people online and believe that media is an essential tool for eradicating injustice. Through consciousness-raising around issues like online harassment, they help people become more responsible media users.

Reproducing the Status Quo or Challenging it

As a creator, you have a choice: the ideas and messages you create can reproduce the status quo or challenge it. Movies and television shows often copy or imitate the standard formulas found in situation comedies, dramas, or reality TV. But in Andy Kavoori's undergraduate communication classes, he encourages students to watch and critique current television shows and try to develop new kinds of programs that dismantle or challenge the many overused stereotypes that are familiar to the medium: blonde bimbos, middle-aged sex-starved cougars, corrupt cops, and bumbling, pathetic dads. One group of students developed a show about a young adult who has been raised at a casino in rural Wisconsin by his single mom who works as a croupier and a group of older men known as "the posse." By the choice of setting and characters, and the strategic decision to focus on intergenerational relationships between younger and older people, this creative idea for a television program offers a clear alternative to more typical comedy programs that feature attractive young people with professional jobs who live in upscale neighborhoods.[16]

In reflecting on his students' creative efforts, Kavoori acknowledged the tensions that exist between critical analysis and creative production. In many disciplines, these practices are even located in different parts of higher education. For example, art history majors critically analyze works of art while art majors create works of sculpture, painting, graphic design, and photography. Literature majors critically analyze classic and contemporary literature while creative writing majors write short stories, plays, and novels. Film majors make videos while media studies majors analyze videos. But these two discourses don't have to be separate. They can come together in ways that advance innovation and new knowledge. When we use our critical perspective as a stimulus for creative expression, what we create has the power to change the world.

Internet Memes for Social Change

Sharing is indeed the fundamental part of how people experience the Internet. We share what others have shared with us. One of the best ways to understand the power of sharing comes from the study of memes. *Memes* have been defined as a group of digital items that share common characteristics. Memes are shared with others, who pass them along from person to person. Some people modify or make their own versions of memes. That's why the term meme was borrowed from biology and applied to Internet culture to capture the way in which bits of content get used, modified, and transformed through social sharing. Through the sharing and repackaging process, some (but not all memes) gradually scale up to become a shared social phenomenon.

At the web site, Know Your Meme, people can track down the history of various memes to provide important background information and context to understand their meanings and how they change over time. Popular ways to circulate memes are through social media web sites like Reddit, 4chan, and Tumblr. People choose to recirculate and modify memes based on decisions that reflect issues of *identity*: the desire to be admired or respected, the need to be loved, and the desire for attention.

People may think of memes as mere entertainment, but they can be effective forms of political communication. In Portsmouth, Rhode Island, a group of adults and teens got together to create memes that could be used to address the problem of substance abuse in their community (see Figure 6.1 for an example). They recognized that tobacco use, underage drinking, and marijuana use were rampant in their community. Even though there have been some drug overdoses and fatal car crashes associated with substance abuse, little attention was being paid to the negative social consequences. Could memes for prevention help increase awareness? And would people feel comfortable sharing memes that addressed such a complex social issue?

Figure 6.1 Memes raise awareness about substance abuse prevention.

In the 2016 Presidential election, campaigns also explored ways to exploit any stumble made by the opposition. As journalist Carl Miller has written, "Memes are the new weapons in digital politics, and campaigns will look to see how they can empower their grassroots base to convert any slip-up from the opposition into a meme that continue to do them damage throughout the race." Parody Twitter accounts, parody blogs, and a whole arsenal of related images bounce around the Internet and may inflict damage by offering humiliating interpretations of political candidates.

Talking Back to Media

Nuala Cabral is a young filmmaker and media literacy educator who works to help people critically analyze and respond to stereotyped media representations of gender and race. Inspired by the work of bell hooks, a feminist scholar and activist, she has created informal discussion groups for adults, called FAAN Mail (see Figure 6.2).

When their group discussed the Netflix series, *Orange is the New Black*, a series about women in prison, attendees were invited to bring books to donate to Books Thru Bars, a non-profit organization which sends quality reading material to prisoners and encourages creative dialogue on the criminal justice system, thereby educating those living inside and outside of prison walls.

Participants described how the show aims to build empathy for the inmates and at the same time it injects entertainment values into the narrative. They compared and contrasted the representation of the characters with their interpretation of the realities of those who enter prison. Ex-offenders may experience chaos after leaving prison as a result of poverty, dysfunctional families and social relationships, and lack of economic and educational opportunity – all factors which unfortunately may lead to criminal behaviors.[17] The FAAN Mail experience provided an opportunity to discuss the television show in ways that inspired a group of people to come together to talk about the treatment of former prisoners and to address some of the legal and political issues around ex-offenders.

Figure 6.2 Talking back to the media as a form of social activism.

FAAN Mail Principles

---

1) Media both reflect and shape society.
2) Media owners should be accountable for the media that they financially support.
3) Artists have the right and responsibility to make the music/art that is meaningful to them.
4) Artists should be aware of who their audience is and how they may interpret the message.
5) Artists can no longer pretend that their selling power is only limited to products like shoes, soda, etc. They sell ideas with their lyrics, videos and other forms of media.
6) Artists should be willing and have a responsibility to have conversations, good and bad, with audiences about what they produce.
7) Audiences are not passive. We interpret media texts based on our world view. Our interpretations shape the meaning of texts.
8) Audiences have a responsibility to question and think critically about the messages we consume.
9) Audiences and consumers have a voice. We too can create our own messages.
10) Audiences are diverse. We are all races, multiple genders, at various places on the class hierarchy, and fall everywhere on the sexuality spectrum. We acknowledge that solidarity across these differences are important when addressing media representations.

Parody, Resistance, and Transgression

One timeless approach to criticism as a form of social action is the *parody*, where a work is created to imitate, make fun of, or comment on an original work. Literature, film, the visual arts, and music all use parody to comment on and critique the world in some way. Literary critics have recognized that parody can be a powerful stimulus to social change. Parody reframes our interpretation of a work in way that opens up imaginative new possibilities. One critic has noted that if creative people want to make art that makes people question the world, "it must question and expose itself."[18] As literary critic Mikhail Bakhtin has noted, parody embodies this kind of *self-reflexive stance* because the creator has a dual function as a critical reader (of the work being parodied) and an author of the work being created.[19] A good parody has a critical edge that captures our attention and invites us to see the world in a new way.

The concept of *intertextuality* is central to understanding how parody works. To understand the parody version of Justin Bieber's "Sorry," it is important to be familiar with the original song and to understand it in relation to his highly publicized screw-ups including run-ins with the Swedish police, beating up photojournalists, being late to performances, and visiting the Anne Frank house in Amsterdam and suggesting she would be a fan.

Transgression may occur, when, in the spirit of creativity, authors bump up against or overtly challenge or disrupt social norms and values. While many positive contributions are claimed for using digital media popular culture for learning, creativity can go off the rails and become utterly inane, politically incorrect, mean-spirited, and even dangerous. Transgression may occur more frequently when people work in teams, where carried away in a spirit of camaraderie, people can produce parodies that may be humorous but may also be really cruel, nasty, or inhumane. Sometimes transgressive media production can happen at school, and when it does, it can damage the shared environment, namely, school life and their teachers, according to art education scholar Paul Duncum.[20]

Given the kind of media we see on cable and broadcast television, we shouldn't be surprised if, for many, flirting with political incorrectness is part of the fun. For example, one group of college students on my campus experienced the pleasure of transgression in their collaborative effort to develop a public service announcement that could go viral. The professor had offered them the chance to make a viral video. In three weeks, if they could get a million views, they would earn an A grade. One group learned about the Random Acts of Kindness Foundation, a resource for people committed to spreading kindness. At the organization's web site, there are ideas for kind actions, ideas for educators and schools, activities and lesson plans, inspirational quotations, videos, and workplace resources. The idea is that people are inspired to small acts of kindness, and in these small acts, they are creating a powerful, synergistic action throughout the world.

Using the acronym, RAK ("random acts of kindness"), students created a short video where a variety of college boys say "show us your RAK" and college girls say things like "mine are pretty special" or "my RAK is huge." The girls proclaim, "We are not afraid to show our RAKs." In an abrupt shift in tone that moves from salacious to sweet, we then see a variety of random acts of kindness, including buying coffee for the people in line behind them.

Although the students' media production effort was well intended and the video reached 45,000 views during the semester it was produced, there was a lot of muttering on campus. The playful, racy video probably did appeal to the target audience, but plenty of people – students and faculty alike – were turned off or disgusted with the sexist tone of the public service announcement. They viewed it as a sleazy bait-and-switch that did not truly represent the core values of the "random acts of kindness" campaign. The students had used sex and sexism to attract attention creating bad feelings among some who viewed the campaign. Lesson learned: a playful approach to media production needs to be balanced with strategic thinking about the purpose, audience, the tone, and values of a message.

By the time students get to college, they often already believe that media has a variety of negative effects on individuals and society. The media is often described as a monolithic object or force, not part of us. But media messages are simply one way we share, interpret, and negotiate cultural meaning. We are free to interpret the meanings in many different ways, but *frameworks of interpretation* that are culturally constructed may limit how we interpret messages. Debates about the relative power of individuals and social forces have been rampant in the field of media studies for many years, but the Italian sociologist Antonio Gramsci's concept of *hegemony* can help us see what contributes to the overall stability of meanings and ideologies in culture.[21] People consciously or unconsciously give their consent to maintain a variety of cultural values in their everyday behavior. For example, we may unconsciously think an attractive person is more competent at their job than a less attractive person. We may form judgments about women who choose to wear high heels and makeup and men who wear ties to work. Symbolic meanings can be powerful in part because we may not always be conscious of how we ourselves have them.

Social psychologists have made an effort to measure how our prejudices and biases may unconsciously shape our perceptions. The Implicit Association Test is an online test that measures attitudes and beliefs that people may be unwilling or unable to report. By presenting a series of images and words, the test examines some of the automatic ways you may associate certain professions with certain genders or races.[22] Even when individuals may cognitively resist the idea of gender, racial, or occupational stereotypes, we are all implicated in systems of meanings that reproduce social norms. It takes a high degree of reflective thinking in order to see how we, through our talk and actions, may inadvertently contribute to perpetuating inequality and injustice.

Social Action and the Multiperspectival Imagination

How do people turn ideas into action? Producers and executives at the Walt Disney Studios have long used a method of creative imagination and brainstorming for their work in the media business community. Working in a small group or team, people move through series of thinking styles. First, the group thinks like *spectators* to gain an analytical, external view of the challenge. They describe, observe, and gather data to understand the situation. They then act as *dreamers* to brainstorm ideal solutions, using divergent thinking to conceive a large number of creative and radical ideas. In the next mode the group adopt the perspective of *realists*, reviewing the ideas they generated, selecting the best idea and constructing a plan for it. Finally, they adopt the perspective of *critics*. They take a hard look at the plans and identify weaknesses, thinking about unintended consequences or other obstacles and risks.[23] It turns out that all four of these identity positions are important to the creative process, and the critical perspective provides especially important insight that enables creative media projects to help transform society.

Disney Brainstorming Process

Spectator's View: What does the problem look like from the outside? What are the facts?

Dreamer: What are some ideal solutions? What could be done if there were no constraints?

Realist: What ideas are most practical under the circumstances? What steps need to be taken to turn the dream into reality?

Critic: What are the risks? What could go wrong? What might be some unintended consequences?

To use the power of communication and information to make a difference in the world, the following actions and habits of mind are key:

- Acknowledge the power of communication to maintain the status quo or change the world
- Participate in communities of shared interest to advance an issue
- Be a change agent in the family and workplace
- Participate in democratic self-governance
- Speak up when you encounter injustice
- Respect the law and work to change unjust laws
- Use the power of communication and information to make a difference in the world

Reflection Activity: Dream It, Do It

Because creative work involves so much effort, digital authors need to remind themselves about why the work matters. This is often accomplished through reflection, as you talk about the project with your family and friends. They may ask naive questions, like "What's this project about?" or "Why does this matter?" that can help you clarify your purpose, goals, and strategy. While some people think reflection is a solitary activity, much reflection is social. By talking with others about your project, you reflect on what's working and what still needs work.

Throughout the production process, your creative project may shift and change. For example, you may start out thinking you want to create a podcast, and then realize that a data visualization will help your work be more memorable and have more impact with your target audience. Digital authors take time to reflect on the evolution of their work by continually comparing their current conceptualization of the project with their original goals and ambitions. They imagine "best case" and "worst case" scenarios as they develop their ideas.

In informal writing or in an oral performance, reflect on these questions by imagining the future:

1) Now that you have conceptualized your project, what does it look like from the outside?
2) What problem does this project help to solve?
3) What is the most ideal way to create this project? What could be done if there were no constraints?
4) What are the most likely circumstances you will face in creating this project?
5) What steps need to be taken to turn the project idea into reality?
6) What might be some risks involved in creating this project? In distributing it? What could go wrong?
7) What might be some positive consequences of creating this project?
8) What might be some negative and/or unintended consequences of creating this project?

Part II

Nine Media Forms Help You Create to Learn

Overview of Part II

When creating to learn, you work with a variety of symbolic systems and a variety of genres to inform, persuade, and entertain target audiences.

In the chapters that follow, you'll create with digital media by accessing, analyzing, evaluating and creating messages in different forms, then use reflection to consider the personal and social impact of your work as you harness the power of communication and information. To begin, take a bit of time to explore some of the many free or low-cost multimedia production tools as you dig into the next chapters. Remember that new digital tools are constantly being developed; the sample below is just a starting place. Check the Create to Learn web site (www.createtolearn.online) for an up-to-date list of free or low-cost digital media tools to explore.

Create to Learn: Introduction to Digital Literacy, First Edition. Renee Hobbs.
© 2017 John Wiley & Sons, Inc. Published 2017 by John Wiley & Sons, Inc.

Blogs and Web Sites

WordPress – Templates make your content look amazing online
Weebly – The fastest way to create attractive web sites with a few simple steps
Wix – A simple-to-use web site creation tool

Digital Audio and Podcasting

Opinion – Free podcast recording tool for iPhone
Soundcloud – Global online tool for uploading, recording, and sharing audio content
Chirbit – Create and share audio simply and easily

Images

Picmonkey – Edit photos, make a collage and more with this simple free tool
Kizoa – Create an image slideshow with music and text on screen
Sharalike – Create an image slideshow on your iPhone, Android, or tablet

Infographics and Data Visualizations

Piktochart – Create and publish visualizations
Infogr.am – Make an infographic
Easel.ly – Create infographics with easy-to-use templates

Vlogs and Screencasts

QuickCast – Make a 3-minute screencast on your computer
Screencast-o-Matic.com – Make a video using your computer screen
Screencastify – An extension for Chrome that makes it easy to create a simple screencast

Video Production

Animoto – Make a video using still and moving images and sound
Videolicious – Make a simple movie using a free app on your smartphone
WeVideo – Simple cloud-based tool for collaborative video production
Shadow Puppet – Make a simple movie using a free app on your smartphone or your iPad

Animation

OSnap – Create stop-motion animation using your iPhone or iPad
PowToon – Make an animation using this free but powerful tool
Moovly – Animation software, free and easy to use

Remix

YouDJ – Free music remix tool lets you mix audio from your library and other sources

YouTubeMixer – Simple digital tool allows you to intercut two different YouTube videos

Storify – Curate social media to present your own perspective using digital media resources created by yourself and others

Social Media

Make a Gif – Take some pictures and make them move with this simple GIF maker

IMGFlip – Make a meme

Vine – Make a 6-second video on your cell phone

Periscope – Live broadcast to the world from your mobile phone and share your work on Twitter

7

Blogs and Web Sites

> **KEY IDEAS**
>
> There's no better way to develop your voice as a digital author than to maintain a blog or build a web site. Blogs can be used as a digital diary or a platform for social activism: the focus is on what you know, think, and feel. When you blog, you make time to think about your thinking, and you use writing to discover and reflect upon your ideas and emotions. When you build a web site, you think about your audience and their needs, organizing content to make it easy for people to find and use it. Free software makes blog and web site production a truly level playing field for publication. Because they are highly flexible forms that can incorporate all other forms of digital media, blogs and web sites can serve as your digital portfolio. All the work that you create as a digital author can be housed in one place.

Tavi Gevinson is just turning 18 and she's finally graduated from high school. When she was a young child, she paid a lot of attention to fashion, experimenting with her clothing and style, and recognizing how fashion is influenced by everything else in the culture. Like about 40 percent of American girls ages 15–17, she started a blog. But Tavi first created her blog, Style Rookie, when she was 11, and as a result of her creative efforts, Tavi got invited to Fashion Week, which generated a lot of attention from the mass media. Then Tavi created an online magazine for teen girls called *Rookie* when she was 15 years old. Like a number of teen bloggers, her distinct voice is surprisingly self-aware and politically sophisticated.

Today, numerous girls and young women represent themselves online in conventionally feminine, gender-neutral, sexualized, or feminist ways. Through blogging, people can gain visibility that leads to career opportunities. To understand the *neoliberal context* in which entrepreneurship of the self becomes important, it's important to see that in contemporary society, everything has an economic dimension, even the self. The philosopher Michel Foucault wrote about this phenomenon, noting that to get attention to the self is to increase one's value in the social and economic marketplace.

Create to Learn: Introduction to Digital Literacy, First Edition. Renee Hobbs.
© 2017 John Wiley & Sons, Inc. Published 2017 by John Wiley & Sons, Inc.

In constructing their online identities, many women and men seek to become *entrepreneurs of the self*, seeking to represent their identity in ways that attract attention and lead to professional success.[1]

Consider the rise of beauty and personal style bloggers as an increasing dimension of *merchandising*. Because some companies will give bloggers free stuff in exchange for positive mentions, even young bloggers may be aware of how their blogging and online communication can communicate a certain stance that will attract the attention of marketers seeking brand partnerships. It's OK to write good (or bad) things about products and services, of course. But bloggers are being deceptive if they mention a product, but do not mention that they received payment to write about it (or got the product for free).

Thankfully, however, blogging is more than just a device for merchandising. As a form of writing, blogging is also a personal journey of discovering your ideas. When you sit down to write, only then do you discover what you really have to say. Jeff Goins admits that he has benefited from blogging: through it, he learned what he wanted to do with his life, because by sitting down to write a blog, he took time to think about his values, goals, and needs. Blogging taught him how to practice, how to edit, and how to write for a deadline. When he says, "Blogging will change your life," it's because he found that his own most passionate interests (and he considers himself the world's foremost expert on guacamole!) could be harnessed to the needs of the larger world.

The terms "blog" and "blogging" have only been used since about 2001, about the time that Jeff Goins was deciding to become a blogger, taking a risk that involved making a commitment to write a little bit every day. He explained, "All writers are risk takers. They just are. Taking risks is how we become better at what we are called to do."

Learning to express yourself on a blog or web site is a process that takes stamina and courage. Today, there is no gatekeeper, no editor or publisher that limits a digital author: anyone can create and compose using these tools for any purpose under the sun. Moreover, there is something magical about blogs and web sites as spaces that are simultaneously private and public. The possibility of sharing one's private ideas with a potential and unknowable audience seems to inspire many to write with authenticity, depth, and precision.

Fundamentally, to understand blogging is to appreciate it as *the unedited voice of a person*, said Dave Winer, who first defined the essential features of the "weblog" in 2003.[2] Bloggers who type as they think don't need to worry about spelling, typos, and other cut-and-paste related mistakes. In fact, errors are part of what distinguishes a blog from a more polished piece of writing. Bloggers have complete freedom as digital authors, of course, but "writing without a safety net" may be stressful because without editors, "you are standing alone, with your ideas out there, with no one else to fault for those ideas."

Who Blogs?

No one knows how many blogs exist in the blogosphere, but the best estimates suggest that blog posts are published 2.2 million times each day. The popular blog platform WordPress notes that over 409 million people read WordPress blogs each month, viewing more than 21.9 billion pages A study of 7,200 blogs found three common types of people who maintain blogs.

- **Hobbyist** – 64 percent of bloggers do it for fun or to express their personal musings. They measure the success of their blog according to their level of personal satisfaction.
- **Entrepreneur** – 21 percent of bloggers blog full time or occasionally for their own company or organization, generally because their blog is a marketing tool that increases their visibility in their industry.
- **Part-Timer** – 13 percent of bloggers devote significant time to their blogs, spending more than three hours blogging each week, and sometimes even updating their blog once a day. They might earn a bit of money from advertising or merchandising but it's not their primary motive.

Blogs as Diary

Blogs can be used as a type of diary. People keep a diary (or journal) for many different reasons, but historians believe, during the Renaissance, the rise of diary-keeping was linked to the practice of silent reading, which emerged as a result of the Gutenberg revolution, where in the space of just 100 years, books began circulating widely across Europe and beyond. Before Gutenberg's printing press made them affordable, books were generally read aloud. As more and more people gained familiarity with silent reading, it encouraged introspective thinking and people were drawn to use writing to capture their response to what they had read. As part of the various Protestant reform movements that emerged throughout Europe from the late sixteenth century on, a "radical new type of personal piety was being cultivated" where people used writing as a form of prayer, meditation, and self-examination.[3]

But diaries were not just used as an aid to spiritual life; they were also used to record people's experience of "the good life." Today people may take photos of their meals and post them to their Facebook or Instagram pages, but the practice of self-documenting ordinary life originated in the seventeenth century with Samuel Pepys, a British diarist who chronicled in detail his eating, drinking, and even his sex life. For Pepys, the "keeping of records was necessary to the art of living." Over the centuries, diaries have been valued by historians, anthropologists, and literary scholars for material concerning social structures and relationships, cultural insights, and even as legitimate narrative forms.[4] Diaries bring us close to the personal experience of an individual and may help us understand history better. For example, nearly every American schoolchild has read *The Diary of Anne Frank*, which captures in heartbreaking detail the day-to-day experience of a 13-year-old girl living in hiding in Amsterdam after the Nazis invaded the country and just before the family was sent to the Bergen-Belsen concentration camp to be killed in the Holocaust.

Typing Matters

How many words per minute can you type? When people type without looking at the keyboard (a practice called *touch typing*), researchers have found that their overall level of productivity on a computer increases dramatically. Typing on a computer is an essential life skill for becoming digitally literate. This is why elementary educators work to help Grade 4 students to learn to type one page of text (250 words) in a single sitting. Sadly, some elementary schools do not teach typing, mistakenly thinking that students already know how to type because of their routine use of digital devices. But without formal training, people may develop idiosyncratic hunt-and-peck approaches that can be hard to change. By contrast, touch typing, because it approaches the speed at which people think, allows people to write more flexibly. Touch typing frees people to focus on what they are writing by activating *cognitive automaticity*, which is the ability to do things without conscious attention or awareness. There are a wide variety of web sites which allow people to take a typing test to check their typing speed and then practice to improve speed and accuracy.

Developing a Personal and Professional Voice

When I was growing up, I was told, "Write like you talk." It's advice that has served me well. I loved hearing the voices of Huck Finn and Holden Caulfield as Samuel Clemens and J.D. Salinger captured the personality of these characters in writing first-person narratives. But the "voice" you use as a writer will depend on your purpose and goals for expression and communication as well as the genre and form of your work. The concept of voice in writing is a complex, hard-to-define idea and it cannot be itemized or evaluated using a checklist. As writing scholars observe, "Voice emerges in the course of the composing process, a by-product of the writer's focus on content, purpose, diction, style and audience."[5] Research shows that readers easily recognize writing with a strong voice and that certain techniques are associated with voice, including elaborated details, sensory language, striking words, and repetition.

Perhaps you have established a writing voice already or perhaps your writing voice is emerging. When people learn to tell their own stories, they move towards *self-actualization*, a psychological concept developed by Abraham

Maslow who conceptualized it as the highest level of human need: the need to find meaning in life.[6] The concept of voice has been of importance to the development of *youth media community* in the United States, England, and around the world. During the 1970s, when the first generation of portable film and video cameras became available, filmmakers and artists and journalists entered schools and began introducing concepts in media and communication arts to students of all ages. As people perceived the need to develop both a personal, professional and civic identity, the focus of youth media production (including blogging) has shifted. During the 1990s, in the writing community, the concept of voice transformed into the idea of a writer's *stance*, a term that seemed more professional and formal as writing teachers explored the power of rhetoric "to get things done."[7] As writing programs grew in reach and scope, they migrated from schools and into the informal learning sector.

Today, youth media programs vary widely: some may focus on *personal self-expression* where media creation was seen as helping individuals (especially those from marginalized communities) develop a sense of identity-driven empowerment. Or they may focus on a more *entrepreneurial and instrumental approach* that emphasizes media creation as a ticket to professional and career success.[7] Still other programs may focus on advancing the *civic competencies of youth*, helping them use expression and communication to make a difference in the world.

In every case, the quest to express an authentic self through writing is a challenge. Too often, it's easier to simply repeat or restate what others have said, doing what is expected, familiar, or socially appropriate. This may not be truly authentic expression, however. In inviting writers to contribute to the online magazine, editors of the *Rookie* blog point out:

> Regurgitating a kewl opinion/Tumblr aesthetic can *feel* like self-actualization, but may actually keep us from learning more about our own preferences and beliefs. Can we use the Internet to express our deepest selves and not just our personal-brand selves (and can we do that without also inadvertently doing brand consulting on all the companies that look to teens on Twitter to learn how to be #modern and #young and #cool)? Is there a truly free way to use all these platforms to communicate new ideas or discover who we are?[8]

The Power of Hyperlinks

When you click on a hyperlink, you move symbolically from one "place" to another online. The hyperlink is now something so common and familiar to us as online readers that sometimes we don't even notice it as a unique and important feature of online texts. Perhaps you have already learned how to use hyperlinks in your own writing. Writers use hyperlinks for many purposes: they can be used as a way to connect texts to each other, to offer a form of citation, to provide additional information, to define unfamiliar words, to promote or market products or services, and to display the relationships between ideas. We know a word is hyperlinked if it is blue (or some other color). Images or other visual objects can also be hyperlinked.

Hyperlinks affect the reading process. Some authors, like Nicholas Carr, writer of *The Shallows*, argue that hyperlinks distract the flow of the reading process.[9] You have probably noticed that, as a reader, you make *inferences or predictions* about what you think the hyperlink will lead to. Your eyes slow down momentarily as you're reading. You may study the *anchor text* (the words or phrase that is linked) in order to decide whether or not to click on it. Depending on the type of reading activity, this inference-making process may be distracting, or it may lead you to consider the author's purpose more strategically.

Hyperlinks are a strategic device used by the author to connect one digital text to another. There are two types of hyperlinks: external links and internal links. *External links* are links to content outside the blog or web site, while *internal links* are links to content within the blog or web site. When search engines like Google evaluate the relevance of a particular web site, they take into consideration the number of web sites that point to it. External links are like a "vote" for the quality of that particular web site, increasing its trustworthiness. After all, trustworthy sites include links to other trustworthy sites. You may have noticed that you unconsciously evaluate the quality of a web site by the quality of the hyperlinks. When you're reading a document and click on a link, and it takes you somewhere you don't want to go, you're likely to have a lower opinion of the author's work overall.

Google's search engine also uses the quality of hyperlinks to determine a web site's relevance and quality. Search engines use algorithms that consider the popularity of the linking page, the relevance of the content between the source page (your blog) and the target page (the document you link to), and even the anchor text you use to create the link. When you use hyperlinks effectively in your blog or web site, your work moves up in the page ranking process, making it more findable online. Therefore, hyperlinks are a key feature of the economic structure of the Internet.

Designing Your Blog or Web Site

There are a variety of free web site platforms. To decide which is best for you and determine which one you'd like to use, you must explore them. Each web site platform has advantages and limitations and your choice will depend on whether you are looking for the easiest to use, the most stylish and professional, or the most customizable.

When you set up your blog or web site, you'll make a set of strategic decisions when you select a template. A *template* is the design frame or structure where your digital content will be placed. Templates are essentially a *CSS style formatting sheet*, which is a coding language that defines the layout of an HTML document. CSS includes instructions about fonts, colors, margins, height, width, and more.

Like everything in life, there are fashions in web design that change with the times. Your decision about a design should consider your purpose, the type of content you will be sharing, and your target audience. If you're creating a blog, your purpose is likely to be more on the side of personal expression, while if you're creating a web site, your purpose may be to inform, entertain or persuade specific groups of people, your users or audience.

Because more than half of Internet users now access content from mobile devices or tablets, check that the template you use is a *responsive design*, which automatically adjusts the layout in order for it to look good on a laptop, desktop, tablet, or mobile screen, regardless of the model or size of the device. When building a web site, you first select a template by considering these issues:

- **Content width:** some web site design templates use the full width of the screen while others use boxes to house the content.
- **Header design:** some templates enable you to show a static image with no content, which is ideal when your web site relies heavily on images that don't require much explanation. Other web site designs use a static image with content that might include a headline and a supporting paragraph that help your reader understand your web site's purpose. You may want to select a template that enables you to use a *slideshow or video header*, if you have different target audiences or ideas that you want to showcase.
- **Menu bar:** the navigation bar is perhaps the most important choice you will make in selecting a template: it's the road map that helps people find the content they're looking for. You may choose your navigation bar to be fixed and at the top of the page if your content is long and requires scrolling. Some people place their navigation bar at the bottom of the page and rely on internal hyperlinks to guide users through the web site. The most important set of navigation decisions have to do with the top-level words used. Many web site authors experiment with these choices and watch how users interact with their content.

User Experience Considerations

When blogging or creating a web site, it's important to think of the needs of the end user in relation to the content you'll include as well as the format you'll use to structure that content. People have been studying how humans interact with computers for over 50 years and we know a lot about how people use digital devices to get things done. When we first began to use computers, we relied on the keyboard and the monitor to give the computer instructions. When the mouse was developed, people were able to use "move and point" activities to tell the computer what to do; by the 1990s, computer technology became easier to use as people navigated the Word Wide Web using a *browser,* which is an application that enables you to access web content. When the iPhone introduced the touch screen in 2007, humans could interact with computers through direct manipulation.

By the early 2000s, the field of *user experience (UX) design* developed as a multidisciplinary field, arising from the practice of ergonomics, or the science of human labor. To create optimal, easy-to-use computer programs, people rely on ideas borrowed from information science, computer science, industrial design, and communication. User experience specialists help with the design of complex web sites for banking, medicine, retailing, and other fields. They study the people who use a web site and how they use it, examining how color, position on the screen, and the design of the web site affect usability. As you design your web site, use some of these UX techniques in the design process:

- **Imagine the user.** Think about the ideal user. Why will they coming to your web site? What are they seeking to find? What will they look for first? Then what will they do next? By having a clear picture of your intended target audience, you can design your web site with this person and their needs in mind.
- **Organize your content.** Make a chart of the different types of content you'll have on your web site. Identify the major categories you'll need for the web site as it grows and changes over time. Ideally, there should be no more than 3–5 categories. Too many choices leads to confusion.
- **Use contrast and size to signal importance.** Important things on your web site need higher levels of contrast between light and dark elements. Size indicates importance. Use size to indicate the most important elements on your web site. Headlines are usually the highest contrast element on a web site.
- **Use color to communicate feeling.** Don't design a web site using your personal favorite color. Instead, consider the psychological meanings of color, as red indicates excitement, blue seems peaceful, and green signals naturalness. Use color in ways that align with the web site's content, purpose, and target audience.
- **Use images of people to appeal.** More than any other kind of image, people pay attention to images of people. Try to get the eyes of the person in the image to be looking where you want people to look on the web page. This will help to draw interest and attention to your web site.
- **Use F- and Z-patterns to support online reading.** When people read, their eyes move across the page in familiar patterns. Web designers help people's

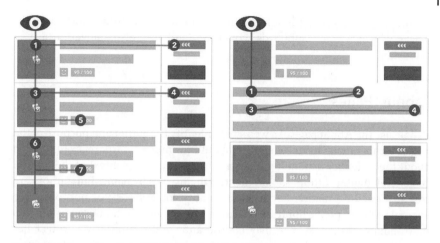

Figure 7.1 F- and Z-patterns (illustration by Dejan Ulcej).

skimming become more efficient. As Figure 7.1 shows, in an F-pattern, people scan through a list, moving down the left-hand side of the screen and moving across the screen to find key details. In a Z-pattern, people move left to right at the top of the page and then down to the next line.

Choosing Typefaces and Fonts

Writers often enjoy picking out just the right typeface for their web site. There are so many cool typefaces and new ones are continually being developed! Designers use the terms *typeface* to describe the design of the letters and the term *font* is used to refer to the particular size and weight of the letters as you choose to display them. For example, if you choose the Verdana typeface, you may select the font to be 12 point bold, regular or italic. But some beginning web designers select typefaces without fully understanding how typography intersects with browsers on cell phones, tablets, and laptops. For example, if you choose a font based on how it looks on your Mac, it may display differently on a PC. The typeface may look different if the page content is enlarged.

Typography is an excellent way to depict a visual hierarchy to help the reader recognize what's most important. In general, designers suggest that you use no more than two fonts on a page. Most recommend a serif font for *headlines* and a sans serif font for the *body text*. The strategic use of bold, italic, and color elements can also be used to help the reader skim and scan more effectively.

Eye tracking studies have consistently revealed that people read only some of the words on a web page. In general, first they scan the whole page, deciding where to focus. Then they skim, reading between 20–28 percent of the words on the page. They read the information at the top of the page most carefully. That's why headlines, subheads, concision, and careful organization are so important.

"About" Pages

People use the About page of a web site to identify the author and purpose of the page. Authors make strategic choices about how much *transparency* to provide about their identity depending on their purpose and the context of their work. In general, digital authors should identify themselves by name. But authors are free to omit information about their identity for a variety of purposes. For example, when a public librarian is writing a blog about her humorous moments or troubling challenges, she may choose anonymity in order to protect her patrons (and her job). When a young father is writing about the delights and stresses of raising a child, he may omit his name and geographic location (and use pseudonyms for the names of his children) in order to protect his family. A student may choose to withhold his or her name on a blog if the contents may interfere with career aspirations, for example. Other times, however, people omit information about their identity in order to mislead others. For example, a person may omit information about themselves on the About page in order to trick people into believing that their organization is more well-funded and professional than it really is. Indeed, a red flag of warning should be alerted in your mind when you come across an About page that does not provide the names of people who are responsible for the web site. Because users make judgments about the veracity and quality of a web site based on the construction of the About page, being transparent about your identity is generally wise.

Killer Headlines and Powerful Subheads

Web marketers, who get paid per click, have discovered many ways to attract and hold attention. That's because users make a decision within 20 seconds after arriving at your web site whether to continue to read or to escape and find other content elsewhere. To hold your attention, there is a standard battery of techniques.

Killer headlines use outrageousness to inspire a reader's curiosity. Headlines like "Why I Regret Getting Straight A's in College" and "How Formal Education Killed the Passionate Career" attract attention by going against the grain of popular opinion (and economic evidence) that college is beneficial to success in life.

Subheads are the short phrases that are often bolded and serve as a form of internal organization for many forms of writing. By using subheads, you tell the reader that you have thought about how you have organized the information and ideas and that you have a plan and purpose. Subheads provide visual organization to help a reader see the structure of your ideas. They're not just labels, however; when used well, subheads inspire curiosity, communicate your personality, and evoke emotion. They make the reader want to read more. Powerful subheads will improve your online writing and your academic writing.

On the web, some formats that rely on subheads have become ubiquitous. For example. the *listicle* (which mashes together the words "list" and "article") is a short form of writing where a list, usually featuring a number, describes content using the structure of a numbered list, as in "The 100 Best Albums of the 20th Century" or "Seven Reasons Why You Should Create a Blog." Because listicles are so easy to create, and because they often recycle information that has been published elsewhere, some critics say that this form of writing is culturally worthless. But others note that listicles are a powerful form of *curation*, where digital authors select information and help us process it by organizing it spatially in the list format.[10]

Clickbait and Online Economics

It grabs your attention. You click on it almost automatically. Sensational content usually has one of more of the following:

- sex
- violence
- children
- animals
- UFOs

The term *clickbait* began to be used frequently to refer to sensational online content beginning in 2014, according to Google Trends, which displays the frequency of online content over time. Clickbait relies on *emotional arousal*, a term used by psychologists to refer to content that engages our deepest, most primal emotions. For example, cute children and small animals are clickbait because humans are biologically predisposed to caring for small helpless creatures (like our children, for example). Similarly, when you click on something, read or watch something that makes you angry, your emotions have been hijacked in the service of profit.

Clickbait still fuels the economics of the Internet, as David Auerbach has noted in *Slate Magazine*. Today, advertising is more tightly woven into the fabric of our everyday use of social media. For example, when Facebook started inserting ads directly into people's news feeds instead of alongside it, people were far more likely to click on those sponsored links. Web sites create promotional articles for advertisers which are then published across a variety of online social media platforms. Online advertising today includes *sponsored content* (sometimes called *native advertising*) where advertising material resembles editorial content.[11] This content shows up on your social media feed, leading to a careful integration of advertising with its surrounding content. Since the goal is to make the advertising look like the other (non-sponsored) content supplied by your friends, outrageous clickbait content can seem out of place, calling attention to itself as advertising, which then diminishes its effectiveness.

Embedding Other's People Media on Your Blog

Depending on your purpose and target audience, your blog may be enhanced when images and multimedia are embedded. Of course, you can use your own photos, infographics, animation, and video on your blog. But sometimes you may need to use other people's creative work in order to express yourself. Copyright law protects the author's right to control the distribution of their work. In making a decision whether and how to use other people's creative work as part of your own blog, use *fair use reasoning* to analyze whether your use of the work is a fair use. Are you merely re-transmitting someone else's creative work? Or are you transforming it and adding value by the way in which you use it? Copyright and fair use are flexible in that they are sensitive to the particular context of how people use other people's copyrighted content in their own creative expression.

Consider your context and situation when making a fair use determination by using *strong-sense critical thinking*, a concept developed by Richard Paul where you step away from self-centeredness, and strive to treat every viewpoint equally.[12] By considering the interests of the copyright holder as having as much weight as your own interests, you should be able to evaluate whether your particular use of a copyrighted work benefits society more than it harms the copyright holder. That's the true test of copyright and fair use.

The Ethics of Blogging

Morten Rand-Hendriksen created a set of ethical principles for digital authors based on his experience teaching people how to use WordPress. He recognized that the role of being a digital author carries with it several responsibilities, noting that "the content you create today will more than likely outlast both the content's relevance and your own lifetime and it is of vital importance that it be a truthful representation of the topic at hand not only for those who access it today but for those who access it in the distant future."[13] Here are 10 key insights, adapted from his list of ethical principles:

1) **Voice your opinion**. Freedom of speech, information, publication, and expression are basic elements of a democracy. As a digital author, it is your obligation to use and protect these rights at all times.

2) **Be critical of everything, even your self**. As a digital author, you are part of the creation of free knowledge creation and discussion. It is your obligation to shed critical light on what goes on in society as well as how other digital authors, including yourself, are presenting these events.

3) **Use your power for good**. As a digital author, you can shine a light on injustices and neglect perpetrated on individuals and groups. Use this power wisely.

4) **Tell the truth**. Words and images are powerful tools that should be used with the utmost care. When publishing content, present the facts as they are, even if you disagree with them.

5) **Your opinion is your opinion**. Your opinion and interpretation of events is important and should be shared. When voicing your own or someone else's opinion or interpretation, always state it as such. Never present opinion, interpretation, or conjecture as fact.

6) **Be transparent about your allegiances**. To preserve your own trustworthiness and integrity as a digital author, always state any financial, personal, or political relationship to the subject or topic you are presenting. Bias, even if it is only perceived as such, immediately discredits your account unless you warn of it first. In simple terms; if you have a political affiliation that colors your judgment, say so; if you are employed by or received money from the subject you are covering, say so; if you were given gifts or preferential treatment in return for a positive review or commentary, say so. By stating these facts of allegiance your opinions gain informational value that would otherwise be lost in suspicion of bias.

7) **Reveal your sources.** In ensuring transparency you lend credibility to your own content as well as provide others to further pursue the facts of the matter. Be critical of your sources and seek independent verification. Before presenting information as fact, always check your source's credibility. If none can be found, state so clearly.

8) **Give credit where credit is due**. Give proper attribution when using, quoting or basing your content on the work of others. In other words, present quotes as quotes and use hyperlinks to original content that you are referencing or re-purposing.

9) **Preserve intended meaning**. When quoting or paraphrasing a statement, always ensure that the intended meaning is communicated. Never edit or change a statement in such a way that the intended meaning is changed.

10) **Admit and correct your mistakes immediately**. When an inaccuracy or error in your content is discovered by you or someone else, correct it

immediately and announce that you have done so to ensure that those who base their opinions and other content creation on the incorrect information have a chance to make corrections as well. It is your duty to uphold the truth and present fact even if that means admitting you were wrong.

Developing a Civic Identity through Blogging

The concept of citizenship has shifted as social media enables a wider range of participation in democratic process. While once civic participation involved a focus on politicians, partisanship and parties, today's citizens do more than simply bask in the media spectacle every four years. We're charged with doing more than simply monitoring our political and cultural environment. As engaged citizens, we pay attention to issues that matter to us, whether that be world peace, respect for diversity, police brutality, excessive government regulation, global warming, immigration, or other issues. We may share information about these topics with our friends and family as a way to express our identity and values. As Clay Shirky has noted, our relationships with others are the most important asset we have in the world.[14] Through blogging and communicating online, we share information that helps us express our civic identity and helps our friends, family, and others understand the issues that matter to us. Together, we appreciate the small communicative actions that bind people together in mutual interests and shared concerns. Indeed, the sense of belonging we feel when reading the blogs of people we know and respect is perhaps more influential and powerful than the work of experts. Today that sense of belonging must be recognized as a form of social power that has the capacity to change the world.

In studying how media literacy affects the civic development of young adults for many years, Paul Mihailidis observes that the journey towards civic responsibility includes the "5 As": *access* to media; *awareness* of authority, context, and credibility; *assessment* of how media portray events and issues; *appreciation* of the diversity of information, dialogue, collaboration, and voices that exist onlin; and *action* to become part of the dialogue.[15] These five processes help us de-center outside of our private interests and move towards the development of more public interests.

Such efforts are inevitably a process of "education as the practice of freedom,"[16] a concept first articulated by Paulo Freire, who recognized that true education was about intellectual curiosity and inquiry in response to the failures, inadequacies, and injustices in the world. This concern and caring, not the need for domination or control, was at the heart of the political and democratic process. All political action is ultimately relational and social. As you become more confident communicators, you are better able to share ideas and take actions that enable you to confront injustice and improve society.

Activity: Create Your Blog or Web Site

Review your Scope of Work that you developed in Part I. Keeping in mind your purpose and target audience, create a blog or web site that includes a Home Page, an About Page and one page of content. As you make decisions and create, compose a journal entry to consider these questions:

- What does your blog or web site title communicate to the user?
- What three adjectives best express the tone or feeling of your blog or web site?
- Why did you select the template you chose?
- Why did you select the images you chose?
- How do you use headlines and subheads to structure the content?

8

Digital Audio and Podcasting

KEY IDEAS

Through storytelling, we pass along bits of human wisdom that might enlighten, entertain, or inspire others. Storytellers use a set of conventions and strategies that bring their listeners into the magic circle, creating a relationship and provoking a strong emotional response. The ability to tell a story and/or read aloud well – with inflection, rhythm, appropriate tone, and energy – must be considered a fundamental competency when creating to learn. That's because most digital media makes considerable use of the human voice. Indeed, listeners gather much nuance about the personality and character of a speaker through the sound of their voice. Digital audio and podcasting also rely on the power of the expert interview, where through dialogue, we participate in a knowledge community. When music is used in radio, audio or podcast production, it can create a mood and inspire people to connect knowledge to emotion, linking thought and feeling in a way that creates a sense of emotional truth. The power of found sound and the use of man-in-the-street interview techniques can also create a sense of "being there." Through the power of spoken language, time and space can be manipulated in highly creative ways, creating an intriguing blend of authenticity and unreality that attracts audiences.

If you've listened to a podcast, you may already understand the power of oral performance as a form of entertainment. In the podcast series, *Love & Radio*, produced by Chicago Public Radio, the topics generally address a range of fascinating and quirky topics. In the 30-minute episode, "The Wisdom of Jay Thunderbolt," we're introduced to the central character, Jay Thunderbolt, AKA Charles Farrell, who was born to a middle-class family in Boston. At 12 years old, he left home and came of age on the street, participating in what he calls "low-life culture." Within the first minute of the broadcast, we hear him blow his nose within close range of the microphone as he comments on his bad sinuses. It's disgusting – but it's attention-getting and it gives us a sense of his character and personality. The podcast also includes a dialogue between the interviewer and his producer, presented as a series of interruptions to the unusual interview. At one point, the producer asks for a description of the setting of Thunderbolt's house. "It's full of 70s furniture and the carpet's matted down,"

Create to Learn: Introduction to Digital Literacy, First Edition. Renee Hobbs.
© 2017 John Wiley & Sons, Inc. Published 2017 by John Wiley & Sons, Inc.

he says. Suddenly, as we listen, we can see the creepy little apartment in our mind's eye.

We then learn that Thunderbolt runs a strip club out of his house, where it's $20 with the G-string on, $30 with the G-string off. We hear music over Thunderbolt's story about how he got involved in the adult entertainment business as a young boy. He describes stories of his encounters with "thugs and low-life" in poor and racially diverse neighborhoods in Chicago. Within minutes, we feel physically present, listening in to the encounter between the interviewer and this unusual individual. The tense and discordant music creates a sense of unease as we wonder what will happen next. "You want to borrow a pistol?" Thunderbolt soon asks the interviewer. An interruption from the producer informs us that, at this point, Thunderbolt has now pointed the pistol "about two inches from the interviewer's face."[1]

Storytellers use a set of conventions and strategies that bring their listeners into the *magic circle* to create a relationship and provoke a strong emotional response.[2] Through storytelling, we tell stories that pass along bits of human wisdom that might enlighten, entertain, or inspire others. Weaving together the audio interview with Thunderbolt with some wry commentary from the producers, combined with evocative music and sound effects, it's riveting entertainment that manages to be disturbing, provocative, and authentic, all at the same time.

Theater of the Mind

It's a powerful idea: the more personal and specific a story is, the more universal its appeal. No one knows this better than Dave Isay, who founded StoryCorps in 2003 when he opened a booth in Grand Central Terminal. Participants entered the booth where they engaged in a recorded interview experience, answering open-ended questions and sharing stories. Isay discovered that ordinary people have insightful, educational, and meaningful stories.[3] We all benefit by learning about people from different backgrounds, cultures, and religions. In listening to the stories of ordinary people, we are reminded of our shared humanity because we inevitably find much of value in the life stories and experiences of others.

The term *digital storytelling* emerged in the 1990s when Joe Lambert developed a method for teaching people how to become storytellers based on his experience with experimental and solo performance. He founded the Center for Digital Storytelling (now called Story Center), showing ordinary people how to create a script based on a personal experience, perform it as a voiceover, and then combine it with still images to create a short video. Lambert urged people to reflect on a particular life experience that was meaningful to them and write it up as if they were talking to a friend.

He found that the experience of creating a digital story affects the artist at least as much as it affects the audience. According to Lambert, "Almost any creative process helps open one's heart, but digital storytelling has a particularly useful combination of intelligences, an interdisciplinary creative form that allows any number of ways to get to people."[4] As well as enhancing the opportunities for creative academic learning, digital storytelling technology can also help people become more comfortable using technology and think more deeply about how to communicate ideas.

There are some risks to the rise of storytelling in contemporary culture, of course. Storytelling may become "a dangerous replacement for facts and reasoned argument" as a way to market products, services and ideas, notes Christian Salmon. Storytelling's inevitable and highly attractive approach to oversimplification, through the creation of a hero, villain and victim, may distort our understanding of history by contributing to the fictionalization of history.[5] For example, people may watch HBO docudramas like *Confirmation* and believe they have a full understanding of the Clarence Thomas confirmation hearings. They may see the HBO documentary *When the Levees Broke* and believe they got the whole story of Hurricane Katrina's impact in New Orleans. Media literate people know that while stories can be informative and educational, they are always selective and incomplete: reality inevitably eludes the story structure simply because reality is far more complex and multivocal than stories can ever be.

Podcasting, Radio, and the Art of the Spoken Word

Today, more and more people are listening to online radio and spoken word broadcasts available through podcasting. People listen to radio in their cars; they listen to online audio on their smartphones, using aggregators like Stitcher, which offers access to more than 40,000 radio shows and podcasts. Perhaps you use a podcast app on your smartphone or listen while you're working out at the gym. Although podcast technology has improved greatly over the years, it's still a challenge to easily share podcasts the same way we share images on Instagram. And while we know how many people download podcasts, we don't know much about how and why people listen to them.[6]

When the popular podcast *Serial* reached a milestone of five million downloads in 2014, it seemed like the success of podcasting was finally on the horizon. As a spinoff of the highly popular *This American Life*, a radio program produced by WBEZ in Chicago, the show chronicles real-life crime mysteries. Its success may be due to the way that listeners become deeply invested in the question that the producer sets out to answer: is this man innocent or guilty? Critics say the podcast illuminates the complexities of the criminal justice system and portrays the police officers, the prosecutors and the defense attorney in vivid and non-stereotypical ways, unlike typical police procedural shows. Everyone involved in the story seems to get to give their point of view.[7]

Entertainment, Emotion, and Social Commentary

It's not surprising that spoken word audio has found a growing audience: *oral performance* offers an extraordinary way to combine the goals of entertainment and persuasion. The ancient Greeks were well aware of the power of the spoken word as a part of theater, of course. They invented the creative forms of storytelling we now call *drama* and *comedy*. They recognized that stories convey ideas about social values and moral order and are situated in local contexts that reflect community opinions. Such messages can be far more powerfully persuasive than the recitation of dry and boring facts.

Ancient rhetoricians like Aristotle and Cicero formulated principles and practices that form the bedrock of our entertainment media today, recognizing that the power of narrative comes from its ability to activate a strong *emotional response*. For example, comedy is often rooted in a high-spirited celebration of human sexuality where endings are happy, despite the many accidents and mishaps that occur along the way. Tragedy occurs on the battlefield, the boardroom or the palace, where through a simple bad decision or a character flaw, people hurt others and experience suffering. We watch and feel anger, sympathy, or pity as the drama arouses our emotions.[8]

Since ancient times, storytellers have continued to evolve new ways for stories to compel audience attention and express social values. In the nineteenth century, writers like Charles Dickens made a fortune by developing dramatic novels using *episodic structure*, telling a story in small sections that were published every month. Each episode was a complete, satisfying story but the episodes fit together in an interesting way. Readers got hooked on the characters and waited eagerly in anticipation of the next installment, just as you may enjoy watching *NCIS* or *Big Bang Theory*.

Dickens was skillful in weaving ideas about the social and political issues of his time into his narratives, including child labor, the hardships of the poor and working class, the consequences of rapid industrialization, approaches to education, and the judicial system.[9] Dickens understood that popular entertainment is a powerful form of *social commentary*, much the same way that television producers like David Simon, creator of *The Wire* explores the American working class in relation to capitalism. The show has explored issues including racism, the drug trade, the Iraq War, the education system, and the paradoxes of reform and reformers. Dickens and his storytelling successors link together a fictional story with a compelling message about contemporary society.

Narrative Persuasion

It was the invention of radio advertising in the 1920s and the need to develop an *indirect revenue stream* for broadcasting that led to the development of two basic formats for persuasion: the pitch and the story. In the pitch, listeners hear an announcer telling you what the problem is and what the solution is, telling you why you want it, and how you should go about getting it. An appliance ad that screams, "You won't believe our low prices! How do we do it? We buy right!" is using a pitch. A pitch directly asks, tells, or even commands the listener to do something. In the story approach, the radio ad drops you into a mini-movie – perhaps a drama or a comedy, where characters have problems and the product is the solution.

Narratives are powerful tools of persuasion. The best advertising presents stories that *connect a product with an important human value.* Values might include the need to have status, to love and be loved, or the desire to make a difference in the world. For example, in the Wells Fargo Bank ad, "Password," we see a handsome and well-dressed African American father as he attempts to enter the imaginary castle created out of blankets by his young twin daughters. "Can I enter the kingdom of the two fairies?" he asks. "You have to say the password," says one daughter. After guessing with some silly phrases, the dad finally announces, "The password is 'Dad's coming in!'" Later, we see dad checking his cell phone in the kitchen as the narrator tells us, "You work hard to protect what matters," informing us about the authentication technology used to protect online banking accounts.[10] In watching this 30-second story, the viewer makes an inference to understand the connection between the dad and his daughters and the story of the bank protecting its customers. The work involved in connecting the story with the pitch increases the likelihood that the ad will be memorable.

In the "Look Beyond Borders" campaign, a public service announcement for Amnesty International, a true story is created. A *social experiment* is used as we see people of different ages and cultural background brought into a room where they are asked to simply look at another person directly in the eyes for four minutes. In the ad, we look into the eyes of these individuals, and over the span of four minutes, we see how they begin to feel and act towards each other, gradually interacting and growing in respect and appreciation. Only in the closing minutes do we see the names of these individuals and get to see their countries of origin: Poland, Syria, Belgium, Germany, and Somalia. On screen, we read: "Over one million refugees crossed into Europe last year. Like every-one else, they all have their stories to tell."[11] This ad persuades by capitalizing on the emotional power of the human need to love and be loved.

Stories for Social Change

Stories can be used to amplify or articulate a policy campaign and when digital stories are shared by ordinary people, they can reach large audiences and impact attitudes and behavior. For example, researchers from the Mayo Clinic worked with a group of immigrants and refugees to the United States who are living with diabetes. Community members were invited to share a story about their experiences with diabetes self-management through medication, glucose self-monitoring, physical activity, and nutrition. People report more positive feelings of self-control after participating in these workshops. In a *culture-centered approach* to health communication, it's recognized that, since health and illness are tied to an individual's cultural identity, through effective use of media, people can increase their sense of belonging and accept guidance about behaviors that improve their own health.[12]

People experience feelings of empowerment when they share their life stories with others, leading to a process called *critical consciousness*.[13] This is an approach to education and social change that takes as its starting point the life situation of the learner. For example, the Silence Speaks initiative uses digital storytelling as a tool for promoting gender equality, women's health, and human rights. In South Africa, the problems of gender-based violence and HIV/AIDS are explored by conducting digital storytelling workshops in urban and rural settings with a range of participants. The stories created by participants help empower them to make changes in their behavior and lifestyle that save lives. It's also worth noting that these digital stories have reached a real audience: since 2009, the project has reached an estimated 16 million viewers a week.[14]

Narrative Momentum: Creating Powerful Stories

How do people create stories that compel interest? Ira Glass of the NPR show, *This American Life*, talks about narrative momentum. In stories, we are introduced to people in situations, and the *plot* is the sequential presentation of events. People are hard-wired to pay attention to the linear, sequential presentation of actions that happens to other people. In a two-hour action film, for example, there are generally 24 beats or plot points. *Conflict* is essential to storytelling as it leads us to become invested in the outcome of the events. In a good narrative, characters experience conflict and stresses that lead us to care about the outcome. When we get inside the head of the storyteller to understand the point of the story, a *message* is revealed. The story has a meaning that transcends the mere revelation of actions.[15]

The Voice

To engage people in the magic circle, an effective storyteller exploits the many characteristics of the human voice. The ability to speak well – with inflection, rhythm, loudness, appropriate tone, and energy – should be considered a fundamental competency when creating to learn. The term *prosody* refers to the defining features of expressive reading, including timing, phrasing, emphasis, and intonation. Through manipulation of these elements, speakers convey aspects of meaning and make their speech lively.

If you're good at reading aloud, you're probably a good reader. That's because researchers have found an association between the quality of oral reading and general reading achievement. Skilled readers pause briefly at commas, raising their pitch at the end of questions, and lowering their pitch at the end of declarative sentences. Enunciation and pronunciation are also elements of prosody. Listening to the prosody of a reader offers a window into many aspects of reading skill.[16]

When learning to read with expression for broadcast radio or television, students generally mark up their scripts to indicate *phrase cues*. A phrase-cued text is a written passage that is divided according to natural pauses that occur in and between sentences. By visually marking how groups of words go together, slash marks are used to indicate the pause length, so that one slash mark is used between phrases and two slash marks are used between sentences. For example:

> A veteran fireman/risked his life yesterday/in a fire on Seventh Avenue/ just below 40th Street/while searching for a mother/and her infant baby/ who were thought to be in the building//The fireman/Mark Smeechone/ was injured on the right shoulder/thigh, and torso/and is in good condition at Memorial Hospital//"He's a lucky guy,"/fire chief James El-Mahaal said,/"and brave, too."//

People's *rate* of speaking varies but on average most people speak about 130–150 words per minute. Many factors influence how fast you speak including how nervous you are, the complexity of the content, mental fatigue, and the reaction of the audience. Good speakers vary their rate, going more slowly through some sentences and more rapidly through others, using pauses strategically to compel listener interests. Researchers have found that people who speak faster are perceived as more competent and more extroverted than those who speak more slowly.[17]

TV news anchors and political speakers usually read from a *teleprompter*. Free online teleprompters can help you practice reading out loud. But for many people, it takes professional coaching or lots of practice to get good at reading a script naturally. At web sites like Voices.com, you can listen to professional voice talent who offer their services for hire. Some voice performers specialize in video games, ads, documentaries, and animation. Some even specialize in voiceovers for pornography!

To become a digital storyteller, it's wise to practice varying the *emotional tones* you use when you speak or read aloud. In the voice talent industry, adjectives are used to define the emotional characteristics of difference voices. For example, John Mohr's voice is described as cool, warm, believable, real, storyteller, man's man, smooth, natural, gravitas, strong, and powerful. Joanna Koschig's voice is described as professional, informative, serious, natural, smooth, sexy, fun, smiling, playful, and energetic. If you close your eyes while listening to people read aloud, you will become more alert to the emotional tone of their voices. You can practice changing your own emotional tone by actively using your imagination as you speak.

Planning an Oral Performance

In planning an oral performance for a podcast, voiceover of other digital media may involve writing a script, performing impromptu or extemporaneous planning. Each of these three strategies, alone or used in combination, can be effective for people depending on your personality, learning style, and the context of your creative work. A *script* is a piece of writing designed to be read aloud. Once you start looking for it, scripted audio and video is all around us. Movies, television shows, news broadcasts on radio and television are scripted and either read from a teleprompter or script. Even late-night comedy shows are partially scripted. Scripting ensures that you'll get the message exactly right, often with precise timing, which can be crucial.

For many forms of media, *impromptu speech* is required. In some situations, scripts are simply inappropriate. For most radio and talk shows, for example, there is a bit of scripted material (especially the introductions, transitions, and conclusion) but most involve impromptu talk, not planned in advance, where people speak freely and have no restrictions or directions for their content. For some people, impromptu speech allows their personality to fully show through. Impromptu speech seems authentic and that's one reason why it is appealing to audiences: people are attracted to those who are presenting something they truly care about. However, impromptu conversations place demands on listeners because speakers might not be as organized and precise when speaking off the cuff. It might take you five minutes to say something that could have been said in one minute with a little more planning and preparation.

That's why most public speaking professionals specialize in *extemporaneous* speech: it's planned and organized in advance but not written out word-for-word. It's often just an outline, with key ideas and phrases in a list format. Extemporaneous speakers create a structure to help them organize and sequence their ideas. This might be a number-type *listicle* format like "Five Ways to End a War" or "Three Kinds of People I Want to Work With," but it could be as simple as a few memorable words, ideas, or phrases. Good speakers begin with the punch line, stating their main idea in the opening minutes of their talk. They acknowledge the audience by connecting their own ideas to the people who are listening. They don't worry about the precise formulation of words; instead, they focus on the ideas themselves.

The Classic Ten: Public Speaking Commandments

1) Exude confidence
2) Relax
3) Slow down
4) Simplicity is key
5) Convey passion
6) Keep your gestures to a minimum
7) Use variety of pace, pitch, and volume
8) Let it flow
9) Look at your listeners
10) Love what you do.

Source: Martha B. Ebeling, "Ten Commandments for Effective Extemporaneous Delivery"[18]

Audio Recording

Your smartphone is equipped with an audio recorder, and it's a surprisingly versatile tool for podcasting. Free apps can turn your iPhone into an audio recording device, giving you more control over sound quality. Inexpensive field audio recorders enable you to get great quality sound, too.

Compared to video, audio recording is unobtrusive but you have to get used to the microphone's proximity and be confident that your equipment will work. Professionals offer this advice: Make a test recording every time before you begin. The secret to good audio is to get the microphone close to the source of the sound. To get quality vocal recording, the microphone needs to be about six inches away from the mouth.

To get good audio, talk with the person you're talking to and don't look at the audio recording device. Don't let the person you're interviewing hold the microphone. Jay Allison, the NPR radio journalist, holds the microphone casually in the beginning, resting it against his cheek to get his source used to the idea of the microphone being close to the mouth. Don't interrupt or overlap your voice with the speaker's. Jay Allison suggests you use head nods and eye contact to encourage your source, rather than saying, "uh-huh."

Think about the location of your recording. A quiet room with carpeting and a couch will absorb sound and create the acoustical qualities of intimacy. A room with hard surfaces will create a more "public" sound. Outdoors, wind noise and street sounds will give your audio the feeling of "being there."

The Art of Asking Questions

When creating to learn, it is highly likely that you will interview a source using audio or video recording. This might be someone in your family, a friend, or a stranger, or it might be an expert that you contact via e-mail, Facebook, or Twitter. As an interviewer, you must acknowledge the power that is embedded in the role. People will often agree to be interviewed because – well, it's flattering to be asked. Appealing to people's vanity or sense of self-importance can often help you secure an interview with an expert.

Of course, it's important to learn as much as you can before inviting someone to participate in an interview. Explain your purpose before conducting the interview as this will affect how your subject responds. You might choose to conduct the interview face to face, on the telephone, or through a video chat tool. When audiotaping or videotaping people for an interview, you should use a *release form*, which is a document signed by the interview subject, where they acknowledge that you are using their voice and image. However, if you are recording sound footage of events happening in a public place, a release form is not needed.

Most interviewers agree that using short questions, offered to the interview subject one at a time, works best to yield answers that can be used for multimedia productions. Listen carefully to the answers and encourage follow-up elaboration by asking "why" and "how" questions that invite deeper thinking. Don't interrupt the interview subject. Invite the interview subject to tell a story and provide concrete examples as these will add interest and appeal to the interview.

If you're listening well, your natural curiosity will lead to ask questions based on the information the subject provides and those questions often are better than the questions you prepare in advance. NPR host Rachel Martin offers an additional piece of advice from her own experience as an interviewer: Don't be afraid of silence. Sometimes the best follow-up question is to say nothing, especially after the person has just revealed something important. She said, "More often than not, if you are quiet and give them the space to keep sharing – they will."[19]

A Release Form Gives Permission to Record Voice or Image

I grant to NAME OF CREATOR the unrestricted right to use and publish audio/video/ images of me, or in which I may be included, for editorial, trade, advertising, and any other purpose and in any manner and medium; and to edit and alter the material without restriction and without my inspection or approval. I hereby release the NAME OF CREATOR from all claims and liability relating to the material collected.

Name and Signature of Interview Subject

The Power of Sound and Music

When he was in college, Jad Abumrad studied creative writing and music composition, specializing in electronic and electroacoustic music. After he graduated, he was lucky enough to get to work with Robert Krulwich, a distinguished journalist, to create a radio program called *Radiolab*. The show offers audio explorations of scientific and philosophical questions.

Created in 2002, the show uses a new aesthetic for radio, blending dialogue, music, and sound effects into compelling documentaries on topics like the nature of numbers, the evolution of altruism, or the science of emergent phenomena within ant colonies and other complex systems. When Jad Abumrad started this creative project, all he remembers is "gut churn," the feeling of being sick to the stomach, which is a type of physiological response to stress. For some people, the creative process literally feels like life or death. "Radical uncertainty feels crummy," said Abumrad. As he sees it, blind panic and desperation are part of the creative process. It's something to live with – you can't let it stifle you.[20]

In designing the sound for the show, Abumrad created little sound signatures, combining snippets of voice, music, and noise. These little sound signatures became like a pointing arrow, suggesting a direction and conveying a particular sensibility. Gradually Abumrad and Krulwich began to see audio storytelling as a deeply personal and musical expressive form. They conducted interviews, layering them with their own reactions and interior thoughts, manipulating sounds like thought bubbles that expressed the emotional contours of the ideas. Experimentation with sound was the key to discovering what they wanted to say.

Sound and music are ideal tools for expressing a mood, attracting attention, and capturing our imagination. Almost any interview is improved with the use of *found sound.* The term refers to the creative use of sound recording at a particular location or scene. For example, Diego Stocco listened to the sounds coming from a local dry cleaning shop. He decided to experiment with recording the different sounds and composed a song made entirely from these sounds. With skillful editing and imagination, Stocco turned found sound into beautiful music.[21]

Some people even turn Internet data into music. At *The World According to Sound* podcast, audio engineers create ways for people to learn by listening to unusual sounds. For example, they created a way to represent the editing that happens on Wikipedia, as users add, modify, delete, or edit text. Whenever someone adds information, you hear a bell. And whenever information is removed, you hear a string plucked. The larger the edit, the lower the tone.[22]

Still other artists specialize in combining music, sound, and the spoken word. The radio show *Fugitive Waves* produced by the Kitchen Sisters uses a rich combination of music, sound, and spoken word. One episode called "Horses, Unicorns, and Dolphins" explores young girls' favorite fantasy animals, offering interviews with subjects including an expert who studies dolphins, the creator of the My Little Pony toy franchise, and a 10-year-old girl who loves horses. As we listen, the interviews are interspersed with horse whinnies, clips from the soundtrack of the film *National Velvet*, and even electronic music from online pet web sites.[23] The layers of music and found sound in this work conjure up mental images for the listeners. The found sound helps create a wide variety of emotional states. Listeners may feel nostalgia for childhood, a deeper sense of appreciation of the natural world, and an otherworldly feeling of the possibility of encountering magical animals like unicorns. All these emotions are well-suited to the theme of the episode.

Music is Magic

Have you ever wondered why music is so important to people all around the world? Music has superiority over language as a way to represent and communicate complex emotions, including celebration, grief, contemplation, anxiety, love, fear, anticipation and even despair.

Evolutionary psychologists believe that music was invented as a means to unite groups of people as a community. Whether we are creating or listening to music, we are participants in a shared experience. The ability to coordinate action through rhythmic beats and simple melodies is sometimes called the *yo-heave-ho* theory, reflecting the belief that music increases people's ability to work together.[24]

Another group of scholars believe that music's origins lie in the territorial defense signals we see in animals: music helps us recognize and affiliate with members of our tribe. Swedish brain researchers have identified six ways that music affects emotion, from triggering reflexes in the brain stem to triggering visual images in the cerebral cortex. When you reflect on the ability of music to manipulate the emotions, it can be pretty amazing to consider: some sounds lead people to feel sadness and other sounds lead to joy. Media may influence our sexuality. Given that adolescents spend about two hours every day listening to music and about 40 percent of pop songs are about romance and/ or sexuality, it may be that music helps channel our sexual impulses. Reviewing the shifts in sexual explicitness in popular music, some researchers conclude that popular music can teach young men to be sexually aggressive and treat women as objects while often teaching young women that their value to society is to provide sexual pleasure for others." For these reasons, music may impact people's sexual behavior.[25]

Vox Pop Interviews

The use of *man-on-the-street interviews* (called "vox pop" from the Latin *vox populi* – "voice of the people") can create a profound sense of "being there." You have heard and seen this genre of media before: it's a carefully edited selection of interviews featuring diverse individuals in public places offering their opinions or responding to a specific question. A short phrase selected by the audio editor is called a *soundbite*. It's a short clip of speech or music extracted from a longer piece of audio. Ideally, a soundbite captures the essence of what the speaker is trying to say.

Today you can collect vox pop material quite easily using an audio or video recorder on your smartphone. But when the genre was new, considerable effort was required to collect audio recordings from ordinary people in public locations. One of the earliest and most famous examples of man-in-the-street interviews occurred in December 1941 when fieldworkers were collecting recordings of American folk music for the Library of Congress's Archive of American Folk Songs. One day after the Pearl Harbor bombing, the assistant in charge sent telegrams to his team, asking them to collect reactions to the bombing and the subsequent declaration of war by the United States. Back then, magnetic audiotape had not yet been invented, so the interviews were recorded using portable instantaneous direct-to-disc recorders that weighed about 100 lbs. During those days, audio was recorded on an acetate disk that looked like a vinyl record.[26]

To construct a man-on-the-street interview montage, it's good to use strong, creative questions that your interview subjects are likely to enjoy answering. The real appeal of a man-on-the-street interview comes from the divergent ways people respond. You might want to ask your interviewee to imagine a hypothetical situation and explain how they would handle it. No two people will give the same answer to this kind of question.

Podcast Production

For beginning audio producers and editors, platforms like Audacity, Reason, and Garage Band enable users to record and layer sound, music, and effects. SoundCloud, Opinion and Podbean are among the many podcasting platforms that make it easy to upload, share, and distribute audio productions, music, and podcasts.

After you have developed your Scope of Work, begin by experimenting with the recording software. You'll need to record audio, edit it, add the music and effects, write a brief summary of your podcast, and select cover art before you upload. Take advantage of the many video tutorials which are available on YouTube or Lynda.com to help you master the fundamentals of the technology. Trial and error is often the best teacher.

Representational Ethics

Through the power of spoken language, time and space can be manipulated in highly creative ways, creating a blend of authenticity and unreality. *Audio editing* is an essential part of the production process, as it is through the careful selection, arrangement, and sequencing of material that meaning is shaped and stories gain the structure needed to compel attention. Editing often compresses longer spoken material into minutes or even seconds. But the spoken word can also be compressed in ways that alter or distort the speaker's intended meaning.

Three common techniques in audio editing raise important ethical challenges for producers, interview subjects, and their audiences. When editing an audio interview, some people engage in *cherry-picking* by selecting an excerpt that oversimplifies and therefore distorts a person's verbal statement. Others *omit the context* in which a person makes a comment, taking a phrase or idea about one topic and editing it to make it appear to be referring to something else entirely. Then there's the *Frankenbite*, where an editor stitches together different phrases to create a new whole. Because interview subjects may ramble, editors may cut out the unnecessary pieces of a sentence to get to the heart of the matter in a timely way. But this important technique can be easily misused. When editors splice together the start of one sentence with the end of another or remove a phrase, they may change the meaning.

It's easy to make people look stupid using this technique. You may have seen the 2013 *Jimmy Kimmel Show* which features a man-on-the-street video, where people were asked if they approved of the Affordable Care Act or Obamacare. Most people didn't realize that the term Obamacare was simply a nickname for the Affordable Care Act so the piece is humorously edited to highlight people's ignorance.[27] We may enjoy laughing at the stupidity of others because it can make us feel superior. In man-in-the-street videos, the short length of the clips may also contribute to a sense of detachment we feel towards the people who are featured. That's also why we may laugh when we see a skateboard accident or those family accidents depicted on *America's Funniest Home Videos*. The context delivers a mood of humor, which can prompt the audience to respond with a laugh. Because it's so easy to make people look stupid, this technique is common on late-night television. But if you have ever been on the receiving end of a "gotcha" question and felt the sting of looking stupid in public, it may lead you to create media messages that, while still funny or interesting, are more sensitive to the people you are representing.

Activity: Create a Digital Story

Select some of the questions below to generate stories from your own life experience. Record yourself alone or with a partner. Then edit the best stories into a 3–5 minute audio recording, using music and sound effects to intensify the emotional experience. Post and share it online.

- Who has been the biggest influence on your life? What lessons did that person teach you?
- What are the most important lessons you've learned in life?
- What is your earliest memory?
- Are there any funny stories your family tells about you that come to mind?
- Are there any funny stories or memories or characters from your life that you want to tell me about?
- What are you proudest of?
- When in life have you felt most alone?
- If you could hold on to one memory from your life forever, what would that be?
- How has your life been different than what you'd imagined?
- How would you like to be remembered?

9

Images

> **KEY IDEAS**
>
> The power of photography is undeniable. Most people can easily recognize an image that "looks good" and consciously base their judgment of the credibility of the content of a web site on the quality of the images and the graphic design. The same thing goes when we look at a YouTube video or a photo posted on Instagram, Pinterest, or Flickr, one that's been made by a professional filmmaker or photographer. But unless you've been trained as a photographer, artist or graphic designer, you may not be able to concretely define the specific qualities that distinguish the "good" image or photo from an "awful" one. In this chapter, we learn some of the fundamental principles of photography and graphic design, the ABCs of good practice that have shared as informal rules or principles for generations. While the best artists and designers know that rules were made to be broken, adhering to these principles helps beginners to put their best foot forward toward successful and effective communication.

If you're like me, you've taken a selfie within the last week. In 2014, researchers found that 93 million selfies were taken per day – just on Android devices alone! Even the word *selfie,* as a genre of amateur photography, arrived into our language within the past 10 years. While some people see the selfie as evidence of rising levels of narcissism and voyeurism, selfies are a form of self-representation, where we depict the *self enacting the self.* In 2010, the artist-critic David Colman wrote in the *New York Times* that the selfie "is so common that it is changing photography itself." Defined as a photographic object that initiates the transmission of human feeling in the form of a relationship, the selfie is both an object and a social practice. In a way, selfies construct an identity "between the self as an image and as a body."[1]

But selfies don't merely record or document an event, a time, a place, or a person. They are powerful tools of expression and communication. By sharing them with friends and making them public, they are a "constant reminder that once anything enters digital space, it instantly becomes part of the

Create to Learn: Introduction to Digital Literacy, First Edition. Renee Hobbs.
© 2017 John Wiley & Sons, Inc. Published 2017 by John Wiley & Sons, Inc.

infrastructure of the *digital super public*, outliving the time and place in which it was originally produced, viewed, or circulated."[2]

Images have enormous emotional power to affect our feelings at the same time that they inform, persuade, and entertain. Perhaps you have grown up documenting your life, using the camera on your phone to capture some of the many experiences, people, and places encountered. Most people enjoy taking photos of their travels. When we think of travel images, pictures of classic buildings, monuments, beaches, and even food often come to mind.

For example, a first-time traveler to Paris is likely to capture images that simply document the marvelous architecture, avenues, and parks that grace the city. But when we compare and contrast two images from any traveler's collection, we can readily identify differences in quality. Some travel images are simply boring, while others hold your attention for a longer period of time, activate feelings, and provoke a sense of "being there."

Photojournalist Mindaugas Kavaliauskas offered a "A Frequent Flier's Photos of Air Travel," selected from his book of photographs, where he captures some of the unexpected moments experienced inside airports and during air travel. See Figure 9.1. What makes these photographs so compelling is their intimate quality; in one, we feel so close to the passenger seated nearby. In another, we sense the overwhelming tedium of passengers on a long transatlantic flight. Such images can metaphorically transport us to places far removed from our experience or represent experiences we have ourselves experienced. As John Culkin put it, "We become what we behold."[3] As screens have increasingly become central to

Figure 9.1 The art of observation. Photo by Mindaugas Kavaliauskas.

our daily experience, photographs can intensify our own perceptual experience. Artists of all kinds reshape experience through various manipulations.

The World in Images

Images have status as legal evidence. They express aspects of *social reality*, conveying a sense of truthfulness, authenticity, and actuality. Eyewitness accounts of hurricanes, accidents, unusual performances, and animal behaviors are part of our social media streams. Citizens use their cell phones to capture police brutality and police wear video cameras to capture the challenges of their jobs.

When Freddie Gray fell into a coma and died in Baltimore in 2015 after having just being arrested by Baltimore police for possession of an illegal switchblade, eyewitness accounts suggested that the officers used excessive force in the arrest, giving Gray a "rough ride" while handcuffed but unrestrained inside a police van. This form of police brutality causes a victim to be helplessly thrown around the interior of a police vehicle as it is being deliberately driven to cause trauma. But, unlike other forms of police brutality that we have seen on TV news and YouTube, there was no cell phone footage of Gray's ride in the police van.

So as part of their efforts to tell the story of Freddy Gray, photojournalist Jeremy Ashkenas and fellow *New York Times* reporters created a multimedia portrait of the Sandtown neighborhood in Baltimore, where he grew up. Here, more than one-third of the buildings are abandoned and high levels of poverty, unemployment, and incarceration exist. The images offer a simple juxtaposition of intersections in the neighborhood paired with a portrait of a person who lives there. A map shows abandoned buildings as little yellow squares, and there are thousands of them.[4]

The power of this work stems from its *simplicity*: it juxtaposes images of various street corners with images of local residents. The caption above the images has names like "Calhoun and Cumberland," with the name and age of the resident who is depicted; underneath the image is shown a short quote from the individual about their experience with police harassment. To see the images, the user moves down the page, discovering the unique personalities of the residents, almost as if strolling through the neighborhood. In this case, the horizontal blocks of images and text mirror the feeling and texture of the urban landscape.

What Makes a Great Photo?

How can you tell the difference between a good photo and a great photo? The art of photography lies in the *art of observation*. A good photographer is observant, attentive, awake, and alive to everything that's around us. Photographers

Calhoun & Cumberland Tavonne Taylor, 25

"It's a peaceful neighbourhood when it wants to be," said Mr. Taylor, who says he has lived in the area his entire life. But he said that the police are a "harassing presence" even when people are not doing anything wrong.

Figure 9.2 Calhoun and Cumberland: Portrait of the Sandtown neighborhood in Baltimore. *Source*: *New York Times* Interactive.

help us to see the world with a freshness of vision that can awaken our emotions and insight. French philosopher Roland Barthes offers insight on the power of photography by describing how photos are always situated in a rich cultural context. He uses the term *studium* to refer to the ways in which photos represent "what is," generating some modest and relatively superficial level of interest in the viewer. But sometimes, something in a photo may seem to pierce us, "provoking a more intense and personal reaction in the viewer," as Andy Grunberg explains.[5] This is the *punctum* of the photo. It's the emotional heart of the image. In the two photos in Figure 9.2, it is the face of Tavonne Taylor, which (turned towards his neighborhood, it seems) reveals a mix of love, disgust, and pain. His face makes us recognize the bittersweet feeling we associate with our old neighborhoods.

The Emotional Truth of Photos

Some photos pull us in, connecting us to the people and places they represent. Amy Toensing, an American photojournalist, is known for her intimate essays about the lives of ordinary people. In 2007, she captured photos to depict the impact of the drought that plagued the Murray Basin region of Australia. One photo, shown in Figure 9.3, features a father and his two children in a desolate landscape, where we see the father and his young son reflected in the mirror of a truck, while the daughter covers her face. The image hints at a story of the physical and emotional challenges the family experiences as part of everyday rural life.

Figure 9.3 *Studium* and *punctum* activate curiosity. Photo by Amy Toensing.

Perhaps this photo makes you wonder about the family relationships; perhaps you notice the flat, treeless horizon and the emptiness of the landscape. Can you sense the grit and the wind on the little girl's face? Do you feel like you're secretly observing a little moment of family life as the father lifts the son off the truck? Do you sense the way that living in a rural isolated place may create complex dependencies in family relationships?

Amy's assignment was to capture aspects of how Australians were coping with the drought. This involved researching the story and interviewing people involved, learning about the water distribution system for farmers, the types of crops in the region, what each crop required, and how the drought was playing out in Australian politics. Amy also had to dig into the topic of climate change and explore differing opinions on whether this drought was part of a shifting global climate.

But to capture *emotional truth*, she needed a different mindset: "a place where I am connecting to the subject on a basic and emotional level: light, shapes, color and raw emotion." We can learn about the art of photography by seeing Toesing's *contact sheet*, shown in Figure 9.4, which displays the whole collection of photos she made at this scene.

Even without technical training, you can take great photographs when you capitalize on your individual perspective and imagination. For many people, photography builds self-confidence and helps them become more curious about the world. The photos people create can sometimes become a catalyst

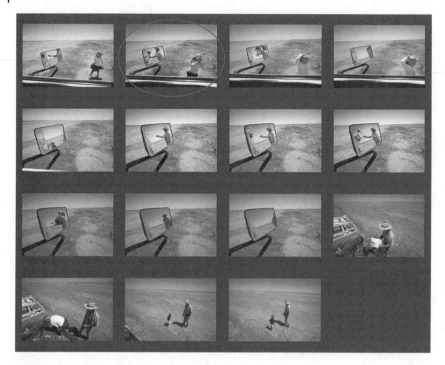

Figure 9.4 Photographers make choices. Photo by Amy Toensing.

for written expression. When a portrait of someone is paired with a letter to a person, for example, the combination can offer insight on a complex human relationship.

Truth, Beauty, and Emotional Valence

Scientists, philosophers, and poets have long explored the fundamental relationship between truth and beauty. The Latin expression *pulchritudo splendor veritatis* translates to "beauty is the splendor of truth." Scientists describe beautiful true ideas or theories as having three qualities: simplicity, completeness, and symmetry.

Things that are simple seem to be more beautiful and true. Ancient scholars once tested mathematical proofs using the concept of Occam's Razor, as Thomas Aquinas wrote about in the thirteenth century, noting that "If a thing can be done adequately by means of one, it is superfluous to do it by means of several; for we observe that nature does not employ two instruments [if] one suffices."[6] *Simplicity* is well aligned with the concept of concision, which was discussed earlier in the book.

According to philosopher George Santayana, something that is beautiful should have "patterns and appearances that offer sufficient novelty to arouse curiosity, but not so much that their complexity is beyond understanding." As Nikhil Ravi explains, it's the balance between the complexity of the concepts being described and the simplicity with which they are described.[7]

Consider the *emotional valence* of the photograph with the charming caption shared by the "Humans of New York" web site, shown in Figure 9.5. Social media researchers have learned that content with strong positive emotional valence is more likely to be shared through social media than content that lacks positive emotional value. Here the creative naming of these elderly nuns as "Mother Joyous" and "Sister Adorable" adds a special warmth and tenderness to the image, which has been shared nearly 3,000 times by Twitter users.

Humans of New York
over a year ago

Mother Joyous and Sister Adorable were seen walking down 14th Street yesterday.

👍 65,518   💬 733   ➤ 2,293

Figure 9.5 Positive emotional valence.

Figure 9.6 The rule of thirds. Photo by Renee Hobbs.

Structure Matters: The Rule of Thirds

There's no simple formula to creating a great image. But still artists have been articulating the math behind their art for thousands of years. One of the best ways to create a good photograph is to exploit the concept known as the *rule of thirds.* The theory recommends that points of interest be placed in the intersections or along the lines that can be drawn when dividing the horizontal and vertical axes into thirds. When viewing images, people's eyes usually go to one of the intersection points most naturally rather than the center of the shot. When you start looking for the rule of thirds, you find it everywhere, especially in photojournalism and online publications. Figure 9.6 shows an example of how photographers can use the rule of thirds in their compositions.

The Power of Sequence: Why People Love Slideshows

In the early or mid-twentieth century, if people were lucky, they got to attend a lecture or talk that included a slideshow. When photographic slides could be projected in a carousel-type projector onto a large screen, it caused a revolution in the lecture hall. Schools and public libraries would sometimes feature presenters who used slideshows to illustrate their visits to faraway places in South America, Africa, or Asia. In the workplace, it was common at the end of the year for the management to host a special event where pictures of workers in action were projected with inspirational music to promote warm feelings among members of staff.

Today, slideshows are a dominant part of our experience on the web. They are often at the top of web sites, functioning as headlines to attract our attention and help us navigate and decide where to click. Image slideshows are important forms of content, where they compel interest and hold attention.

Today, you may scroll through Instagram or other social media to encounter images, choosing for yourself which ones to look at more closely. You may also scroll through a series of images that are embedded on news or information web sites. Image slideshows are an important twenty-first century form of expression for information, entertainment, and persuasion.

Why do people love slideshows? A linear sequence of images enables the creation of a journey of sorts. Slideshows are also great for communicating about a process or a specific time period. We can see the power of sequence when searching for a recipe online at those web sites that show us the steps in the process of stir-frying vegetables or making a soufflé. The creator has selected some images to illustrate strategic points in the cooking process, and in doing so, has helped us visualize the entire process. Another example of narrative sequence occurs on travel web sites, where we might see images that represent a long weekend trip, as in "36 Hours in Madrid." In this case, the choice of which images to use in the sequence is vital to viewer response. Even though we have seen only a few frozen moments, a sequence of images can help us reconstruct or imagine the entire process or experience in our mind's eye.

Do Your Photos SCARE?

Nicole Dalesio, a teacher in the Los Gatos-Saratoga Union High School District, introduces principles of photography by telling learners they need to "SCARE."

Simplify. Remove all unnecessary objects from the frame.

Close and Closer. Move close and closer to the subject. Don't rely on zoom.

Angle. Use creativity in designing how your subject appears in the frame by exploring high and low angles.

Rule of thirds. Center your subject on the right or left third of the image, not in the direct center.

Even lighting. Avoid shadows on people's faces. Don't shoot a subject in front of a window – ever.

Ambiguity and Specificity

Photographs are both specific and ambiguous. They are so specific in depicting a particular event, situation, or individual that the viewer is left to fill in the details about their meaning. We do this by connecting the image to our own life experience or imagination. It's a bit ironic that the very specificity of photos creates *ambiguity*, a type of uncertainty of meaning. When we look at a photo, several interpretations are plausible. Your interpretations of the photos in this chapter, for example, may be different from the interpretation I provide in my writing. The context of the photographer and the context of the interpreter may play a role in resolving ambiguity.

It's worth wondering how photographs and photography may awaken our empathy or deaden it. Photographs can evoke strong emotional response. For example, when we see an image of a child crying on the sidewalk, near a fallen bicycle, we may experience a memory trace of our own childhood traumas and make an emotional connection. But critics like Susan Sontag believed that the photographer is a *divided witness*, someone who cannot fully participate in an experience or event because they are documenting it.[8]

Some photographers believe that the ambiguity of photographs comes from the limitations of the *frame.* There are no edges or hard boundaries in the real world – you can always turn your head to get additional context. Photographs intentionally shape your perception and interpretation of them by deciding what to omit and what to emphasize. As Ming Thein writes:

> But what you see in a photograph is all you get: and there is an implied limitation to the composition delineated by the edges of the frame that forces the viewer to consider only what lies within it. It is the spatial relationship between not just the elements within the frame but the frame itself that has implications on causality and story: forced empty space in the center of the frame suggests deliberate avoidance; proximity suggests collaboration. This is both an important storytelling tool as well as a visually balancing one.[9]

When we see a photograph, we should notice how the photographer is drawing our attention inside the frame. Most people tend not to think much about what's not inside the frame. But what's omitted is as important as what's included when it comes to interpreting photos.

Representational Ethics: Headlines and Captions

Ever since the invention of the photograph, creators have used *headlines* and *captions* to offer descriptive, informative detail that situates the meaning of the

Figure 9.7 Comparing headlines to identify point of view.

image in context. Media educator and author Neil Postman believes that images need language in order for them to make them truly valuable for information and learning.[10] In the newspaper business, a photojournalist is assigned to document an event and bring back photos. Then the photojournalist works with an editor to compose the words that accompany the photos we see. Words can radically alter and reshape our interpretation of photos. For example, consider the hypothetical media coverage of Dakota Fanning at the airport, which is shown in Figure 9.7. How does the meaning of the image change as you read Captions 1 and 2?

This image was created when editors at *The Vagenda*, a UK-based online magazine confronting sexism in the media, held a challenge to its Twitter followers to "take a snarky headline and turn it around." The online magazine was created in 2012 by Rhiannon Lucy Cosslett and Holly Baxter, two British women who like to laugh at women's magazines, with their sexist headlines, like "Inside His Sex Brain: Find Out Exactly What He's Thinking." They thought it was funny the way that celebrity magazines made fun of the appearance, clothing, relationships, and minor weight fluctuations of actresses. They also recognized that headlines and captions essentially tell people how to interpret an image. Learning to recognize how headlines shape our interpretation helps in your evaluation of the quality of information. Providing a *counternarrative* or alternative interpretation through rewriting headlines can help to challenge the dominance of many different types of stereotypes in the media.

The Damage a Headline Can Do: A Research Study

Misleading headlines can have devastating effects on how people interpret an image. Ullrich Ecker, a psychologist and cognitive neuroscientist at the University of Western Australia, researched the cognitive impact of the relationship between headlines and images. In one study, subjects read newspaper articles where headlines mentioned either the victim or the perpetrator, with photos that featured either the murderer or the victim. For example, in some cases, the photo of the perpetrator matched the headline that read: "Man charged over Thornlie murder." In other cases, the same photo of the perpetrator was accompanied by a headline featuring the victim: "Grandfather killed in Thornlie." After the students read the articles, they were asked to rate the faces that they had seen based on attractiveness, trustworthiness, dominance, and aggression. Then, students were asked to rate the faces as "good" or "bad."

As expected, the criminal received more negative ratings and the victim more positive ratings when subjects saw photos that matched the headline. But when the headline diverged from the photo, the victim was rated more negatively when the headline had been about the criminal.[11] Similarly, the criminal was rated more positively. As Maria Konnikova explains, "misinformation appears to cause more damage when it's subtle than when it's blatant." She describes a 2013 *New York Times* article with the headline, "Selling a Fake Painting Takes More Than a Good Artist." Alongside the article, there is a photograph of an innocent gallery owner who was the victim of a scam. However, the pairing of the headline and the photo seems to implicate the victim, visually suggesting that he was the perpetrator of the crime. "Even well-intentioned readers who *do* go on to read the entire piece may still be reacting in part to that initial formulation," noted Konnikova. Thus, great care is needed when composing headlines and captions to consider the potential ethical issues that arise in context of image–word relationships.[12]

Staging, Photo Editing, and Image Manipulation Ethics

Ever since the invention of photography, people have been finding ways to manipulate images. *Staging* or setting up a science is the primary way that photographers manipulate reality. They may set up a shot by orchestrating a scene to fit a particular narrative. Santiago Lyon, Vice President of the Associated Press, a news aggregation service, says photojournalists may ask subjects to do things they would not ordinarily do, or ask them to repeat things they were doing prior to the photographer's arrival. He said, "For example, the photographer who might ask a combatant to fire their weapon so they can capture a more dramatic image. Or the photographer who agrees when the subject proposes doing something solely or primarily for the benefit of the camera – burning a flag or chanting during a demonstration."[13]

But it's not just the photographer who may stage or set up a scene. The organizers of media events may create a *photo opportunity*, where the subjects are asked to pose for the photographers – politicians shaking hands for the cameras or victorious athletes holding up their trophies. While these scenes actually happened, they're not the same type of reality as when photographers document events as they happen, as *found moments*, without staging.

Staging practices must be understood as situational and contextual. For bloggers creating a how-to sequence on fancy cake baking, staging practices are essential. For news photography, some staging of the subjects may be necessary depending on the subject and the context. Depending on the photographer's purpose, goals and genre of the media outlet, these practices may be considered appropriate or inappropriate by professional photojournalists.

It's important to consider the changing economics of photography in a world where everyone can be a photographic witness just by using a smartphone. In the 2015 World Press photo competition, a large number of photographs were disqualified for excessive staging. A survey of more than 1,500 photojournalists from around the world found that most were *freelancers*, that is, self-employed men and women. The majority earn under $30,000 annually by selling the rights to their photos to professional mass media organizations.[14]

The Market Value of Photographs

Freelance photographers make money by selling the rights to reproduce a photo in a newspaper, magazine, or online. Here are some sample rates of the fees they receive, as of 2016:

Magazines

Vanity Fair: photographer for Paris Fashion Week
Fee: $2,000
Bon Appetit: photography for an article about restaurants
Fee: $1,500

Television

NBC News: breaking news photo
Fee: $100

Online publications

Stereogum: photographer for music festival
Fee: $200
Mashable: news photograph
Fee: $450
Real estate firm: photographs of a house for sale
Fee: $200
Small web site for a local company: images of the company and employees
Fee: $25 per image used

Photojournalists have a wide range of perspectives about their craft: 75 percent regard photo manipulation as a real problem but 25 percent admit they sometimes alter the content of images. Half of the photojournalists in the survey say they staged photos by asking subjects to pose, repeat an action, or wait for the photographer to get ready.[15]

Photo editing is another common type of manipulation. Three types of photo editing include cropping, color correction, and image manipulation. *Cropping* can really improve your photos. Your smartphone enables you to resize, edit, cut, or crop a photo. Other free online tools enable you to add rounded corners and create a drop shadow for your image.

Color correction used to be something only for the experts. But today most people experiment with color correction by using filters on Instagram or Snapchat. For example, if you apply the Moon filter to a photograph you have uploaded to Instagram, it transforms it into a black-and-white image, giving the subject a vintage feel. If you use the Lark filter, it brightens and intensifies all the colors in your photo except red. Image manipulation, cropping, and color correction are considered acceptable practices of professional photography in almost all image-making contexts and 90 percent of professional photojournalists say that they manipulate an image hue, saturation, or tone through digital image manipulation.

More substantial forms of *photo manipulation* involve transforming or altering a photograph to change the image using various methods and techniques. This is sometimes called *airbrushing*. In a portrait, facial lines can be softened and body parts can be slimmed down. In an event photo, people and objects can be added, adjusted for size, shape or placement in the frame, or even removed. In some forms of mass media, photo manipulation is a common practice. Nearly all the images we see on the covers of magazines have been manipulated using professional tools like PhotoShop or Illustrator. The graphic designers who specialize in this work are artists who create an idealized glamour portrait using digital editing.

But critics say that the prevalence of glamour photography distorts people's expectations about their own body. *Social comparison* is the term used for people's tendency to compare themselves to others. This phenomenon combines to create what is called *thin-ideal internalization* when women's exposure to media images of models, actresses, and celebrities inspires them to want to be thin. Researchers have documented how media affects people's attitudes and behavior, including the predisposition to eating disorders. When everyone you see on TV and in the movies looks glamorous, young females may feel pressure to achieve the thin ideal that is depicted. It's not just women who are affected: young males may feel pressure to have bulked-up muscles and may engage in unhealthy eating behaviors as well.[16]

Even celebrities themselves may object to the distortion that occurs as their images are altered. For example, Kate Winslet spoke out against photo manipulation after *GQ Magazine* published an image of her, making her look unnaturally thin. Other celebrities have released un-airbrushed images of themselves.

The Instagram Revolution

The ubiquity of the smartphone and the rise of photo sharing platforms like Flickr, Instagram, and Snapchat exposes tensions between professional and citizen photojournalism. Smartphones are more portable than larger, more delicate traditional cameras. As a result, today, everyone has the capacity to become a news photographer. Researchers have found that 75 percent of Instagram photos use an applied filter. As Meryl Alper explains, "Not only does Instagram make photos look better, but it also makes anyone's photos look better."[17]

Posting and sharing on Instagram can activate both a deep sense of envy and the *fear of missing out* (FOMO), which is the desire to stay continually connected to what others are doing. Researchers have found that heavy smartphone use is associated with FOMO and contributes to lower life satisfaction.[18] Constantly seeing beautiful images of others who are appearing to lead the good life can have a negative impact on your own feelings of self-esteem.

Everyone can use a filter to make their images look better. But even as Instagram has grown, so has the term "#nofilter" as a popular hashtag or textual marker. People who use this tag are claiming that they not have altered the image's appearance using a filter.[19] As you have read this chapter, you've gained knowledge that helps you both as a consumer and as a producer of images. By being aware of the impact of images on attitudes and behaviors and by using images strategically to learn and communicate, you gain digital literacy competencies.

Activity: Document a Place, a Person, or a Process

Make a list of 3–5 concepts and ideas from the chapter that you want to experiment with as you create to learn using photographic images. Then, create a series of five photographs, each with a headline and caption, to document a place, a person, an experience, event or a process. Share your work online and solicit feedback to see how others interpret your work.

10

Infographics and Data Visualization

KEY IDEAS

Information is power. There are many ways to create information but people find statistics, data, and facts especially compelling. When data is presented visually, it can compel our interest and illustrate complex ideas. Simple online tools make it easy to design infographics, and online aggregation services can help these images go viral. Much important data is publically available from online databases but it isn't always easy to use. Digital tools help people access data but these can be behind expensive paywalls because they are presumed to have competitive value in the business marketplace. Infographics are compelling ways to share information but they always have a point of view: like all media, they are inherently selective and incomplete. Infographics are often used for persuasive purposes because people find information that is presented in visual and numerical form to be trustworthy. For these reasons, infographics and data visualizations can be used as a form of beneficial or harmful propaganda.

When Anna Rosling Rönnlund wanted to represent human social, economic and ethnic diversity, she did not want to rely on national or ethnic stereotypes. She asked photographers in 37 countries to collect images of the lifestyles and everyday possessions of more than 200 families to create Dollar Street, a visual tool which employs photos of everyday life as a type of data, using the images to represent a community's socioeconomic conditions along a spectrum from poorest to richest.

In her TED talk, Anna said, "Imagine if the world lived along a single street, with the richest households on one end, the poorest on the other – and every door flung open to the public." She was curious about how to visually represent the diverse lifestyles and daily habits of people around the world. For example in analyzing the astounding variety of "toothbrush" photographs, she displays the different types of toothbrushes used around the world in a sequence from the most humble to the most ostentatious. See Figure 10.1. When we see these photographs, we understand this sequence visually represents the levels of poverty and wealth around the world. For example, in middle-class families each member of the

Create to Learn: Introduction to Digital Literacy, First Edition. Renee Hobbs.
© 2017 John Wiley & Sons, Inc. Published 2017 by John Wiley & Sons, Inc.

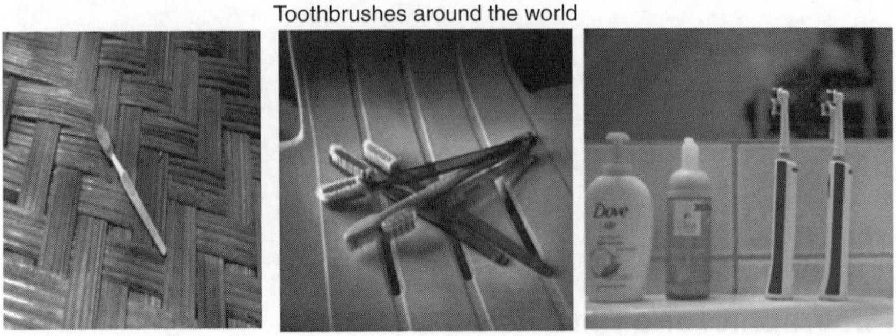

Toothbrushes around the world

Figure 10.1 Images as data: Toothbrushes around the world. Illustration by Anna Rosling Rönnlund.

family has an individual toothbrush. Among the poorest people of the world, teeth are cleaned with a finger, using gentle rubbing and a bit of dirt as an abrasive; among the richest people, a personal electronic toothbrush is the norm.[1]

Anna works for the Gapminder Foundation, a Swedish organization helping to fight ignorance with the use of facts, statistics, and the creative presentation of data. It investigates what the public knows and doesn't know about basic global patterns and macro-trends. Through this, Anna's father, Hans Rosling, founder of Gapminder, aims to reduce global ignorance. They use clever ways to visualize data and information, presenting facts in an entertaining way. They believe that people in rich countries have preconceived ideas and outdated concepts about the health and lifestyle of people in less well-off countries. Rosling notes, "Most people understand the world by generalizing personal experiences which are very biased." Our life experiences shape our world view. And at school, teachers may transmit outdated knowledge about people who live in other countries; in addition, the news media, because it exaggerates unusual events, may underreport slow and gradual changes in economic development around the world. These factors combine to produce *systematic bias* that affects our ability to really understand what is happening around the world.

The communication process that Anna uses by showing examples of toothbrushes around the world is called *data reduction*, which is an approach to analyzing data by simplifying it in order to determine essential patterns. Data reduction may sound technical but it's actually a type of storytelling. By representing people's lifestyles through photographs of their toothbrushes, Anna uses *synechdoche*, a type of metaphor, letting toothbrushes represent or symbolize the larger and more abstract concept of wealth. Synecdoche is a device used in effective communication that involves letting the part stand for the whole.

Why Infographics Work

There's no doubt about it: infographics are eye-catching, engaging, and informative. They are easily shared on social media networks and have grown in popularity in recent times. According to Google Trends, which reports the frequency of keywords, the term, "infographic" became much more common beginning in 2011.

But infographics are not new. Before the rise of Internet culture, infographics were created by graphic designers who worked for the newspaper industry to add interest to dull pages. Even further back, statisticians during the Victorian era used graphs and charts to explain the relationship between variables and represent numerical information visually. The most famous scholar of infographics and data visualization is Edward Tufte, who began teaching journalists about statistics in the 1970s and wrote an influential book, *The Visual Display of Quantitative Information.*[2] Tufte's work spawned a generation of graphic designers specializing in the creative and informative display of information.

Infographics are powerful because images are highly effective forms of communication and expression. We have long known that people process words and pictures differently. The concept of *dual coding theory* explains why infographics are effective for informing and persuading. Dual coding refers to the cognitive process involved in comprehending visual and verbal information.[3] These forms are processed somewhat differently in the human mind. With an image, one sees the whole thing all at once; with words, we must move sequentially through a linear arrangement. Researchers still do not fully understand all the cognitive processes at work, but they have discovered that the brain does not differentiate between real-life experiences and still or moving images. We process images as if they were experiences.

Language is processed differently than images. Researchers who conduct eye-tracking studies have found that readers actually read 28 percent of the words on a computer screen. Simply adding color to a page increases readability. For reasons that are probably rooted deep in evolutionary history of the human mind, people find images to be easier to process than listening to or reading words.[4]

Among the many approaches to visualizing data that are possible, graphic designers use dynamic content and comparison/contrast to control people's attention and aid in their comprehension of numerical data that is presented visually.

Infographics vs. Data Visualization

These terms are sometimes used interchangeably but some important distinctions are worth considering. According to Hjalmar Gislason, founder and CEO of DataMarket, *data visualization* is the graphical representation of quantifiable data, usually by means of a chart, graph, or map types.[5] Although they can be created by hand, they can also be generated by applying automated methods on top of the data. For example, when using Excel to examine numerical data, you can easily create a pie chart, a bar chart, or a line graph to explore patterns in the data that might be hard to notice only by reviewing the numbers.

An *infographic* combines one or more data visualizations with some graphics or text to point out relationships, show a process, tell a story, or persuade. To create an infographic, an individual must have a communicative purpose and an intended target audience, applying a creative process with some understanding of the underlying data and its context.

Controlling Attention with Dynamic Content

Infographics and data visualizations can be presented in static or dynamic formats. In a *dynamic* format, information is presented in ways that change over time or enable people to interact to display data in a particular way. For example, at the Faces of Fracking web site, photojournalist Sarah Craig profiles the people and communities on the front lines of fracking, including those in favor of it and those opposed to it. Fracking, or hydraulic fracturing, is the industrial practice of extracting oil and gas by blasting water, sand, and chemicals at high pressure underground. In one data visualization about fracking in California, created with her colleagues Anna Flagg and Antonio Bruno, as you read the article, a series of interactive animations are revealed that illustrate key ideas using a map that displays various types of data.[6]

The movement on the screen, in the form of a dynamic animation, really underlines the key ideas. As you look at a map of greater Los Angeles, home to more than 500 oil and gas wells, you see black dots representing the number of times (477) that high-intensity fracking techniques have been used in the past year. As you read that 72 million pounds of toxins were released as a result of local fracking in 2013 alone, an animated chart displays the increase in toxins over a one-year period. In this way, dynamic data presentations *control attention* by using the power of interactivity and animation to build a tight connection between verbally presented information, numerical data, and visual representations. Figure 10.2 provides a still image from the web site.

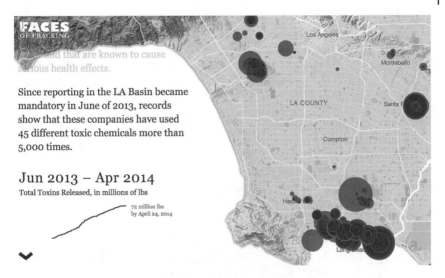

FACES OF FRACKING

...nd that are known to cause s...ous health effects.

Since reporting in the LA Basin became mandatory in June of 2013, records show that these companies have used 45 different toxic chemicals more than 5,000 times.

Jun 2013 – Apr 2014

Total Toxins Released, in millions of lbs

72 million lbs
by April 24, 2014

Los Angeles
Montebello
LA COUNTY
Santa F
Compton
Harb
Long Beach

Figure 10.2 The faces of fracking: Dynamic data visualization.

Controlling Attention with Comparison/Contrast

Comparison and contrast is a timeless rhetorical tool to advance an argument, represent ideas, or develop a persuasive message. Nathan Yau, data visualization expert and author of *Visualize This*, used data from Google Maps to compare and contrast the number of bars as compared to the number of grocery stores in the United States. In the *legend*, shown in Figure 10.3 and reproduced in black and white, colors are used to represent a ratio. When there are more bars than grocery stores in a particular location, that region is colored in brown (to remind us of a beer bottle, perhaps?) When there are more grocery stores than bars, that region is shown in green. Dark brown represents that there are three times more bars than grocery stores. A legend is an essential component of data visualizations because they help us understand how to interpret the visual symbols. In this case, the map's use of color is the primary way that numerical information (the ratio of bars to grocery stores) is represented.

Yau discovered that in many parts of Wisconsin, there are three times more bars than grocery stores, as Figure 10.4 clearly reveals. In the southeast, the presence of many bright green dots shows that there are far more grocery

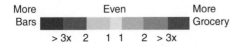

More
Bars

Even

More
Grocery

> 3x   2   1 1   2   > 3x

Figure 10.3 A legend helps readers interpret the visualization.

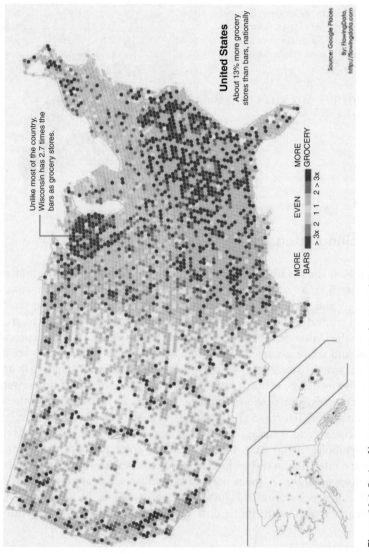

Figure 10.4 Ratio of bars to grocery stores in the United States.

stores than bars there.[7] By developing a creative way to compare and contrast using ratios, he was able to reveal patterns that offer insight on American culture and geography.

People's Engagement with Visualization

People who create infographics as a career often have a background in art and design, media and communication, computer science, or statistics. Many designers are transparent about their creative processes, offering explanations of how they created various infographics and data visualizations on their blogs or web sites. For example, at the website Flowing Data (www.flowingdata.com) you can see examples of information scientists, statisticians, designers, data scientists, and others who explain their strategies for analyzing and exploring data using visualization techniques.

While we know a lot about the people who create infographics and data visualizations, we know much less about how ordinary people use, interpret, and understand them. Researchers have examined what factors influence why people engage with some visualizations and not others. Researchers have found that the content of a visualization may affect the *engagement level* and the emotions activated in responding to it.[8] People need a broad range of skills in order to interpret the content of data visualizations, including reading skills, a conceptual understanding of statistics and mathematical concepts, motivation and critical thinking skills. When we interact with a data visualization, we bring our background knowledge, beliefs and interests to the interpretation process.

People tend to find infographics to be more believable when they confirm what is already known. This phenomenon is called the *confirmation bias* and it's the tendency to search for, interpret, favor, and recall information that matches our pre-existing beliefs. It's one of many cognitive biases that shape the way we interpret information.[9] Because it takes time to read and make sense of an infographic, some visualizations can be challenging. Busy people may not be willing to take the time required to interpret a visualization. However, people can have an *"aha!" experience* when they encounter information in an infographic that contradicts their pre-existing knowledge, especially if it is high in novelty and surprises them in some way.

Can You Trust an Infographic?

People tend to trust data visualizations from a university or think tank more than news sources that are not thought of as "quality" newspapers.[10] Of course, not all infographics are trustworthy. It's been said that humans process visual information much faster than verbally presented information. Of course this makes sense. But how much faster?

There's an infographic online that claims that people process images 60,000 times more quickly than verbal information. But this turns out to be a very good example of how easy it is to lie with infographics. Darren Kuropatwa, an information literacy specialist, tried to trace the origins of this claim. He used advanced search strategies to find the origins of the term and was able to trace the information back to a presentation made by a woman from a college in the Philippines in the late 1990s who did not identify the source of the claim.[11]

This story reveals the second reason why infographics are so persuasive compared to other media forms. It's precisely because we don't generally have the same standards of *verification* for infographics as we do for other forms of expression and communication. Verification is the term used when the accuracy of information is checked by comparing it with multiple sources.

But even when information on an infographic is true, the visual presentation of it can still be highly misleading. At his web site, a law student, Tyler Vigen, has created compelling data visualizations, using publically available sources to show some crazy patterns. For example, in one chart he shows that since 1999, the amount of US federal government spending on science is closely correlated with the number of suicides by hanging, strangulation, and suffocation. Figure 10.5 shows the strong (but goofy) correlation between people who drowned after falling out of a fishing boat and the marriage rates in Kentucky. Another chart shows the strong correlation between the number of divorces in the State of Maine and the per capita consumption of margarine![12]

How to Make an Infographic in Five Easy Steps

First, study the best infographics in order to gain clarity about your own preferences for the relationship between images, data, and language. You may review examples at the Best Infographics of 2015 and select one that serves as your mentor text. As discussed in Chapter 3, a *mentor text* is simply an example of a well-constructed form of media (in print, visual, sound, or multimedia form) that informs your own creative work.

Second, review the affordances of a variety of free and low-cost digital tools for creating infographics. Some examples include Infogr.am, Piktochart, and Easel.ly You can also make charts and graphs using Excel or Google Sheets. You can find links to these (and other) digital tools on the Create to Learn web site. Experiment with a couple of different tools first, before deciding which one to use. This will help you see how the digital platform structures the production process. If you're looking for advanced tools for visualization, consider exploring Tableau, a platform for analyzing data.

Third, consider what *data and information sour*ces you want to visualize in relation to your target audience and your purpose. Today there are many free datasets available from the US government and other sources.[13] Be sure you

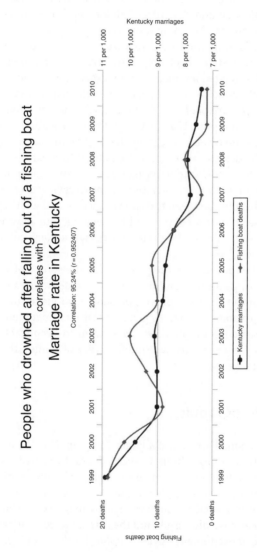

Figure 10.5 Spurious correlation.

can clearly explain how people will encounter your infographic and your expectations for your audience's behavior. What do you want them to know, think, feel, and do after interpreting it?

Fourth, consider your message content, audience, and purpose as you decide on an appropriate format and structure. Think about how you will attract and hold your viewer's interest. You may want to create a *style sheet* for your infographic, where you identify the colors, fonts, and typefaces that you will use to create your project. A style sheet helps you ensure that your infographic is consistent with other related media you might create. For example, if your infographic will be embedded on a web page, you will want the colors and fonts to be consistent. If you are beginner, you might want to use a template to help develop your first infographic. Using a template can be a good way to appreciate the many choices involved in creating an effective message.

In this part of the design process, don't be afraid to create several different versions of your infographic or data visualization. Professional designers generally create three (or more) versions for a client to review. In the design process, consider the balance between text, images, icons, and white space and the message. Of course, at all times, you will be keeping your message, purpose, and target audience in mind as you select images, graphics, colors, and fonts for your infographic.

Finally, you need to develop a strategy for citing the source of your information and data. By using citations and hyperlinks, you demonstrate the credibility and authority of the information you present. Also make sure to include a legend, title, and explanatory text. It's generally wise to document the creative process used to create infographics; you may want to keep track of the decisions you made as you work through the discovery of finding the "story" that your creative work reveals.

Analyzing an Infographic

Figure 10.6 shows a small section of a larger infographic by NeoMam Studios entitled "13 Reasons Why Your Brain Craves Infographics," which offers a good example of what makes infographics so powerful. The image of an eye with electrical plugs coming out of it (like digital eyelashes perhaps?) has a lot of *novelty*, because it's unlikely that you have seen an image exactly like this before. It illustrates the term "visually wired" and the bright red *color* attracts attention and creates a sense of excitement. As a *metaphor* for the brain's predilection to attend to images, this graphic design is effective.

Underneath this image, the *sequence* of three smaller *graphic elements* and information builds an argument using a combination of images, numbers, and words. Because of the *principle of threes*, the series of images looks balanced on the page. The *font size* gives clues to what's important: those numbers tell the story.

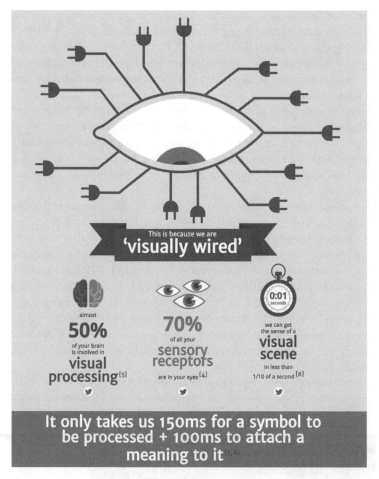

This is because we are
'visually wired'

almost
50%
of your brain
is involved in
**visual
processing**[5]

70%
of all your
**sensory
receptors**
are in your eyes [4]

0:01
seconds

we can get
the sense of a
**visual
scene**
in less than
1/10 of a second [6]

**It only takes us 150ms for a symbol to
be processed + 100ms to attach a
meaning to it**

Figure 10.6 An infographic about infographics. Created by NeoMam Studios.

The *source* of the information is suggested through the footnote, which adds credibility to the infographic by alluding to the information source without cluttering up the image. The use of *mathematical shorthand* (ms stands for millisecond) suggests that the creators of this infographic expect their target audience to have basic familiarity with scientific measurement.

Information Economics

While many people think that data is factual and unbiased, it's a product of human creativity and therefore inevitably inflected by the point of view of the people who created and collected the data. Gathering data involves selection and interpretation, which are subjective processes. Because most people are unaware of how data visualizations are designed, however, they are vulnerable to perceiving them as neutral or unbiased. But recall that a key principle of media literacy is that all media messages are selective and incomplete, so the ability to recognize and critically analyze the constructedness of infographics and data visualizations is more important now than ever.

Undoubtedly, the increase in visual information is occurring because of its overall perceived value in the marketplace. But because so much information is available for free, many people do not have a good understanding of the scope and scale of aspects of the information business. Many do not recognize the biases of the data that are embedded in the processes of gathering and collecting it.

As a college student, you have access to a wealth of information resources from your college or university library. You may not be aware that the most valuable information lives behind a *paywall*, a digital fence that is a system designed to monetize online digital information by limiting access to people who have paid for information or have been authorized to use it. For example, if you want access to Nielsen ratings data to write a paper about the rise and fall of the Nickelodeon TV show *iCarly* by looking at the viewership data, you'll need to attend a university whose library has paid $4,000 a year for subscription access. Some university libraries may pay as much as $40,000 per year for one scholarly journal on a specialized science topic in fields such as biology, pharmacy, medicine, engineering or law.

Visual information has tremendous value to users. As Figure 10.7 reveals, there has been significant growth over time in the use of visual images in books,

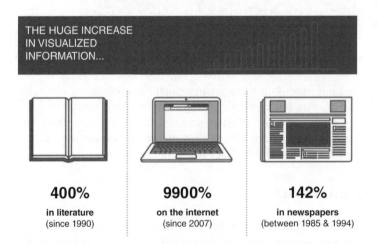

Figure 10.7 Increase in information visualization over time. Created by NeoMam Studios.

online, and in newspapers. When you compare a high school history textbook that your grandmother used compared to the one you may have used, you'll notice right away the use of graphic design elements: photographs, charts, bulleted lists, and other elements designed to increase novelty and compel viewer attention while simultaneously conveying information.

Where Does Data Come From?

The rise of big data has created a data deluge, as Hans Rosling describes it. It's a flood of information, that's for certain. The term *big data* first gained traction in 2013 and it is a term used to describe all the data that is produced by businesses, national, state and local governments, and even by people themselves as part of ordinary life. Data gets produced whenever you get a driver's license or go to the doctor's office. If you get arrested, a whole lot of data is created all through the process of your arrest, sentencing, and trial. When you comment on a YouTube video, your comment can be analyzed and contribute to big data by companies trying to figure out how to better market to you.

Hans Rosling uses data visualization to help people understand the world's problems. Data about local crime, for example, can be presented on a simple chronological list, or it can be mapped to show patterns of crime in various neighborhoods. Data like this is extremely valuable but only if we can interpret and make sense of it. That's why we need statistics and data visualization tools, because they help us "see" the patterns in the data that otherwise would be unavailable. For example, Google has created a tool called Montage that helps researchers sort, map and tag YouTube videos. Such tools may have value in using videos more strategically as a data source.

The Ethics and the Economics of Information

Data is a new kind of commodity. That's why some people refer to the idea of *data mining*, where people extract value from data by discovering the patterns that it holds. But the economics of information are still evolving. Who owns the data that you produce through the use of social media?

Researchers and business professionals use the term *passive data* to refer to the information that you produce without much conscious awareness, simply by purchasing, moving through digital spaces and being connected to social media. One kind of data gets created simply as a byproduct of our everyday life with digital media and technology. For example, when you use your smartphone or laptop, of course you throw off data about your location, your relationships, your favorite types of music, your shopping and purchasing decisions, and other online activities. Your browser history which is collected by Google and other companies, offers a treasure trove of information about how you spend your life online. This information has intrinsic monetary value but it often goes unnoticed by Internet users.

What makes big data different is the way in which information from many different sources, collected at different times and different places, can be combined through algorithmic analysis. Because data can be connected easily now, big data has the potential to change the relationship between businesses, organizations, governments, and individuals.

In 2012, the passive data you created in one single year was valued at about $60, a figure that represents the scale of the data-mining industry, which generated $156 billion in revenue in 2012. With users of the Internet expected to rise to five billion people by 2020 and a corresponding rise in the use of smartphones and devices, the data-mining industry is likely to increase dramatically in the coming years.[14]

Scholars recognize that these new forms of data require new thinking about ethical considerations, including surveillance as well as individual and group discrimination. It's also possible that big data will lead to *privacy harms*, where the aggregation of data leads businesses or governments to make predictions and generalizations about you based on inferences from the coordinated use of multiple datasets. For example, perhaps your geolocation data from your smartphone and your grocery store receipts and your credit card data all lead to the conclusion that you're consuming a lot of alcohol. If the data looks like you're en route to becoming an alcoholic, that information might be valuable to a potential employer.

Are you likely to be able to profit from the data that you create? Sadly, individual users have little power in this economic model if they do not understand that the information they provide has value. Internet users can find ways to take control, however. Facebook users can export their personal data – but right now, there's no retail market available for individual users to sell their data. Some people believe this approach – giving users more control – would reduce people's fears about privacy violations.

Activity: Create an Infographic Resume

Create an infographic resume that depicts your life history, talents, and work and life experiences. First, identify key data, facts, and information and organize this information chronologically. Then select an online infographic tool from the resources provided at the Create to Learn website. Experiment with different ways to represent your information and create three versions. Post and share the infographic online and get feedback on how your work is interpreted by others.

11

Vlogs and Screencasts

KEY IDEAS

This chapter introduces two common forms of video production that can be developed by a single individual or a small team quickly and without professional equipment. Vlogging is a genre that relies on the ethos of the host. In vlogging, authenticity and authority are constructed through spoken oral performance but sensitivity to setting and story structure is important. Screencast videos display a movie of one's computer screen, often combined with narration and music. Both are simple video production formats that require careful planning if they are to accomplish their goals. Vlogging and screencasting can be highly effective in informing, entertaining, and persuading. To make effective use of these forms of creative expression, a good understanding of the power of performance is needed.

When Hank and John Green started the Vlogbrothers back in 2007 as an experiment in brotherhood, they vowed to communicate to each other only by video blogging for one full year. They couldn't have imagined that they were influencing an entire generation. When they began their experiment, they had been inspired by the work of the performance artist Ze Frank, whose videos, posted online in a pre-YouTube world, included talking directly into the camera in episodes that were just three minutes long. The episodes also featured an unusual style of editing, where right in the middle of a point, Ze Frank would move a few inches to or away from the camera, accompanied by a jump cut that is now a standard feature of vlogging.

Hank once commented that videoblogging is "about turning the camera on and off and talking," noting that vlogs are a profoundly personal form of direct address by an individual to an audience. The pleasure in viewing vlogs can be understood by noting that they are a form of *interstitial media*, something we generally use for a little bit of time in between other activities. Vlogs fit "the cognitive style of Web browsing because they are made with the tacit assumption that no activity claims the computer user's total attention for long."[1]

Create to Learn: Introduction to Digital Literacy, First Edition. Renee Hobbs.
© 2017 John Wiley & Sons, Inc. Published 2017 by John Wiley & Sons, Inc.

Figure 11.1 The Vlogbrothers.

Part of the appeal of the Vlogbrothers was undoubtedly their nerdy and distinctly amateur identity (Figure 11.1). Today, the divide between producers and consumers of media has eroded nearly completely. As Nick Couldry writes, "Professional and amateur cultural production are not distant, but closely overlapping, regions of the same vast spectrum."[2] As media becomes more social, amateurs become more central to the enterprise and the social compulsion we feel – the need to keep up with "the media" – is not so much based on watching television as in being part of online mediated interpersonal relationships.

Long before *Big Bang Theory* made nerdy guys into television celebrities, Hank and John Green were just two ordinary guys, sharing their love of computers, Harry Potter, sledding, hair, science, and happy dances. As of summer 2016, the brothers still post two videos per week onto their Vlogbrothers channel. John Green posts a video on Tuesday, and Hank Green on Friday.

These two talents have parlayed their vlogging into a creative enterprise, creating YouTube videos on channels that include SciShow, CrashCourse, How to Adult, Mental Floss, and other channels. Both Hank and John use vlogging as a way to perform a constructed identity that offers self-disclosure in an authentic, vulnerable, and personal way. They make a good living from their creative work, including YouTube advertising, which pays them more than $5 per 1,000 views. They also get money from putting on conferences. Their fans also pay small sums of money using a crowd-funded platform called Patreon, which enables people to support creative artists online.

Vlogging and Screencasting

Vlogging and screencasting are genres of moving image media that are now commonly found online, produced by both professionals and amateurs and ranging widely in content, form, length, and tone. Today, these forms of video production can be created without expensive video cameras, microphones, or special equipment.

Vlogging is a first-person style of episodic video production that is tied to the rise of YouTube. It is characterized by a charismatic host who speaks directly to the camera, offering ideas, information, and usually humor or charm, using a conversational style to create the sense of a *parasocial relationship* between the host and the audience, where viewers feel emotionally and socially connected to a celebrity, character, actor, or host, even in the absence of face-to-face contact. We derive some of the pleasures of a real relationship from the familiarity of feeling "in touch" with another human being we see on video. These feelings of emotional warmth are intensified when characters are people we can relate to, or when they perform with charm and grace. Vloggers and their viewers have an interdependent relationship that helps create a feeling of social connectedness through participation in an online community. One of the most globally recognized vloggers is PewDiePie, a Swedish comedian and YouTube celebrity, age 27, who, with 51 million subscribers on YouTube, has the most viewed YouTube channel of all time.[3]

Screencasting is another type of video production that involves the use of moving images displayed on a computer or laptop. A screencast may take the form of a demonstration or explainer video, where a combination of still images and moving images are captured from a computer screen (through screen capture software and the computer's webcam) and combined with narration and music.

Since YouTube is such a brand new medium, of course, these genre labels are provisional and still in formation. YouTubers may mix vlogging and screencasting with animation and live action in a single video. Because these formats are useful for creating to learn, we'll focus on them in this chapter, recognizing that the insights gained from producing vlogs, animations, and screencasts are useful for all forms of media. But to put things in context, we must also consider the historical, political, and economic significance of online video.

Developing an Argument

Great vloggers demonstrate fine qualities of carefully structured argument. Sometimes, you can see and hear them move through three distinct phases where they present, develop, and share their ideas:

- The claim that answers the question: "What do I think?"
- The reasons that answer the question: "Why do I think this?"
- The evidence that answers the question: "How do I know this is the case?"

Vloggers don't always present claims, reasoning, and evidence in the kind of structure you might find in a written document. Sometimes they begin with the evidence and then use reasoning to discover their claim. This is similar to the way writers work out their ideas. Even though the written claim is presented first as the thesis statement, the writer arrived at the claim as a result of careful reading and analysis of the source materials. Most of us discover our ideas in the process of writing and creating to learn.

In a video entitled, "What's Wrong with Monopoly?" John Green creates a screencast that starts with the opening line: "Today I will be reviewing the mobile app Monopoly, and what I'd forgotten or perhaps just never noticed, is that Monopoly is a terrible game. The basic idea that you buy property and then charge rent when your opponent lands on that property is distressingly similar to real contemporary human life." As we listen to this thesis statement, presented upfront, we view moving images from the mobile version of the Monopoly game, which is an animated and interactive version of the actual game, as shown in Figure 11.2.

But Green is doing much more than offering a review of the mobile game, as it turns out. As evidence that the game is awful because it's too similar to real life, John Green describes some details about playing against a nonhuman

Figure 11.2 "What's Wrong with Monopoly?" screencast.

opponent (the artificial intelligence) who proposes increasingly more desperate trades as the game continues, leading the human player to take pity on the machine. By examining his emotional reactions in agreeing to ridiculous trades, John Green supplies a form of evidence rooted in his own response to the game. By analyzing the game's values, Green notes that although getting rich is celebrated, such success is a random thing, being dependent upon the role of the dice. Thus, the game offers "a convoluted self-contradictory analysis of capitalism." Green then reviews the history of the inventor of Monopoly, a guy named Charles Darrow whose story is described in the game's instruction manual. Then Green surprises us with a twist: "Turns out, 30 years earlier, a woman named Elizabeth Magie invented a game called 'The Landlord's Game' that demonstrated how capital tends to become concentrated in fewer hands." This game was even played at business schools; over time, thousands of collaborators modified and improved the game. Green said, "The game was really created by a community and the free market failed to reward that community, instead wrongly assigning most of the value to one contributor." To deepen this argument, Green notes that the mobile Monopoly app was created by Hasbro, the multinational company that bought Parker Brothers, suggesting that "the history of Monopoly turns out to be a far more interesting study of capitalism than the game itself." He concludes by returning to the premise of the 4-minute screencast, rating the game a 2 out of 10 (not recommended).[4]

In constructing this neat little argument, Green began by observing specific features of the game. After sharing his emotional response to the game, he summarized information about the game, using facts and evidence about the game's origins. From that process, his thesis statement emerged. Green's short screencast managed to both inform and entertain while offering us a brief but persuasive critique of capitalism. It satisfied the expectations of those expecting a game review but went far deeper by offering a larger and more critical perspective on the question, "What's Wrong with Monopoly?"

A Short History of Online Video

Since the first videos were uploaded in 2005, the rise of YouTube has been revolutionary in helping democratize media culture. In 2007, researchers found that about half of the most popular videos on YouTube were excerpts from traditional mass media – television shows, advertising, informational programs, celebrity interviews, and Hollywood movies. User-generated content was a term that first came into use in 2005 to describe any form of content that is shared online using social media. In only 10 years, we've seen "Evolution of Dance," "David After Dentist," and "Grumpy Cat" videos reach millions of viewers. Today YouTube videos are a fascinating kind of popular culture created by ordinary people and media professionals alike.[5]

You have been part of the origins of user-generated content. You probably remember young Justin Bieber's rise to fame and his discovery as a 13-year-old boy, as teens watched him on YouTube playing the guitar and singing from his bedroom in Canada. It was a viral sensation.

Of course, social media has been increasingly a vehicle of communication for marketers and mass media. YouTube has become a primary vehicle for *talent discovery* of all kinds. YouTube videos are a part of mainstream entertainment media now, competing with cable and broadcast television and film. For example, you didn't need to wait for MTV to broadcast Psy's "Gangnam Style" music video – the song was available online to people all over the world. Many were inspired to create remake videos, versions of the song that include people recording themselves singing and doing the horsey dance moves that captured the world's attention in 2012.[6]

User-generated content is an important way for social change activists to reach, inspire, and mobilize audiences. YouTube has enabled activists to be independent of mainstream mass media to a greater degree than ever before. As a result, YouTube has also become an extraordinary tool for spreading both beneficial and harmful propaganda. "Kony 2012," the documentary about the Ugandan warlord, Joseph Kony, reached 100 million views in just seven days, becoming the most viral video ever. People shared the video, in part, because it blended art, human rights advocacy, and journalism in a skillful way, tapping into people's strong feelings about fatherhood, family, and social responsibility.[7]

But you don't have to be a talented performer or filmmaker to reach a large audience on YouTube. Some ordinary people have found an audience for their ideas about almost any topic. Some are using it to present information about what's happening in their communities, workplaces, and schools. *Citizen journalism* is a form of newsgathering and reporting that functions outside mainstream media institutions.[8] As the smartphone became a ubiquitous part of life, people all over the world were able to upload eyewitness news, enabling anyone and everyone to be a citizen journalist. Ever since the videotaping of the 1992 beating of Rodney King by Los Angeles police ignited riots, we continued to learn about police brutality in African American neighborhoods through the documentation of abusive treatment via smartphones. In the spring and summer of 2016, in the months leading up to the election of Donald Trump, these videos dominated the news media as citizen documentation of police shootings became almost routine.

Choices, Choices

Perhaps you will comment on the ideas of others, in developing a media review. Or you'll share information and present or explain ideas that you are learning in a specific course. You may even choose to reveal yourself, with all your warts, contradictions, paradoxes, and inconsistencies. Whatever you do, you will find that vlogs are, from a technical point of view, pretty easy to produce. Most people can produce a 5-minute vlog or screencast in 3–5 hours from start to finish. As in all forms of public speaking, the main message of a vlog is communicated by both the verbal content and the nonverbal behavior of the vlogger. Vlogs remind us of face-to-face conversation, and the sense of immediacy and intimacy we experience when viewing them is a big part of the appeal.

Beyond the ideas and content that a vlogger chooses to talk about and the qualities of their performance, vloggers make many other choices that shape how they convey ideas visually in a vlog. The location, physical place, and lighting all represent choices that communicate a message. These choices are sometimes referred to as *mise-en-scène*, a term used in film theory that includes specific issues such as setting, location, lighting, camera position, and performer position.[9] Because the vlogger is usually performing all the roles of performer, cameraman, and producer, vloggers make personal decisions about how to depict themselves: where and how to be standing (or sitting) and whether to include face, upper body, or whole body in the frame. They make decisions about the length of the video and choose production values: whether to publish their videos as unedited video files or edit them to include introductory and closing sequences, music, other video content, title credits, sound effects, and more.

Ethos and Performance: The Power of Personality

The ancient Greeks knew that the performance of identity was a crucial factor in whether a speaker was perceived as competent, believable, and trustworthy. They used the term *ethos* to refer to all the ways in which the personality of the speaker affects the audience. In speaking about the power of personality in the context of communication, the use of the term "performance" doesn't necessarily mean what an actor does on a stage. The sociologist Erving Goffman used the term *impression management* to refer to our tendency to present an acceptable image to the people around us.[10] Thus we perform various kinds of identity through many forms of ordinary social interaction.

Four fundamental video production techniques can have an impact on how the speaker is perceived. First, to achieve a sense of emotional intimacy in video, many vloggers use the *close-up*, focusing attention on the performer's face. Because YouTube videos are generally low resolution, close-ups become effective devices to create visual intensity. The close-up has long been used in film as a way to establish the main character and to capture aspects of thought and feeling through facial expression. In narrative movies, close-ups help create a sense of identification with a character, while in documentaries, close-ups communicate authenticity, which is a sense of the message's "realness."

Secondly, *direct address* to the camera can shape how audiences respond to the ethos of the performer. Direct address occurs when the performer looks in

► ►I ◄)) 0:03 / 3:43   cc ⚙ ☐ ⌗

So, I Ruptured Both my Eardrums! (Also, NerdCon: Nerdfighteria)

vlogbrothers ☑

▶ Subscribe 2,858,325

118,108 views

✚ Add to   ↱ Share   ••• More   👍 7,695 👎 39

Figure 11.3 The emotional power of direct address by the Vlogbrothers.

the direction of the audience and seems to be looking directly at the viewer, as shown in Figure 11.3. In narrative fictional movies, this technique is seen infrequently because it is understood to be breaking the fourth wall, the metaphorical window that separates viewers from the imaginary world of the drama or comedy. When direct address is used in movies, it's usually to complicate the viewer's relationship to the characters or story. Direct address when used in a vlog elevates the role of the viewer because we become directly part of the performer's story. Direct address conveys a sense of immediacy, so, for example, we can watch a performer's direct address and feel like they share the same time and space as us, even when we know the video was made years ago in a remote location.

Third, whether to use a static, shaky, or *moving camera* is another important decision that affects ethos. Derek Muller, who created the YouTube channel Veritasium, sometimes uses a selfie stick while walking around in a city, creating a moving camera effect as he and talks, walks, and films simultaneously. Although this is a challenging performance to master and produce well, the technique combines the excitement of action and unpredictability that is appealing to viewers.

Finally, another characteristic of ethos can sometimes be found the quality of the *framing* used by vloggers. How is a character depicted visually and specifically positioned within the frame of the camera? In Karoliina

Talvitie-Lamberg's study of confessional vlogs, she found that poor quality video actually seems to make the video performance itself seem more intimate. She explained, "The rough image quality helped construct the impression of the situation as an authentic and real one." In one video she examined, half of the vlogger's head was framed out of the image. Still, the effect was powerful. The camera angle communicated the private nature of the confession, as if the camera was "only a witness" of the situation.[11] When video production techniques are used to enhance ethos, vlogs don't feel "produced" as much as simply created.

Parasocial Relationships

In the 1950s psychiatrists began noticing that some people were obsessed by celebrities, engaging in fandom as a type of one-sided relationship. Feelings of attachment with celebrities, organizations (such as sports teams), or television stars are common. When you pay attention to a particular athlete, musician, or political figure, you're investing emotional energy, interest, and time. But the other party, the living persona, is unaware of your existence. Celebrities are aware of their fans en masse, as in Lady Gaga's recognition of the "little monsters."

There are reasons why people form parasocial attachments to media figures. During childhood and adolescence, young people may form attachments to celebrities or media figures as a part of the identity development process. The pleasure of parasocial relationships comes in part from *uncertainty reduction* as relationships develop over time through a process of moving from uncertain to more certain. In the beginning, you experience uncertainty in your encounter with another individual. Over time, as uncertainty decreases, liking increases because you are better able to predict the other's behavior.[12] Parasocial relationships are relatively low-risk relationships: you enjoy the feeling of "knowing" someone without having to reciprocate by sharing your own identity, needs, ideas, and values. Thus, there's little personal risk in forming attachments to media figures.

Participatory Complications

Many people experience real delight in creating and publishing a vlog. They experience a sense of creative flow. Vloggers may also experience a profound sense of making a meaningful personal, social, or political contribution by addressing topics and issues that are important to them and to society. It may be that the performance of identity enables vloggers to make an authentic connection to their audiences. But make no mistake about it: when vloggers share personal stories, they may be more or less authentic. Actors are very skillful at creating performances that seem quite real even though they are not. Of course, some vloggers may be simply seeking attention or using fake intimacy to make a superficial social connection with the viewer. We shouldn't assume that the very format of the vlog inherently makes people truthful or brings authenticity to the fore.

There are a variety of complications that come from performing one's identity online in a highly social online context. Vloggers are often part of a community and their vlogs are a form of conversation. For example, the hashtag #smallyoutuber links together a group of people who are making vlogs for fun. They are often fans of more highly visible YouTubers but enjoy adding their own voices and creativity to the mix. By commenting and responding other vloggers, this helps create a sense of community.

Scholars who study marketing and media recognize that people may adopt a number of stances towards online participation, taking on the role of devotees, tourists or minglers.[13] Consider your own interactions online: they may vary from one context to another, as you have different levels of participation with family, friends, coworkers, online friends, and even brands or products. You may be a *devotee* if you possess a strong interest in a particular online activity, but have few strong social ties to other members of the online community. For example, you may use Twitter frequently but without engaging in much personal conversation with individual users. Insiders also have a strong personal interest in a consumption activity along with strong social ties to other community members. For example, you may feel connected to some (but not all) of the people who are your Facebook friends and feel a sense of obligation to participate in social interaction. Sometimes, you might take on the role of *tourist* if you lack strong ties with either the online activity or with other members of the online community. For example, you may use Quora to scan for interesting questions and answers, but without contributing to the platform. Finally, in some online interactions, you may be a *mingler* by maintaining strong social ties with other members of the online community just for fun but without much passion for the topic or activity being discussed. If you use Instagram as a mingler, you only view the images shared by friends and are not otherwise engaged with other content.

Interaction between vloggers and their viewers is semi-structured and creative. Vloggers often directly ask the audience to subscribe to their channel, like, or comment on their work as this builds reputational status and provides financial support. Sometimes interactivity is designed into the video itself. For example, in the video entitled "Epic Rap Battles of History," this highly produced and hilarious music videos feature rap battles between historical figures, actors, and celebrities. In "Austin Powers vs. James Bond," we hear Nice Peter, epicLLOYD, and Dave McCary offering their taunts to each other in clever rhymes. At the conclusion of the video, viewers are asked, "Who Won? What's Next?" and the comment thread is filled with opinions about which historical rapper was best and suggestions for future pair-ups.[14]

How to Create a Vlog

First, plan what you want to talk about – and plan to talk about something that interests you. Use impromptu, extemporaneous, or written manuscript techniques for planning the content of your vlog. Have a clear purpose and audience and keep this firmly in your mind throughout the production process. You may want to have friends serve as your studio audience, to increase the feeling that you're actually talking to someone, or you may prefer to perform alone, speaking to an imaginary audience – it's up to you.

Select a location and arrange the space. Be attentive to the background. It's best to have some depth to the background. If you are standing in front of a wall, the flat background makes you look small and trapped in the frame. If you're standing in a room, with light from a window shining on your face, the depth of field behind you helps create an aesthetically pleasing shot. Lighting is important to video production because people look best with diffuse white light shining on their faces – this makes everyone look better and there is no substitute for great light. Don't shoot at nighttime in a dark room without good light and never film yourself in front of a window.

Vloggers may use a variety of different types of video cameras, from expensive DSLR cameras to smartphones or the webcam on a laptop. When using a video camera, a tripod is essential to ensure that the camera is steady. Camera placement is important for vlogging. When you place the webcam or camera on a tripod, just slightly higher than your eye level, you look up to it a bit, creating an attractive jaw line, according to MissFenderr, a vlogger. Warm up and practice to get used to talking in front of the camera. "If you mess up, just say it again," says MissFenderr.[15] Once you hit record, use vocal energy and enunciate. Many vloggers stand to perform because standing up helps your voice sound more lively and energetic.

When it's time to edit, you can use video editing software to edit your work. You may even explore collaborative free online video editing tools like WeVideo where teams can share footage and work together on a project. Many people have created screencast videos to explain how to use these tools – and you'll find that if you run into a problem, it's likely that someone has described how to solve it via a screencast video. For example, the keyword search "WeVideo help" yields over 10,000 videos where people created short tutorials or advice on using the basic and advanced features of the online video editing tool.

Many vlogs use *jump cuts*, a distinctive style of editing. Figure 11.4 shows an image from a video tutorial about how to edit jump cuts. Jump cuts remove

Figure 11.4 Editing jump cuts.

pauses and speed up the rate of speech by removing some of the nonspeaking time that occurs between sentences. While some people find these cuts jarring, they do focus your viewer's attention. Jump cuts can add rhythm and accentuate the informal, playful feel to vlogs. Jump cuts are a distinctive feature or convention that distinguishes vlogs from professional productions. Online tutorials demonstrate how to edit jump cuts by listening for pauses.

One common technique is the use of a jump cut to communicate a humorous aside, a remark that is not directly related to the main idea. Other people use jump cuts to intensify small movements. For example, John Green may move from the left side of the frame to the center in a jump cut, creating a shift that disrupts the viewer's sense of time.

Although it's not very difficult, some people may need assistance or benefit from a video tutorial when first learning to export video: uploading these files can be confusing to beginners. The quality of the image is related to the size of the digital file. If your video files are in a high resolution video format, they will take longer to upload.

Screencasting in Education

Tutorials are an important genre on YouTube. When Kimberly Turner decided to create the video, "Vlog Virgins," she developed a series of videos where she demonstrated how to create and edit videos.[16] By creating a screencast tutorial, she was able to demonstrate how to use iMovie to record webcam video. This is a fine example of informal digital learning, the kind of learning that happens online as self-directed learners provide assistance to others using Create to Learn principles. When watching a screencast tutorial, we can see a process in action, as when we see Kimberly selecting video clips to assemble, using simple drag-and-drop techniques to add sound effects and music. She combines her screencast with a web camera where she explains her work, talking directly to us via the camera in her laptop. As a viewer, I watch and learn from such screencasts, as I watch, then pause and copy. Repeating this process enables me to learn at my own pace, by observing and imitating, as apprentices have done throughout the ages. What a great way to learn!

Screencasts are a simple but versatile video production tool for both informal learning as well as for formal education at the elementary, secondary, college, and university levels. In one classroom, a college professor created math screencasts that demonstrated how to solve problems. Because people can pause and replay a screencast, it can help learners handle ideas at their own pace. One study found that students who used screencasts to clarify misunderstandings, supplement the lecture material, and review for exams helped them to perform better at a college level math course. Students in this study preferred instructor-developed screencasts to those provided online, with one student noting that "having the lecturer create them also means that you're shown the method on how to solve a problem just as you have seen in the classroom."[17]

Teaching others has always been a great way to learn something. Eric Marcos, a middle school teacher in California, discovered the power of screencasting when teaching math to sixth graders. One of his students was struggling with how to solve a problem, so he made a screencast video to demonstrate a problem-solving strategy. Another of his students, inspired by her teacher, spontaneously created her own math screencast at home, sharing it with Marcos. "There are multiple ways to solve math problems," she explained. "Plus, kids like learning from other kids." Mr. Marcos shows students how to use Windows Journal to demonstrate their problems and Camtasia to record their screencasts. Mr. Marcos even teaches kids how to add special effects to their screencasts including adding yellow highlighting or enhancing the audio quality.[18]

One student, Tiana Kadkhoda, actually discovered that she had an interest in math only when she began creating interesting visuals and collaborating with friends on math screencasts. Figure 11.5 shows an example of her work. "By explaining difficult concepts on video, I was forced to confront and clarify my understanding of the topics," she wrote. "Through these videos I have learned how to clearly communicate visually and verbally, study more effectively, become a leader among my peers and take control of my education by extending learning beyond the classroom."[19]

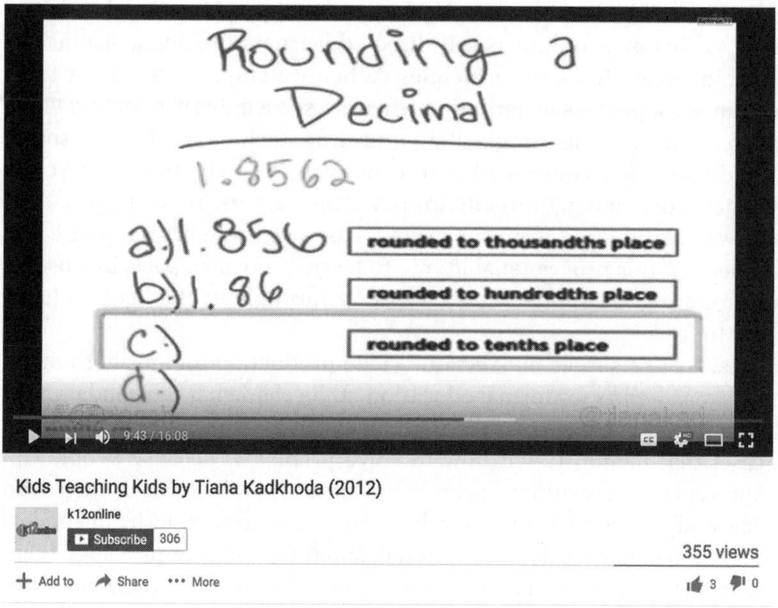

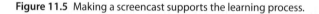

Kids Teaching Kids by Tiana Kadkhoda (2012)

Figure 11.5 Making a screencast supports the learning process.

Some Types of Academic Screencasts

Demonstration. A presenter demonstrates a process using a digital media platform or with a series of images or other content presented on a computer screen.

Slideshow. A presenter discusses content accompanied by a series of PowerPoint slides.

Conversational. Two or more presenters discuss and comment on content using a combination of webcam, PowerPoint slides, and screen capture.

Whiteboard drawing. A presenter narrates a whiteboard session, using digital ink to write and draw on blank PowerPoint slides or uses another drawing application like Explain Everything.

How to Make a Screencast

Screencasts enable you to inform, persuade, and entertain. Have a clear purpose and audience and keep this firmly in your mind throughout the production process. As you develop ideas for the content of your presentation, you'll want to decide whether to use impromptu, extemporaneous, or manuscript speaking. If your content is complex, you may want to create an audio recording of your content in advance of creating a screencast to give you greater control in editing.

Choose a screencast tool from the many choices provided at the Create to Learn website and familiarize yourself with the digital tool. Each tool will enable you to record your screen by using a sizing tool to select which part of the screen you want to capture. It will have a button for starting, pausing, and stopping the recording. Some tools will enable you to switch between recording via webcam (depicting your face) and the screen recording. Others will enable you to combine webcam and screen recording, displaying the webcam in a little box at the left-hand side of the screen (or making the webcam display in full screen).

Your presentation should have a strong opening line that attracts attention and helps people understand what they will be seeing and hearing. Practice your presentation and make a short test recording. This will help you determine if the content presented on the screen looks good: you may want to increase the font size, make your icons bigger, or increase the size of your mouse arrow. When you save your recording, you may publish it directly to YouTube or save the file to your computer and then upload. Depending on your purpose, you can choose whether to share your video with the world or limit access using the Unlisted or Private functions of YouTube. If you want people to see your video, remember to add tags to help increase the findability. By adding 6–10 keywords and offering a concise summary of your video, it's more likely that your work will find an authentic audience.

Ethical Issues: Dealing with Feedback

Vloggers and screencasters sometimes create media for the fun of it. They may or may not be aware of their audience and the choices they are making in representing their own identity. Some people find that their work receives little attention and few people view it and other times vloggers and screencasters are surprised when people like, comment, or share their work. Comments can be hurtful. PewDiePie, one of the most famous YouTube celebrities, decided to disable the comments on his YouTube channel after the quality of the comments, along with spam and self-advertising overwhelmed him. Instead, he uses Twitter to interact with his 30 million subscribers.

In any case, interaction among online viewers can be robust, visceral, raw, and sometimes disturbing. Some vloggers find creative strategies for dealing with criticism. When studying the work and lives of YouTubers, researchers acknowledge that "circulating personal information to a vast Internet audience creates risks that range from humiliation to emotional and physical harm."[20]

In their quest for attention, some vloggers and screencasters have discovered that the mass media formula of *sensationalism* is just as effective on YouTube as it is on CBS, NBC, or MTV. Offensive content attracts attention and gets people talking. That's why trash talking in the comment threads of YouTube can often lead to increasing video views. Some people even claim that the *rant* should also be considered a sub-genre on YouTube, Reddit, and other online communities. When you define your work as a rant, listeners expect that you're going to be biased and emotional. Patricia Lange notes: "It is as if marking harsh criticism with the term 'rant' makes it socially acceptable to its audience."[21]

Once you have uploaded a video to YouTube, you may receive feedback on your work. But remember that only about 12 percent of people who view videos actually use the commenting function of YouTube. Registered users may post a text or video response to what they have viewed. For some videos, there are so many comments that they flow across multiple pages. As a video creator, you can choose to enable or disable comments on your video. You can moderate comments, choosing which ones to display on your website and remove comments that you do not wish to see displayed on the video. Users can also flag inappropriate comments or suspected spam for moderation.

If you read comments on YouTube videos for more than a few minutes, you'll find considerable *flaming*, a term that originated in the 1980s in the early computing community to refer to people who "speak rabidly or incessantly on an uninteresting topic or with a patently ridiculous attitude."[22] Flaming is the exchange of strong and inflammatory opinions, including the use of offensive language such as swearing and insults. It's a simple way to draw attention to yourself online.

Humiliating other screencasters and vloggers, criticizing others, and talking insensitively about people, places, ideas or events are cheap shots, an easy way to attract attention. Some people even choose not to exchange feedback and interaction about YouTube videos because they anticipate their comments will be criticized by haters. In her video, "Stop Supporting Media Trolls," Kat Blaque notices that viewers' attraction to conflict and controversy is part of the economics of YouTube.[23] Getting to be the "Most Discussed Video" is actually aided by the presence of haters, who may displace their own unhappiness through making mean comments. The advice most commonly offered is "Don't Feed the Trolls." Trolls are an Internet menace: their comments seem designed to deliberately anger people, or disrupt a discussion. They use abusive language, or pretend to be profoundly ignorant because, like all human beings, they crave attention, which is why ignoring them usually makes them go away.

Activity: Create a Screencast or Vlog

Create a screencast or vlog that addresses a specific topic of interest and simultaneously informs, persuades and entertains. Consider your audience and purpose carefully in deciding whether to create a vlog or a screencast. Apply some of the concepts you learned in this chapter to your work. Share your work with others and ask them to offer their interpretations. Then write a short essay that describes your creative process. Consider these questions:

- How did your ideas develop in the process of creating the vlog or screencast?
- What techniques did you use to ensure that your work was both informative and entertaining?
- Which ideas from this chapter informed your strategy or message?
- Reviewing your completed work, what did you like best? What might you have done differently or improved?

12

Video Production

KEY IDEAS

Video is among the most powerful of communication tools because it combines the power of image, sound, music and editing to express ideas, share information and offer a point of view.

The widespread availability of video production tools on smartphones continues to blur the continuum between everyday users, amateurs, and professionals. Many people acquire the knowledge of video production without going to film school, using free resources available online. "How-to" and educational videos have become increasingly popular as a result of YouTube. Eyewitness videos have a particular appeal because they seem to record reality as it happens. Although documentary video is a nonfiction genre, it uses a variety of techniques to creative narrative structure. To advance their cause, activists can evoke viewers' strong emotional response to manipulate information and ideas. As a result, people need robust critical thinking skills to recognize forms of video propaganda that may be beneficial or harmful.

What happened when a group of soil erosion graduate students met up with undergraduate students at the University of Rhode Island? Working together, they created a 17-minute documentary that chronicles the unpredictable and authentic learning experience of the young scientists and young communicators — before, during, and after Hurricane Sandy wreaked its havoc on the south coast of Rhode Island. Created through a collaboration supported by the URI Provost's Technology Initiative, students enrolled in Roy Bergstrom's FLM 445 course worked with graduate students at the URI Graduate School of Oceanography to create a film about coastal erosion.

The film opens with the words "Sea Level is Rising" in stark black-and-white text. Then the viewer hears the soft warm sounds of the summer beach, with waves lapping the coast and seagulls calling. We see two guys on the beach with surveying instruments. "What we're doing is measuring beach erosion on the southern coast of Rhode Island," said Cameron Morrissette, an oceanography graduate student. "It's probably one of the longest-running data sets of its time, running continuously since the 1960s. The beach changes a lot

Create to Learn: Introduction to Digital Literacy, First Edition. Renee Hobbs.
© 2017 John Wiley & Sons, Inc. Published 2017 by John Wiley & Sons, Inc.

Figure 12.1 *Ocean Tales* by Daniel Larsh.

every year, but when you look at it over a half century, you can see the changes over time."[1]

As the undergraduate students shoot video of the graduate students making measurements of beach erosion (Figure 12.1), they are learning about science from young scientists in the field. "Being out in the field, learning about erosion and making a film about it is such a different experience from reading from a book," said Daniel Larsh, a URI student who participated in the project. We see the scientific team measuring beach erosion at a number of spots where houses and businesses are precariously close to the sea, where sandbags are piled up to protect building foundations, driveways, and roads.

But quickly, the film's music shifts to signal something ominous. Chris Knowlton, a marine geochemist, points to a satellite picture of Hurricane Sandy, still west of the Bahamas. Hurricane Sandy extended 700 miles up and down the East Coast. "It's going to arrive in New Jersey, making landfall on Tuesday," he says. When the storm surges and winds started blowing at 60 miles per hour, the young filmmakers head out with cameras in hand. The images show driving rain and fast-moving wipers, downed trees, and police "Do Not Cross" signs along the side of the road. "Oh my God," we hear one young filmmaker say as they are driving along the coast during the storm, "We're going to get arrested making this film."[2]

It was a solemn experience for the young filmmakers to see people's houses and property destroyed in just under 24 hours. Aerial footage taken immediately after the storm showed extensive damage to beach houses and roads. "In terms of climate change, everything happens slowly," one student noted. "But the devastation after Sandy was terrible. Seeing these beaches before and after the storm magnified my appreciation for these special places and the need to address climate change." As Bill McKibben writes, "When that ocean is hot – and at the moment sea surface temperatures off the Northeast are five degrees higher than normal – a storm like Sandy can lurch north longer and stronger, drawing huge quantities of moisture into its clouds, and then dumping them ashore."[3] A close look at how scientists create new knowledge increases people's respect for the scientific consensus that climate change is an urgent global concern requiring immediate action.

Amateur and Professional Video

Today 5.2 billion people around the world have a mobile phone and 82 percent of those phones have a video camera built into it.[4] But well before the advent of the Internet, video has been recognized as a means to empower ordinary people. When amateur footage of the 1991 beating by police of Rodney King in Los Angeles was first broadcast on US television networks, the cultural and political power of eyewitness video became obvious. Consumer-grade video camcorders have reconfigured the relationships of power between producers and consumers and between professionals and amateurs. Using their camcorders, ordinary people could document current events and communicate to a mass audience.[5]

But during the 1990s, instead of contributing to improving public knowledge, the video camera's popularity was used primarily to document family life. Consider the rise of television shows that featured crazy stunts and embarrassing family moments. Shows such as *America's Funniest Home Movies* represented the private, domestic world of the family, rather than the representation of more social, political, artistic, or public issues. Cultural critics were concerned by this trend, having long suggested that "popular or mass culture destroys high culture, critical thinking and the political potential of the public sphere, replacing these noble activities with false consciousness and propaganda."[6] As John Berger notes, the blurring between information and entertainment genres, which turns everything into spectacle, compromises political action and turns consumption into a substitute for democracy.[7]

Still, plenty of everyday users are satisfied with using the video function of their smartphones not as a tool for political advocacy but as an ordinary part of daily life. It has become a tradition in many families for parents to videotape their children as they grow up. They are not interested in communicating to an audience beyond the family, so there's no need to add titles, music, special effects, or do any editing. For these users, video-making is a form of play that's not linked to any particular form of communication practice – it's purely in the realm of the creative, the exploratory, and the expressive. Many people just want to have fun by documenting everyday life.

But as video production equipment became cheaper and simpler to use, a continuum developed between the point-and-shoot approach used by everyday users and the more intentional, artful, and strategic approach used by amateurs, who may (or may not) be aspiring to be professionals.[8] Amateurs who are hoping to get paid for their work as professionals make short films on tiny budgets that attract attention and help them get hired. You can see many examples of this on Vimeo, which is the online video community for aspiring professionals. For example, Fede Alvarez, a Uruguayan filmmaker, created *Panic Attack!*, a five-minute film featuring giant robots destroying a city. Only months after it was uploaded to YouTube, he was invited to direct *Evil Dead*, a supernatural horror film.[9]

When people want their videos to have greater impact, reaching a larger audience, they put more time and effort into creating an attractive, compelling video. To achieve this more polished look, they seek out ways to learn about lighting, shot composition, film grammar, and editing. They want to use video equipment that more closely approximates the tools that professionals use. The market has responded to this continuum, providing a range of video cameras at different price points. Cameras have gotten smaller and lighter for everyday users while continuing to have better image quality, as evidenced by the rise of digital video, high definition formats, and even wearable point-of-view camcorders and video drones.

As video has become more dominant as a means of sharing knowledge and ideas, people are now expected to have a significant amount of knowledge about filmmaking even if they are not aspiring to be professionals. David Buckingham and his colleagues note:

> Becoming a serious amateur is seen to involve a learning process; and one key aspect of this entails the need to reflect on professional filmmaking practices. Improving one's work involves learning and applying "film grammar" and techniques (e.g. the "rule of thirds," the "180 degree rule," continuity, camera angles, lighting, editing) as well as paying close attention to planning and scripting.[10]

Fortunately, it's easier than ever to learn about the art of filmmaking. Thanks to the rise of "The Making of..." films, which showcase the behind-the-scenes professional film production process, you can see how Peter Jackson made *King Kong* or how Stanley Kubrick created *The Shining*. But even more interesting and informative than looking behind the scenes of a big budget film is seeing how a low-budget film is created. Robert Rodriguez created the classic work on the subject, entitled *Rebel without a Crew*, a film diary telling of the making of *El Mariachi*, a narrative film he made on a $7,000 budget and later sold to Columbia Tri-Star for $250,000. The behind-the-scenes film he created, *10-Minute Film School*, illustrates the many creative strategies he used for low-budget filming and editing.[11]

Young children get a basic sense of filmmaking thanks to shows like *iCarly*, which features a team of children making a web television show. Another way to learn filmmaking is to create a remake adaptation in your backyard. Perhaps you remember making movies when you were growing up? In 1982, when video equipment was just becoming available to consumers and years before movies became available on VHS, Chris Strompolos, Eric Zala, and Jayson Lamb created a shot-by-shot adaptation of *Raiders of the Lost Ark*, the first Indiana Jones film, beginning when they were only 12 years old. Over the course of seven summers, the boys made an illicit audiotape of the film, memorized the dialogue, and created sketches of the costumes and props. As Figure 12.2 shows, they reconstructed 649 shots from the movie in a spiral-bound notebook, drawing out each shot. They borrowed equipment to recreate each shot, even building a large boulder out of bamboo sticks and paper mache. Using a Sony Betamax video camera rented for the boys by their parents, they recreated many scenes from the film, including the one bar sequence in their basement, where they intentionally set a fire to reproduce the film effect (which nearly burned down their parents' house).[12] After many years, the film was screened to an audience in Austin, Texas when the boys were in college. Since then, it has become a cult classic.

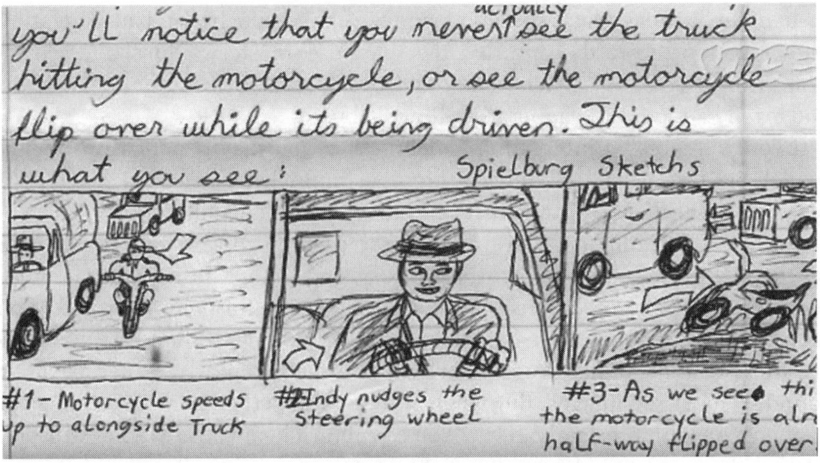

Figure 12.2 Storyboard for the shot-by-shot remake of *Raiders of the Lost Ark* by Eric Zalan.

The Personal Video Essay

Abby Kent wears glasses. She's been wearing them every since the third grade. In a video essay, Abby reflects on the function of glasses in her life in a four-minute video entitled *Spectacles*. In it she describes how corrective lenses have shaped her experience of the world. In her film, we see images of Abby at the optometrist, where she explains that her eyeballs are "too long." In one sequence, we see Abby in a montage of images of herself wearing glasses of all shapes and sizes. In a lyrical transition, Abby explains that one her greatest fears is getting lost in the woods without her glasses. Over a montage of blurry images of trees, rocks, woods, and sky, she makes a list of her specific fears: "Even if I had a map, I wouldn't be able to read it."

Abby then explains the science of spectacles: they bend light in order to create a sharper image. As we see her putting on contact lenses, Abby explains about how the images produced by the eye are actually upside down. Each eye sees a slightly different picture as "our brain stitches together a composite." As a filmmaker, the lens on Abby's camera is an extension of herself. In the closing moments of the film, she reminds us of the surreal pleasure of seeing the world without glasses, as "a smear of blurry, colorful shapes. I like to think of it as my own personal Impressionist painting."[13]

As the viewer of this personal essay film watches these out-of-focus but gorgeous images, we're not exactly sure what they represent. But their strong composition and lovely colors are evocative. In the film's conclusion, the viewer feels a bit more sensitive to the many different ways in which we all see and make sense of the world with our unique pair of eyes.

The video essay is a fascinating genre. Professor Kelli Marshall at DePaul University gives her undergraduate students the option to create a video essay in her film history classes, helping move scholarship beyond just creating knowledge and towards capturing the "pleasure, mystery, allure, and seduction" of intellectual discovery. She requires that the video essay be based on and extend a required reading from the syllabus.[14]

If you're interested in creating a video essay, you may benefit from seeing models of a somewhat unfamiliar genre. The filmmaker Chris Marker is recognized for creating one of the greatest film essays with his film, *San Soleil*, created in 1983. The film uses travel footage and other moving images to meditate on the relationship between truth, memory, and time. The video essay often relies on a complex relationship between language, image, and sound. The viewer must gather up the elements, listen, and look with the heart, to grasp the film's true meaning. Words don't capture the complexity – neither does sound or music or images. But when combined together, something magical happens. As John Bresland puts it, "You can almost hear Chris Marker whisper, 'Here is the problem of being alive right now.'"[15]

"How To" and Educational Videos

It's an eye-popping headline: "Facebook Food Videos are the New Porn." All around the world, television cooking shows have been growing in popularity, even as cooking and eating at home has decreased. Cooking is but one of many forms of "how to" videos that have grown in popularity since the turn of the millennium. Over the years, they have shifted from being more educational to becoming more entertainment-oriented. Shows like *Iron Chef* combine competition with cooking; other shows include a focus on travel, relationships, science or culture. Celebrity chefs like Jamie Oliver (famous for his British television show, *The Naked Chef*) proliferate on television networks around the world.

Cooking videos are now becoming designed for mobile platforms. One example is *Tastemade*, which reaches over 100 million users per month with its food, lifestyle, and travel videos. The format uses extreme time-lapse techniques to show how to make a specific recipe. Videos are usually only 30–60 seconds in length, designed to be viewed on your Facebook or mobile phone (with or without sound). For example, in "Potato Pizza," with over 90 million views as of 2016, you see a speeded-up picture of a potato being thinly sliced, placed in a frying pan, covered with grated cheese and simmered. Tomato sauce is then added along with mushrooms, fresh mozzarella, and an egg cracked over top. With some thin slices of prosciutto, the dish is finished and served in a video that is just under a minute. Besides cooking, home improvement and beauty are the most searched for "how to" videos.[16] In 2015, Google reported that the number "how to" searches are increasing by 70 percent each year. Perhaps you have searched for videos on how to fix a washing machine, how to style a "man bun," or how to build a treehouse.[17]

YouTube is a powerful tool for learning that's both practical and academic. YouTube's Teacher channel shows teachers how to transform their classroom into student-centered learning environments through the active use of educational videos. Video is a good way to learn. Students can become familiar with topics including plate tectonics, figures of speech, legal principles, electrical engineering and thousands of others.

At YouTube's *Veritasium*, Derek Muller creates videos that inform wile intensifying a sense of wonder about the world. In one video, "World's Roundest Object!" viewed 19 million times as of 2016, Derek holds the roundest object in the world, a pure polished silicon sphere. It helps solve an important measurement problem – how to define the kilogram. Since the atom spacing of silicon is well known, the number of atoms in a sphere can be accurately calculated. Using the number of atoms in a sphere as the standard for the kilogram is superior to other measurement standards.[18]

At *Mathalicious*, video and popular culture are used to apply mathematics concepts and skills. In one activity, after watching and analyzing a video that illustrates the history of video games, students examine changes in video-game processing speeds over the decades. They write an exponential function based on the Atari 2600 and research other video-game consoles to determine whether they've followed Moore's Law, the principle developed by Gordon Moore in 1965 that predicts that computer processor speeds will double every two years.[19] Clearly, there are many different ways to learn from watching YouTube videos.

But don't believe for a minute that learning from film and video is all about YouTube. In fact, practical how-to films have a long and distinguished history. In 1926, the Amateur Cinema League was established to support the work of amateur filmmakers who created practical films for learning about all kind of subjects, including geometry, how to fish herring, and even ceramics. These films were commonly viewed in schools, libraries, factories, and settlement houses. In fact, it was a film about making a clay pot, produced in 1933, that experts tell us that the aesthetic of industrial filmmaking was born. The ceramics film was both informative and beautiful to watch: it imbibed "the spirit of the artist craftsman" reinterpreted by the filmmaker's visual eye.[20]

The same people who created industrial films also advanced the genre of the social problem film, demonstrating advances in medicine, public health, and social work. One film, *The Forgotten Frontier*, created in 1930, depicts the work of health care professionals who visit Appalachia to provide services to the rural poor.[21] These docudrama films were influenced by the work of John Dewey, a philosopher who explored the relationship between art and everyday experience. They were true stories that manipulated reality in order to intensify a compelling narrative within the context of a problem–solution structure. By combining the practical and the beautiful, such films could inspire and renew the human spirit.

Top 10 "How To" Searches 2012–2015

1) How to kiss
2) How to tie a tie
3) How to draw
4) How to get a six pack in three minutes
5) How to make a starburst bracelet rainbow loom
6) How to make a cake
7) How to curl your hair with a straightener
8) How to make a bow
9) How to make a paper airplane
10) How to dance

Source: Ten Years of YouTube.

Documentary Structure

When we think about documentary films, we believe them to be truthful. But because all media messages are constructed, they always communicate a point of view. While all documentary films have a subject, not all of them have a clearly identifiable story. When we encounter characters who move through events in a forward direction, with increasing levels of conflict, action and reaction, this story structure often includes heroes, villains, and victims. Documentaries use story structure because it's so effective with audiences.

Some documentaries don't tell a story but use order and structure to develop an argument by the sequential placement of facts and opinions. But don't confuse this with the idea that documentaries are more truthful than fiction films. As the Canadian International Documentary Festival organizers explain, "It is crucial when watching documentaries to be aware of the intentions of the filmmaker and to test their ability to convince you of the truth they are trying to convey."[22]

Although they are works of nonfiction, documentaries tell us what to think about a subject, whether to see someone or something as good or evil, desirable or undesirable, normal or abnormal. Documentaries may even construct an "us vs them" relationship to inspire us to feel or think a certain way towards individuals or groups in society. When you watch a documentary, you might feel good about yourself. It's like you are part of the solution: you care about the issues and people involved and you want to understand them better. But documentary filmmaker Jill Godmilow notes that documentary films exercise power by their deliberate attempt to alter their viewers' relationship to a subject.[23]

For example, the 2009 documentary, *The Cove*, about the methods used by Japanese fisherman to capture dolphins, shocked viewers with its disgusting and graphic depiction of animals being killed. The only animal film to ever win an Oscar for best documentary, this advocacy film combines drama, adventure, suspense, and humor to support those concerned about the rights of cetaceans (whales, dolphins, and porpoises). Created by filmmaker activists who surreptitiously gathered the footage from offshore villages in southwest Japan, the film provokes audiences to feel sympathy for the dolphins and extreme anger towards the Japanese fisherman – without ever including the point of view of the fishermen themselves.

Because people experience strong emotions watching advocacy documentaries, they sometimes may mistake the "immediacy of emotions as proof of their unmediated truth," says Melissa Haynes.[24] Documentaries like *The Cove* activate disgust, an emotion that simultaneously attracts and repels us. The film

Police Brutality Captured on Cellphone Video

Even the most desensitized individual was moved by footage shot by Diamond Reynolds, who livestreamed the moments immediately after police shot and killed her boyfriend, Philando Castile, while she sat in the driver's seat of her car with her five-year-old daughter in the back seat. We were compelled to recognize the power of eyewitness video to mobilize people towards political action. Figure 12.3 captures the fear and shock that Diamond experienced in that moment.

Figure 12.3 Livestream: Police shooting of Philando Castile by Diamond Reynolds.

New York Times television critic James Poniewozik describes the surreal experience of watching cellphone video of the aftermath of the murder of Philando Castile at the hands of police officers in Minnesota on July 6, 2016. He describes the experience:

> More officers, guns drawn, tell her to get out of the car and get on her knees. Someone puts the phone on the ground, and you see blue sky and utility wires. You hear the click of handcuffs, sirens, a male voice shouting, cursing. Then a hand picks up the phone, and there's blackness. But you can still hear. You hear Ms. Reynolds cry out – "Please don't tell me my boyfriend's gone!" – hear her pray for Mr. Castile's life, hear her testify for him: "He's never been a gang member, anything."

Witnessing is an affirmative act. However, for all of video's power to bring us directly into a moment, it can't help but remind us of the gulf between virtual and physical. As Diamond Reynolds sits in the back of a police car, handcuffed, with her daughter, she tells any friends watching live that she's going to need a ride. Finally, she loses her composure and screams. "It's O.K.," we hear her daughter say. "I'm right here with you."[25]

humanizes the dolphins and dehumanizes the rural, working class fisherman, and it inspired a wave of anti-Japanese racism on social media. By relying on emotion as the primary tool for social change, *The Cove* suggests that rational political debate is increasingly supplementary to the activation of strong feelings. Regardless of your position on the topic of cetacean rights, such approaches to the use of film for social change can be dangerous.

Eyewitness Video: The Power of Actuality

When you witness a crisis, you can't help but want other people to care. With people's increasing access to video cameras, eyewitness video footage of political and social events has become a routine feature of mainstream news coverage, expanding and transforming the way journalists report the news. Sometimes those eyewitnesses are journalists working for a news organization. Ordinary people might become eyewitnesses if they're able to use their smartphone videos in a breaking news situation. And some newsworthy events are captured by the more than 30 million surveillance cameras in the United States alone.

Today, professional journalists depend upon the work of citizen journalists. The public sharing of amateur images of the Arab Spring uprisings in 2011–2012 demonstrated the power of amateur video footage to increase the visibility of political crises around the world. When an earthquake struck Japan in March 2011, millions of people learned about the natural disaster through YouTube. Japanese people themselves, in the middle of the crisis, documented the earthquake and the tsunami that killed more than 18,000 people. Recorded and uploaded by citizen eyewitnesses who found themselves caught in the tragedy, these videos were then broadcast by news organizations. The most watched video of all was shot by what appeared to be fixed closed-circuit surveillance camera at the local airport.[26]

As researchers point out, "Journalists involved in crisis reporting need to constantly negotiate this paradox between the traditional normative constructions of journalism and the committed narration that underwrites the idea of witnessing."[27] In reporting on crisis, journalists navigate the inevitable tension between bearing witness to the intense emotions activated by exposure to human tragedy and providing an impartial narrative of it. The capacity of film to activate and channel an emotional response is at the heart of its potential as a powerful form of propaganda.

Scientists also have benefited from large-scale public access to video cameras. Video recordings by eyewitnesses offer tremendous value to science and society. The 2004 Sumatran tsunami resulted from a magnitude 9.0 earthquake and the flow of the tsunami waves was captured by two survivors who took video footage of the event. Although they were 3 kilometers from the open ocean, scientists were able to use the eyewitness video to calculate the velocity of the water flow.[28]

Eyewitness video has some distinctive *formal features* that enable viewers to recognize it as a distinct genre or form. *Hypermobility* is the shaky camera, with its sudden and seemingly aimless camera movement, where the videographer is trying to capture footage but does not draw viewer attention to a particular point of interest. *Opacity* is the typically blurry and grainy quality of eyewitness video, which may include poor lighting and other interferences within the field of vision. *Non-narrativity* is the term used to describe the chaotic, fragmentary, and incoherence of "raw" audio and video, where sound is unedited and the camera is just rolling, pointing in all directions with central events often taking place off-screen. Eyewitness video communicates *authenticity* by these formal features as well as the context in which the work is screened.

In analyzing the eyewitness video that depicted the 2011 murder of Colonel Muammar Gaddafi, a Libyan revolutionary, researchers recognized the video's "deeply subjectivist insight into the brutal drama of the former dictator's capture as it was enacted by, and impacted upon, his fellow citizens who, just like him, were an integral party to the political crisis in Libya."[29] Unlike professional journalists who are detached from events, citizen videographers are involved *partisans*: they are attempting to get a particular message across. As Kari Andén-Papadopoulos explains:

> Citizen imagery that acknowledges its invested perspective is thus often perceived as more truthful and sincere than the "professional" appeal to a principle of detachment which underpins the news image's claim to reality.

Eyewitness videographers are implicated in the events they depict. They are simultaneously reporters and participants, and this subjectivity is in distinct contrast to the role of the journalist. Viewers experience strong emotions when viewing eyewitness video. Even if we hate Gaddafi, the video's depiction of his bloodied face, "his brutalized, confused and agonizing look almost inevitably humanizes him, urging us to identify with his helplessness."[30]

How to Film a Live Event

The international human rights organization, Witness, created a comprehensive manual for creating eyewitness videos of rallies and public events in 2009 as part of the Pledge to Protect anti-genocide campaign.[31] They offer this advice:

1) **Safety First**. When filming a live event, be aware of your own safety. Bring someone with you to watch for potential problems so that you can focus on filming.
2) **Location Shots**. Get wide shots at a distance from the event as well as close shots from within it. Wide shots establishing a sense of the place where the event is taking place – that's why they are called establishing shots.

Close-up shots have more emotional impact as the audience will be confronted more powerfully with the expressions of the participants. Close-ups are good for capturing the sound of action happening immediately around the camera.

3) **Mix of Angles**. Eye-level shots offer the same perspective as we see them in real life. With this kind of perspective, viewers focus more with the content of what's shown than on the camerawork. *Belly-level* shots are good for following a character's movement. Pressing the camera against the belly gives it more steadiness, which is especially good when filming and walking at the same time. The *cowboy shot* is used to follow a person, ideally from the knees up. Never use the digital zoom or any digital effects while filming.

4) **Content**. Make sure to get footage that provides comprehensive information to the future viewer. Images of the leaders of the demonstration, rally or event are important. *B-roll* footage should include many different images and activities that communicate feeling of the demonstration. B-roll also helps in the editing process to create continuity. *Vox pops* are spontaneous interviews with participants who state their views on a subject.

5) **Narration**. Narrators can play a very useful role in helping to structure the film and fill in gaps in information. However, for some audiences, narration may be perceived to be manipulative or indicative of a particular point of view. Narration is a mediating presence between the audience and the film characters. That's why people generally perceive the narrator's voice to be the voice of the film itself.

6) **Editing**. Revisit your audience, purpose and goals. Log and label all your footage, planning the sequence of images as you view. Choose your digital editing tool and remember that shorter videos are more likely to attract an audience than longer videos. As you edit the footage, be truthful to the situation you experienced. Don't abuse the power of emotion in a way that misleads people.

7) **Share**. Decide how to share your work and carefully title and tag your work so that people can find it.

Logging Footage

After you have gathered video footage, you must review it and decide which images and sounds to use. The best way to do this is to develop an organizational system that supports your ability to find and retrieve the clips you need. As you upload digital files to your hard drive, use a file folder system that helps you keep track of your work. Being organized can make a big difference in your success as a video editor. As you watch and review the footage you've shot, take time to describe the clips you're watching. Your notes will be most useful to you as you edit, helping you find and sequence images during the editing process.

The Ethics of Contemporary Propaganda

At the 2015 Grammy Awards, many viewers saw an advertisement that looked like a music video about the use of Tinder, a popular dating social media app. The music video featured popular musical artists Becky G, Fifth Harmony, and King Bach singing about "left swiping" people who smoke, communicating the message that people who smoke are unattractive. Created by Legacy, a public health marketing firm known for its innovative approaches to prevention, the music video and the #leftswipedat campaign was an award-winning example of beneficial propaganda.[32]

Perhaps you don't think that propaganda can be beneficial, but actually, the origins of the word are testament to its intent for good: The term came into common use in Europe as a result of the missionary activities of the Catholic Church. Propaganda has been part of social organization for hundreds of years. As the American Historical Association notes:

> The conflict between kings and Parliament in England was a historic struggle in which propaganda was involved. Propaganda was one of the weapons used in the movement for American independence, and it was used also in the French Revolution. The pens of Voltaire and Rousseau inflamed opposition to Bourbon rule in France, and during the revolution Danton and his fellows crystallized attitudes against the French king just as John Adams and Tom Paine had roused and organized opinion in the American Revolution.[33]

In our times, as concerns about the rise of the Islamic State have grown, newspapers accounts revealed the story of three British teens who traveled to Syria to join ISIS. ISIS and other extremist groups use platforms like Twitter, Facebook, and WhatsApp to reach their target audiences. We learned that the British girls were exposed to a variety of messages, including persuasive videos using high-level production techniques. One video looks like a trailer for an action movie, with slow-motion explosions and flames engulfing American troops.[34]

Contemporary propaganda is ubiquitous, as public relations and marketing have become core dimensions of the global media and communication system, affecting all forms of personal, social, and public expression. Propaganda may be beneficial or harmful, of course, depending on your point of view. Video has become a key medium for disseminating propaganda in all forms and flavors as we experience content that routinely conflates entertainment, information, and persuasion.

According to French scholar Jacques Ellul, propaganda involves the intentional sharing or facts, opinions, and ideas designed to change behavior or motivate action.[35] Most definitions of propaganda focus on the concept of intentionality and motive on the part of the author, impact on the receiver's actions and behaviors, as well as the receiver's level of free will in accepting or rejecting the message.[36] The pleasure and power associated with the ability, as George Orwell put it, to "deceive the world" is ever more evident as easy access to the tools of communication enable everyone to be a propagandist, manipulating messages and meanings for fun and profit.[37]

My interest in teaching and learning about contemporary propaganda was piqued when I worked as a consultant to the United States Holocaust Memorial Museum on their special exhibit, "The State of Deception," about the history of Nazi propaganda.[38] As part of this work, I talked with a number of high school and college students and discovered that many had never even considered that propaganda was still part of contemporary society. In the minds of those students, propaganda was something that happened in the past, back in twentieth-century Germany. I was surprised to find that much contemporary scholarship on civic education does not include reference to the nature of the diverse forms of messages we receive in the increasingly complex media environment that surrounds us.

Learning about propaganda is not easy. Many teachers feel unqualified to teach about this subject while others have concerns about the potential backlash of bringing controversial subjects into the classroom. In talking to teachers, some explained that they could do little with the topic beyond identifying the common rhetorical tropes of propaganda, including glittering generalities, name calling, and so on in instructional practices that were developed in 1939.[39] It's possible that some may consider propaganda education to be a little old-fashioned, with its focus on avoiding the risks and harms of being duped or misled by persuaders who may appear to be friends, entertainers, or even experts.

But with the rise of "fake news" in the United States and around the world, the need for people to develop a sense of "crap detection" is ever more essential. As Howard Rheingold explains, "Unless a great many people learn the basics of online crap detection ... I fear for the future of the Internet as a useful source of credible news, medical advice, financial information, educational resources, scholarly and scientific research."[40]

Film and Video as Forms of Advocacy

As citizens, we scan the horizon for issues that concern us and look for where we might be able to make a difference. Advocacy relies on the power of creating, consuming, and sharing compelling stories to inspire people to take forms of personal, social, and political action. True stories can be powerful, but so can stories that mix truth and fiction.

Filmmakers can play an important role as agents of social change. In *Fruitvale Station*, a docudrama film, Ryan Coogler dramatizes the events leading up to the death of a 22-year-old African American man from Oakland, California, Oscar Grant, who died at the hands of a police officer in 2009 on New Year's Eve. The train station shooting was documented by many witnesses who used their cellphones to videotape the conflict. The film uses the power of docudrama to capture the 24 hours immediately preceding the murder and viewers are captivated by the tender, frank, and dramatic events that unfold. By learning about Oscar as a complex individual, we identify with his tragic death at the hands of police officers.

But the power of media is not limited to filmmakers. Film viewers can also become important change agents. Co-founder of the Black Lives Matter movement, Opal Tometi had just gotten out of the movie theater after watching *Fruitvale Station* when she learned that George Zimmerman, a white man who had been charged in the murder of 18-year-old Trayvon Martin, had been acquitted. In August 2015, one day after Michael Brown's death at the hands of a police offer in Ferguson, Missouri, protests and riots began, as people objected to police brutality targeting African Americans, the militarization of police, and school segregation. The U.S. Justice Department found that the Ferguson police were guilty of discriminating against African Americans and applying racial stereotypes.[41]

In recent years, political and social advocacy has helped to spur other important shifts in attitudes about the rights of gays, lesbians, and transgender individuals. In 2010, alternative newspaper columnist Dan Savage filmed a video about harassment and abuse that he experienced during his youth. He was inspired to address the problem of suicide by lesbian, gay, bisexual, transgender, and queer (LGBTQ) youth. More than 75 percent of LGBTQ-identified students report experiencing verbal harassment and these youth are four times more likely to commit suicide as their straight peers. People were invited to contribute similar user-generated messages to the "It Gets Better" campaign. Over 1,000 videos were created within one week, and today, more than 50,000 videos have been created. In 2015, people in Ireland voted to allow gay marriage and the U.S. Supreme Court ruled that it is legal for all Americans, no matter their gender or sexual orientation, to marry the people they love.[42]

Video is a powerful tool for developing the capacity for critical dialogue. But we need practice to recognize, analyze, and freely choose to accept or reject the film and video propaganda around us. Today, videos are created by individuals, activists, governments, and the military agencies. They are used by political parties, lobbies, advertising, public relations, foundations, sponsored research from corporations, think tanks, and other sources. As you master the competencies of creating to learn, you begin to see yourself as a political being, someone whose ideas matter, someone who is able to exert influence.

Activity: Create a Video of an Event

Create a video of an event, using good production techniques to get a variety of images and interviews. Review the footage and edit it into a 2–5 minute overview, using narration and music if necessary to capture key information and ideas. Use one of the Evaluation Rubrics available on the Create to Learn website to make strategic choices about the content and format of your production.

13

Animation

KEY IDEAS

Rooted in drawing and the visual arts, animation is the oldest of the genres and is an important part of the history of film. In animation, two-dimensional drawings or three-dimensional objects are presented in sequential order at 12, 18, or 24 frames per second, which creates an illusion of movement. Animation creates meaning through the imaginative use of symbols that move in time and space, creating a suspension of disbelief that compels viewer attention. Powerful story structures explain why some animated films seem timeless. Branded animated videos are widely used in the online marketplace to promote products and services. Non-narrative videos use rich content, visual style, and clear structure to attract and hold viewer attention to promote learning. Today with simple drag-and-drop digital tools, anyone can create a simple animation. Animation is perhaps the most powerful way to represent the uncontainable diversity of the human imagination.

Launched in 1997, *Daria,* an MTV cartoon depicted life through the eyes of a witty and sardonic teen with glasses who was actually quite well adjusted to the stresses and pressures of adolescence. Of course, her family was absurd, especially her vain younger sister and her trying-to-be-too-helpful parents. Her school was absurd and her peers were also absurd (with the exception of her one girl friend Jane). Daria's basic conflict in life was with everyone and everything.

If you had a favorite cartoon growing up, you know the warm and fuzzy feelings that are associated with the genre of animation. But cartoons are not just for kids: they appeal to people of all ages. As created by Glenn Eichler, *Daria* was designed for teens and young adults, but parents of teens could find it enjoyable too. We reveled in the depiction of the misfit: Daria was, in fact, a one-dimensional character, who could be counted on to adopt the outsider pose towards every aspect of daily life. Her predictability was part of her appeal.

In the nineteenth century, the poet Samuel Taylor Coleridge used the term *suspension of disbelief* to describe the mental state in which a reader

Create to Learn: Introduction to Digital Literacy, First Edition. Renee Hobbs.
© 2017 John Wiley & Sons, Inc. Published 2017 by John Wiley & Sons, Inc.

could regard a character as real, regardless of their out-of-the-ordinary characteristics.[1] Animation can give the illusion of anything being alive – from a toothbrush, to a car or a children's toy, and even a Minion. What makes a character believable? Their behavior must be *coherent*. Since we don't actually see their thoughts and feelings, the character's actions must give clues to its internal state. An animated character's actions must express what it is thinking and feeling. Believable characters *change with experience*, that is, they learn and grow over time. They must show *awareness of the world* – Daria's character relied heavily on this quality of believability, since she was perpetually offering her commentary about others. A character must be *recognizable as an individual* and their behavior patterns have to have some (but not too much) *predictability*.[2]

But characters also need *conflict* for stories to emerge. In animation, conflict can be expressed through language. Glenn Eichler relied on this when creating *Daria*, because the visual action of the episode was not always compelling. Many *Daria* episodes attempt to create visual *novelty* by placing Daria in unusual settings: visiting a fortuneteller, for example, or playing paintball. But because animation is a powerful tool for visual storytelling, dramatic conflict is often rooted in the physical actions of the characters.

Life as Story

We spend most of our lives involved with stories of one kind of another. According to Christopher Booker, author of *The Seven Basic Plots*, one of the oldest story structures is sometimes known as *overcoming the monster*.[3] Many times, the stories we see in the media have been inspired by something in real life. For example, when Mike Lacher created the animated short video, "Ballad of a Wifi Hero," he did it by taking a simple family story and transforming into a "once upon a time" narrative with himself as (who else but) the epic warrior hero. In this video, the narration begins with noting that "a great darkness descended over the wireless Internet connectivity of the gentlefolk of 276 Ferndale Street." We are then introduced to the elderly grandparents, whose mundane and ordinary Internet activities were disrupted when "Internet Explorer 6 no longer loaded The Google." In a sequence of charming images, the narrator describes how the grandparents tried to fix the problem themselves by minimizing and maximizing the browser and installing the old mouse to replace the new mouse.

Fortunately, "a suitor of the gentlefolks' granddaughter" arrives to save the day. As we watch, the viewer knows there is a monster here somewhere, creating the problem, but we're not sure who it is. The visual design of this particular animation borrows from the 16-bit video game look of the 1980s, with characters drawn from a fairy tale. The noble warrior indeed goes on a quest to fix the grandparents' wifi. By casting the story as a "once upon a time." The pleasure of video comes in discovering that the monster is the router and the quest involves going behind the recliner, past "great mountains" of old *National Geographic* magazines, to a "terrifying thicket" of wires "threatening to ensnare all who ventured further."

Our hero finally discovers where the router is buried. "Gripping the cord tightly, he pulled with all his force." When he unplugs and replugs the cord, hooray! "The Google did load." Lacher transformed the quite ordinary experience of fixing a router (by unplugging it and plugging it back in) into a humorous version of the warrior's epic quest (see Figure 13.1). Lacher created a great video animation by choosing a genre (fairy tale quest) and a visual style (video games of the 1980s), then creating a *hero* (the warrior), a *victim* (the grandparents), and a *villain* (the router).[4] By establishing these core story roles, the narration was written and the graphic designer created the images for the story. Charming writing communicates the playful intent. The editor selected music and sound effects to intensify the emotional mood of the quest and complete the story.

Ballad of a WiFi Hero (McSweeney's and Vulture Exclusive)

New York Magazine

Subscribe 56,388

460,175 views

Add to   Share   ••• More

10,198   134

Figure 13.1 The heroic warrior unplugs the router by Mike Lacher.

Animation and Disney Culture

All over the world, when people think of animation, they think of Disney. As the third largest media corporation in the world (just behind Comcast and Google), it earned more than $55 billion in revenue in 2016. The Disney Animation Studios has produced 55 animated feature films since 1937, with the launch of *Snow White and the Seven Dwarves*. Disney pioneered the multi-plane camera, which enables the manipulation and filming of layers of acetate cels of hand-drawn animation simultaneously. When it acquired Pixar in 2006 for $7.4 billion, it became a leader in 2D and 3D animation. The release of *Tangled* in 2010 was the first time Disney used 3D CGI animation to tell a classic fairy tale.[5]

Gender, race, ethnicity, and occupational stereotypes have long been part of Disney storytelling. One common stereotype that is built into Disney films is the belief that "the beautiful is the good." In Disney films, most of the villains are ugly and most of the heroes and heroines are beautiful, with the exception of Shrek.[6] Some people have criticized *Moana* for representing the demi-God Maui as fat, while others see the Polynesian hero as solid, strong, and capable.

Drawing as Abstraction

How do people transform life into stories? If you're like me, you might be someone who thinks with your hands. When I'm encountering new ideas, I find myself sketching. It's usually circles and squares and arrows and little objects of all sorts. For many years I thought everyone did this, but then I remembered being surprised when someone called out the practice and described it as "weird." According to Nicholas Carr, "The act of drawing is not just a way of expressing thought: it's a way of thinking."[7] He describes how architects use sketching as a fundamental part of the thought process of architectural design. Because the physical act of drawing aids in the formation of long-term memories, sketching is the essence of the creative design process.

Most people appreciate that animation is a process that involves sequential presentation of images, creating the illusion of movement. But animation is also created with a computer, as objects are created and instructions are coded about how these objects move upon a certain command. In animation, 2D drawings or 3D objects are presented in sequential order, 18 or 24 frames per second, which creates an illusion of movement (called the *phi phenomenon*), a perceptual trick that is at the heart of film and video. Hand-drawn animation, puppet animation, claymation, computer animation, and machinima are all approaches to the craft.

Because animation lets you visualize the impossible, it taps the limitless imagination of the human being. When Scott McCloud's book *Understanding Comics* was released in 1993, I remember that it changed the way I looked at art, animation, and the imagination. Here was a book-length comic, a set of drawings, that page after page unlocked the secrets about how drawings and visual art in general work as an imaginative system of representation. In the book, McCloud shows that comics are a visual form of expression and communication that, while historically tied to the visual arts, embrace all art forms, including sound, music, and narrative.[8]

Drawings abstract our experience of reality through *representation.* Through pictorial images, we can appreciate how the formal structure of representing objects and events shapes our understanding of the world. Graphic novels and comics present images in sequence, creating an illusion of time on the static printed page. Across history, many cultures have tried to present time through visual depictions. In American comics, it is presented sequentially in a left-to-right reading sequence, generally with word balloons and captions.

Comic artists make choices when they draw pictures: what moment of the narrative to depict, how to frame the subject, how to use a combination of images and words, and how to sequence the flow of panels. It's possible that the abstraction or non-realism of drawings may invite the viewer into *psychological identification* with the characters depicted: McCloud shows how simple, abstractly drawn characters connect to some universal impulses to identify with the person represented in an image.[9]

Education and the Imagination

Schooling expands thinking, but it also limits it. Think about how your own education has shaped the way you think. Scholars and critics of education have observed how the structures of school, with its demands for compliance, competition, order, and control, emphasize some aspects of intelligence and marginalize other features of our humanity. Elliot Eisner explained, "When we look at school curricula with an eye towards the full range of intellectual processes that human beings can exercise, it quickly becomes apparent that only a slender range of those processes is emphasized."[10] Eisner observes that children and young people get very little exposure to topics in anthropology, the arts, communication, law, and economics before they go to college. They get limited opportunities to collaborate and create. The premise of this book, the one you are now reading, is that creating media as a way to learn activates the imagination and deepens critical thinking. This is an idea that has long been suggested by education scholars throughout the twentieth century.

When Jasmine Huang was invited to create media for her "Theory of Knowledge" class, she decided to make a simple stick-figure animation about

▶ ▶| ◀)) 0:40 / 3:06   ✿ ☐ []

The Imagination Animation

DaRiceCooker

▶ Subscribe 31   3,274 views

➕ Add to   ➤ Share   ••• More   👍 28   👎 0

Figure 13.2 Stick figure animation by Jasmine Huang.

the power of the imagination, as Figure 13.2 shows. Using the song, "Pure Imagination" sung by Gene Wilder in the film *Willy Wonka and the Chocolate Factory*, her short animated story features a man sitting on a park bench. As he watches the clouds, his imagination turns on and the clouds transform into a spaceship, a whale and a horse. There's a ninja fight scene, a pirate adventure with a treasure chest, and a cowboy lassoing a dinosaur. In the end, we see a man who is drawing a fish on a piece of paper, which then starts to move – it's an animation, of course. In the final lyrical moments, the man folds the paper animation into an origami crane, and it transforms into a real crane and flies away.[11]

This animation reveals a powerful truth: the things we create have a life of their own. Jasmine's lyrical and reflective stick-figure animation reminds me of the work of French philosopher Jean-Paul Sartre, who noticed the difference between imagining something completely non-existent in the real world and imagining something that exists (like a horse or a cowboy or a paper crane) but transforming and deepening it by adding layers of meaning through symbolism. Sartre insists that through the imagination, humans are always free to create meaning; but we are also equally free to deny meaning through meaninglessness.[12] This essential freedom to-be-or-not-to-be is celebrated in animation.

For these reasons, creating animation is an empowering experience. "Students have to believe that what they have to say is important enough to bother writing," says Anne Rodlier, a high school teacher in Manassas, Virginia. "They have to experience writing for real audiences before they will know that writing can bring them power." Anne uses animation assignments with her social studies and history students because she finds that it is an excellent motivator for disengaged students. "Through animation, students convey an idea, concept, or thought in a way that words, still pictures, and audio can't," she notes. Anne can adapt the project to address the unique needs of her young students with special needs or for those who are just learning English.

Anne believes that animations help students internalize the information they are expected to learn. "As they develop the story and script for an animation, students are naturally encouraged to write narratives that include descriptive details and clear event sequences." When students create storyboards, it helps them master sequencing, visualization, details, conflict, and narrative structure.[13]

Some Types of Animation

Flipbook Animation. Using a small book, animators draw a series of images, with small variations to the image so that it appears to move when the pages of the book are flipped.

2D Animation. A limited number of drawings are created using software and the computer is used to make variations that create the illusion of movement.

3D Animation. Many animated films use this style where computer software is used to create characters that appear to have depth and often look highly realistic.

Stop-Motion Animation. Static objects are moved, a little at a time, to create a fluid sense of movement. Moving puppets, clay objects, or cut-out pieces of paper all use this style of animation.

Whiteboard Animation. This style can be produced simply by videotaping a person using a whiteboard, but there are also a variety of free or low-cost software tools that can be used to create this style of animation.

Typography Animation. When letters and words are animated, different font faces and types, plus the use of color and space, create a visual look that captures viewer interest and often accompanies the spoken word. This style of animation can be made with PowerPoint.

Animation Styles

There are many different styles of animation, but some require more professional training in art, design, and technology. For example, to create computer-generated animation, you may need years of experience with specialized software. But other styles of animation can be created by non-professionals. In 2013, a former housemate on *Big Brother* named Sam Pepper uploaded a video called "Draw My Life," where he used an erasable white board to draw the story of his life. The crude drawings are combined with a narrative which combines childhood stories including memories of his favorite teacher in high school and some of his many jobs. Now the genre has become quite popular on YouTube and many celebrities have participated in creating this genre of video animation (see Figure 13.3). Since then, counselors and mental health professionals have even used the concept as a tool to promote healthy communication, inviting people to draw people and events that were significant in their lives and explain their choices to a therapist.[14]

Many Draw My Life video animations make use of the *rags to riches* plot, which is a powerful story structure. It's rather simple: we meet a character in

Figure 13.3 "Draw My Life." *Source*: Markiplier.

childhood, and this somewhat ordinary and insignificant person is revealed to be someone truly exceptional. Something happens to create an *awakening*: the hero is compelled to move out into a larger world, where adventures may occur. In some rags to riches stories, there is an *antagonist,* a dark figure, a villain or someone who thwarts the hero's efforts. In the middle of the story, there is always a *point of crisis,* where the hero's efforts are derailed or things fall apart. There is a reversal where the hero discovers in himself or herself something fulfilling.[15]

If you have watched the Draw My Life videos, you've probably noticed that although people draw differently, there is a distinctive *style* that is evident. Many illustrators use agents to find their clients with a distinctive visual style. At Illustration Ltd, the web site serves as an agency for hundreds of professional illustrators and animators, each with a particular visual style. If you're writing a children's book or creating an animation, it's worth exploring this web site to help you decide what look and feel you're seeking for your own project. Illustration style is generally conveyed through the use of adjectives that express aspects of the visual look and feel of the art. Illustrators often have a *signature style* but also are able to adapt their style to different projects. For example, take a look at the two images in Figure 13.4. Can you identify which one describes his style as *cheerful, fun, and clean* and which one describes his style as *musical, romantic and sensitive*?

The Power of Animation

Every sector of the marketplace is discovering the power of video animation, it seems. The term *branded videos* refers to videos used as part of a marketing effort, and the growth in the variety of these is impressive. For example, at health web sites, video animations are used to explain about diseases and drugs for treating them. Video animations are effective in persuading people to take action – 90 percent of online users say a video is effective in making a decision about purchasing a product or service. In the first three months of 2015 alone, viewers watched over 4.1 billion branded videos.[16]

Animation is a powerful tool for persuasion and propaganda. Some of the most persuasive YouTube videos are video animations, including "Dumb Ways to Die," which had more than 132 million views as of 2016. This catchy song, which lists silly and realistic ways to get injured ("do your own electrical work" or "sell both your kidneys on the Internet") includes cute little creatures with roundish shapes and minimal personalities that are suggested by their hats, hair, or facial expressions. We see them die in dumb ways. Shared virally through social media, this video animation was created by an Australian advertising agency aiming to promote safety on commuter trains.

Figure 13.4 Animation styles by Illustration Ltd.

Hundreds of publications wrote feature stories about the campaign, magnifying its influence. The "Dumb Ways to Die" campaign had an impact on the behavior of Australian train riders. According to Metro Trains, six months after the launch of the campaign, there was a 30 percent reduction in near-miss accidents.[17]

Using Copyrighted Music

Many beginning creators are eager to use popular music in their animations. When you use popular music in your own creative work, sometimes you are using it for comment or critical analysis. For example, you might be making a historical examination of the development of Beyoncé's career in relationship to the representation of African American women in music and media. Using short clips from many different songs is essential to show the themes developed in her music over time. In these cases, you can rely on the doctrine of fair use, which considers such uses to be fair use, or exceptions to copyright. When you claim fair use, you can use copyrighted materials without payment or permission because the courts generally recognize that the social benefit of your creative work outweighs the smaller cost to the copyright holder.

But when you are using a longer excerpt or even the whole song because of its popularity, appeal, and familiarity, then you should request permission from the producer. In this case, you're not really repurposing or adding value to the original song. You may even be retransmitting the song without permission, which is violation of copyright. When you want to use a whole pop song, you generally ask permission and/or pay a license fee, which allows you to use the song as part of your own work. You may also consider using royalty-free music from platforms like SoundCloud, where emerging musicians make their original songs available at no cost.

Non-Narrative Animation

"The School of Life" is a London storefront and online shop created by Alain de Botton which offers short courses and workshops for how to live a good life. The program is devoted to developing people's emotional intelligence through the help of culture. A group of short animated videos offers insight on handling the challenges of living, including issues like "How to Remain Calm with People" and "Why Children's Drawings Matter."

In one video, "Being a Good Listener," we learn about the secrets of being a good listener (see Figure 13.5). Listening is not often taught formally and so many people don't know exactly what makes a good listener. But good listeners egg us on, encouraging us to elaborate, with words like "Go on" or "Tell me more." They ask "why" questions to invite us to reflect on our ideas – and they remember what we say, stitching together the pieces of information they receive and connecting the dots.[18]

Somehow the little animated figures that accompany the video help us pay attention to the narration in a personal and self-reflective way. As you watch these animations, you may find yourself thinking about your own relationships

Being A Good Listener

The School of Life

Subscribe 1,210,047

313,084 views

+ Add to → Share ••• More

👍 11,539 👎 68

Figure 13.5 "Being a Good Listener" by The School of Life.

and your own behavior as a listener. Good listeners care about the deeper issues in our lives and by their active listening they may help us clarify or better appreciate underlying issues that we may not have noticed ourselves. One key idea in the video is clear: conversations are not just a matter of swapping anecdotes; they are about the building of relationships. Good listeners recognize and accept our follies, enabling us to express honest reactions.

The Physics of Movement

Animators say that the most important principle of animation is *squash and stretch*, where objects seem more realistic if changes to their shape are used to suggest weight and flexibility. For example, a bouncing ball is drawn with a more squashed oval shape when the ball hits a flat surface and it assumes a more elongated shape when it bounces back. As long as the volume of the ball doesn't change (only the shape), this will look realistic to the viewer. Another animation principle addresses the *principle of inertia*, where movement of a person's body looks more realistic if the hair, for example, continues moving forward in space even after the character has stopped moving. Animators use mathematical calculations to ensure that the physics of motion work appropriately on different parts of the bodies and objects in motion.[19]

Computer-Generated Animation

Computer programmers use a variety of platforms for creating animations, but even if you are not a programmer, you can still use some simple coding platforms to create animations. Digital coding platforms can be used by non-programmers as an entry-level experience to the world of computer programming. As a visual programming language, the user manipulates *sprites,* which are objects, characters, or images. By using simple commands, the sprites can be made to move and speak in ways that are contingent on the user's actions, as in a simple videogame. To create a simple animation using a coding platform, you simply select a background and some characters, and then use programming blocks to add movement and interactivity. If you want to embed simple animation on a web site, you can create animated, interactive content using HTML, HTML5, CSS, and JavaScript.

Children who grow up making virtual worlds in Minecraft recognize the range of creative practices at work in computer-generated animation (see Figure 13.6). Computer animation is essentially a digital version of stop-motion animation that enables a graphic artist to produce scenes at the computer without the use of actors, sets, or props. Today the tools of computer-generated animation are available in low-cost versions that even young children can learn

Figure 13.6 Minecraft animation.

to use. For example, working with a group of 11 year olds in England, Andrew Burn explored the creation of *machinima*, a form of animation that uses the imagery of video games. Using a 3D digital animation tool called Moviestorm, students began by watching examples of machinima animations. Then students used the software, selecting from a variety of ready-made sets, including space ships and famous places. They customized their sets with props of their own choice. Students then created avatars for their characters, selecting costumes, faces, and body types.

During the directing phase of the 3D video animation activity, children made the avatars move in the 3D space and interact with each other. Characters can be made to talk by typing in dialogue and, using a drag and drop tool, they can perform a wide range of movements and gestures. In the filming stage, students selected establishing shots, camera movement, and close-ups to show the characters in action. After assembling a set of shots, the rendering process enabled students to add visual effects, music, titles, and credits.

To create their machinima animations, one group of middle-school students in England worked collaboratively over six weeks, starting by imagining a story featuring a teenage computer games geek who one day finds himself inside his own game. He tours ancient Egypt, meets Cleopatra, and stops an alien from trying to take over the world. Such film animation activities offer a bridge "between the well-established traditional cultural practices of film and the media cultures of young people," who are highly familiar with animation as a feature of video game design.[20]

Animated Interviews

Animation is both a genre and a production technique that is incorporated into many different genres of moving image media. Many short interview clips have been illustrated using animation. In "The Function of Music with Jad Abumrad," a four-minute video interview with the radio producer is illustrated with stop-motion animation that features the use of everyday objects. In the opening moments of this short film, when the interviewer asks, "What is sound?" we hear the interview subject say, "Uh…" and we see a piece of paper being crinkled up into a ball, as if to throw in the trash. This simple and powerful opening establishes a tone or sensibility of playfulness, as if the animated objects on screen are themselves providing a kind of comment and critique of the spoken word interview we're hearing throughout the film. The film combines video interview footage with the animation of objects including a 1980s style audio cassette recorder, and an old-fashioned phonograph.[21]

To understand music as "an emotional communication system," the interviewer plays samples of music and asks Jad to describe his feelings. We hear audio clips and listen to Jad's language as he explains how the music makes him feel, with video interview footage layered with animation overlays. For example, when Jad says the music makes him feel like "getting out and storming the streets," a storm cloud seems to burst from his head. As Jad explains how music gets underneath our cognitive thoughts and connects to our feelings and memories, we see a highly manipulated montage of objects, including metronomes, music notation, and more. Using stop-motion animation, the objects move across the screen in ways that suggest both the emotional depth and sheer evanescence of music as it affects our conscious understanding as beings in time. The filmmaker makes a visual connection between the genres of music and animation in order to express the wildness and uncontainable nature of the human imagination.

Activity: Create an Animation

1) Develop a Scope of Work where you identify your purpose, your audience, and your point of view.
2) Identify a mentor text that you admire, one that influences your thinking about the design of your work. Study how it has been constructed, paying special attention to the use of time.
3) Select an animation production tool from the many free and low-cost tools available. You may enjoy exploring drag-and-drop or photo animation tools. You can see a complete list of easy-to-use animation tools on the Create to Learn website. You may find it useful to experiment with different tools until you find one that works best for your purpose.
4) Use storyboarding as a planning tool for moving image media. A template of four or six rectangles per page can be helpful in visualizing what the viewer will see and hear. Storyboarding helps you design visual interest into your project while enabling you to think more deeply about the content, sequence, and structure of your project.
5) Produce the images you need for your production, editing as you go. Add language, music, and sound.
6) Show your production to some people who can offer you frank and candid feedback. Check to see if the messages and feelings they get from your work are aligned with your purpose and goals.
7) Revise and edit as needed, adding titles and credits. Choose how to distribute your animation and use a well-written description and metadata to help it become more findable.

14

Remix Production

KEY IDEAS

Because we are swimming in a sea of media, we quote from and refer to movies, television shows, music, and current events as part of everyday social interaction. Digital authors use these materials in their creative work. Remix creativity relies on the overabundance of images, sounds, and digital media texts that circulate in contemporary culture. By manipulating and juxtaposing these forms of content, people exercise creativity, create, critique, and share new ideas. Through creating remixes and mashups, you can share your appreciation and love of film, music, photography, and other aspects of culture. You can comment upon entertainment that depicts social norms, current events, and human relationships. You can critically analyze social issues that have political, economic, and environmental consequences. Creating a remix is a very good way to understand the form and structure of media more deeply: by taking something apart, you can actually see how it works.

Jonathan McIntosh is a pop culture hacker, a media critic, and remix artist who created the web site, "Gender Advertising Remixer," which offers a sample of television ads for toys aimed at boys and girls. At the web site, you can experiment with creating combinations of the images and sound tracks. For example, you might select the audio track from "Battleship," a toy ad aimed at boys and combine it with the video track "Barbie Island Princess," from a toy ad targeting girls.

When you click a button, the audio of the boy's commercial plays while we see the images from the girl's commercial. An adult male narrative says, in an aggressive-sounding voice, "The battle lines are drawn. Can you bring down your enemy? The battle lines are drawn. Destroy your enemy. Rule the seas!" While this sound track plays, animated cartoons and photographic images of Barbie Island Princess depict icons of musical notes coming from around her throat area and a young girl demonstrates the toy by pressing a button on the doll, which then unfolds a peacock-like plastic fan attached to her back.[1]

Create to Learn: Introduction to Digital Literacy, First Edition. Renee Hobbs.
© 2017 John Wiley & Sons, Inc. Published 2017 by John Wiley & Sons, Inc.

Figure 14.1 Gender Advertising Remixer for toy ads by Jonathan McIntosh.

As Figure 14.1 shows, the weird juxtaposition of highly gendered images and soundtracks is effective: it seems to intensify awareness of the strategy and effort involved in the construction of toy advertising. All the ads have a three-second *hook* at the opening that calls out for attention. "It's a fashion runway in the sky!" announces the Polly Pocket Jumbo Jet ad. Then there are phrases that communicate key ideas about how to play with the toy. This is accompanied by a sequence of rapidly edited images: boys play with boy toys and girls play with girl toys. There are close-up shots of the toys. There's always energizing music throughout, with the last five seconds used to reinforce the name of the toy and offer a *disclaimer* about what is actually included. For example, "Lego Castle Playsets. Each toy sold separately" or "Polly Pocket Jumbo Jet comes with all this. You put it together."[2] In developing this digital interactive for media literacy, McIntosh used the copyrighted content of toy companies – their television advertising – to create an online platform that uses the power of remix to expose the completely absurd levels of gender stereotyping found in many children's television commercials. The Gender Remixer helps people break down embedded gender messages in toy advertising.

Swimming in a Sea of Media

Unless you go through one of those television *turn-off experiments* where you disconnect fully from all media – your cellphone, your television, your laptop, the radio, newspapers, movies, and social media for a day or even a week, it's hard to fully appreciate the extent to which we are swimming in a sea of media. Some researchers estimate that as much as one-third of our conversations with others concerns media. Young adults, often termed the *millennial generation* (born between 1980–2000) are actively participating in media culture, using smartphones to access the Internet. You may watch television and use social media at the same time, using two or even three screens (television, smartphone, and laptop). Many use streaming services such as Netflix, YouTube, and Amazon Prime. In a study of 47,000 Internet users around the world, it was found that people check in with an average of five social networks (including YouTube, Instagram, Snapchat, Facebook, and Twitter) about five times a day. People use social media for 1 hour and 40 minutes per day.[3] When you use social media, you are receiving content that has been created and shared by others and you are likely composing and uploading content of your own.

Researchers are challenged to measure the sheer quantity of media people use each day, but tools are available to measure your online media consumption. An app on my smartphone tells me that I picked up the phone 47 times yesterday and used email, music and social media for about three hours. If you keep a log of the movies you watch for just one month, for example, you'll see how quickly the list grows. The sheer volume and variety of entertainment, information, and social media have contributed to the rise of remix culture.

Fans as Active Audiences

While it may look like a passive activity, sitting in front of a television or computer screen, media use is an active process. The concept of the *active audience* is based on the recognition that the process of comprehension and interpretation of media involve cognitive and emotional competencies as well as significant social interaction.[4] But because we use media to satisfy many needs, the way we are active with media can vary widely. You may be a news junkie, while your friend is a music geek, for example. Researchers have discovered that people have different motivations for using media, including entertainment, relaxation, information, social affiliation, and escapism. Even television viewing can provide different pleasures and satisfactions to people, as Sonia Livingstone has noted:

> People are emotionally engaged by television; they talk of television meeting personal identity needs such as the legitimation of their values or gaining insight into themselves; they feel television keeps them connected to the rest of the world through a shared imagined community, through knowing what is happening in other places and through having common topics to discuss with others in their everyday lives.[5]

For example, if you're a sports fan, you may know the pleasure of experiencing the game on a big HD screen from the comfort of your living room. You may get feelings of companionship by being part of a shared experience. There is an emotional thrill to both winning and losing. You may even value acquiring information about a player's health, for example, because it aids in your interpretation of the game. And of course, sometimes watching a game is a great escape, a time-filler and a form of procrastination that takes you away from performing everyday chores.

Cut-and-Paste Culture

Everyday life is replete with images, music, sounds, and interactive media. Naturally, these *artifacts of culture* become objects that fuel the creative process. In Lawrence Lessig's book *Remix*, he explains that a cultural shift has occurred as we have transitioned from a read-only culture (then media came exclusively from professional sources) to a read/write culture (where amateur production is normative).[6]

The terms *remix* and *mashup* are sometimes used interchangeably in reference to the reworking or adaptation of an existing creative work. However, experts conceptualize the two terms differently. While these terms originally referred to music genres, now they apply to any media, including image, sound, and even data. A remix creates an alternate version of the original, sometimes by adding new content. The most typical remix is an extended dance version of a pop song. A mashup is a type of remix that involves the intentional juxtaposition and recombination of two or more works that may be very different from one another.[7]

If you have searched for music on YouTube, it's highly likely that you have run into music remixes. There are dozens of apps that now enable people to easily mashup, remix, and share music online. The rise of big data has even helped to create new genres of remix music. One musician worked with IBM to create electronic dance music using data from the US Open tennis matches by using a computer algorithm. The album, *Remixes Made With Tennis Data*, sounds a bit like avant-garde electronic dance music.[8] Undoubtedly, it's a wildly creative idea to take the data from tennis competitions and transform it into music.

New types of sports entertainment can even be understood as a type of remix. For some, viewing sports is part of an active process that includes fantasy leagues. Fantasy Football combines people's interest in professional football with their interests in gaming and gambling: by creating an imaginary or virtual team through a draft process, you collect points depending on how the player performed in the real-world football game.

Some fans engage in creative writing as part of their engagement and play with media, producing *fan fiction*. They use the characters or setting from one or more movies, television shows or books and create new plots, new characters, and new conflicts to resolve. They may upload these works to a web site. *Vidders* are people who use bits of images from films, video games, and music to create multimedia. Fans of the television show *Smallville*, for example, have made music videos that use sequences from the television series re-edited to their favorite music. Vidders have remixed scenes from *iCarly* to construct a romantic relationship between the characters of Sam

An Online Creative Remix Community

Created by Joe and Dan Gordon-Leavitt, HitRecord is an online community where people make things together. It's a crowdsourced production company that publishes books, creates films, and television shows. Contributors get fairly paid for adding their content to the web site if their material is used in a commercial production. Since 2010, they have paid $2 million to contributors.[9]

At the HitRecord web site, you can upload a piece of writing, an image, a sound loop, an infographic, or a video. You can participate in a creative challenge and issue your own challenges. When you upload, everyone has permission to use your work. A singer might contribute a vocal. An animator might take a still image and make it move. Curators decide how these creative works might be suitable for a commercial production. The web site is a great way to explore how to be a collaborator and how many contributions can accelerate the possibilities of online creative communities.

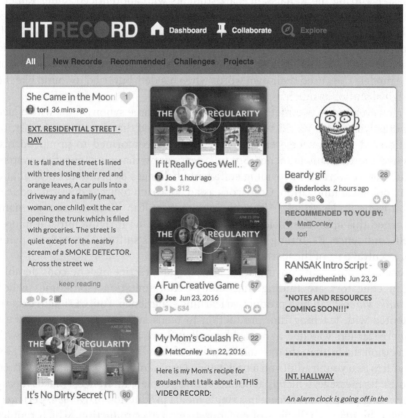

Figure 14.2 HitRecord: An online creative remix community.

and Freddie. Some people discover their interest in film editing through watching YouTube videos created by other vidders. Researchers have studied the reaction videos made by people in response to Korean pop music including Psy's "Gangnam Style," which gained popularity in 2012. Reactors often simultaneously take on multiple roles as a *consumer, critic, producer, and performer*. In doing so, they gain recognition from the more established YouTubers and, as researcher Yeran Kim notes, they advance their own brand, building up their own positions in the cultural network of the *attention economy*.[10]

Learning Through Imitation

Copying is a part of remix practice that can promote or inhibit creativity. Artists throughout history have mastered their craft using a learning practice known as *copywork*, which involves carefully copying the works of an expert or master. During the Renaissance, art students who apprenticed under Rubens or Michelangelo copied and imitated great works as part of their learning experience. Writers including William Shakespeare and Charles Dickens also developed their writing skills by first copying passages from classic literature and then trying to write the same passage again from memory without looking at the model. They used their own words when needed, but tried to sound like the original author as much as possible.

However, in the twentieth century, copying became synonymous with a lack of creativity. After World War II, sociologists noted that the rise of the corporation led to risk-averse employees who easily conformed to group norms. When the Russians launched *Sputnik*, fears grew that our education system and culture were not providing sufficient challenges to promote cultural and technological innovation. Copywork as an approach to art and writing education came under attack. Although copying is still in place in schools, many scorned this approach, believing that it destroys the imagination and injures self-confidence. Beginning in the 1960s, educators shifted away from copying as a central part of the learning process.[11]

Still, the merits of copying as an educational practice may be considerable. Film educators are finding that shot-by-shot imitation (sometimes called *remake videos*) can be a productive learning experience. Yonty Friesem experimented with teaching film production to teens and tweens using a process where learners watched a short video called "Love Language" and copied with precision the format, theme, and structure of the video.[12] The film's simple plot features two young adults on a park bench communicating by means of written notes. Its message, which is about accepting people's differences, makes it easy for young people to replicate in a single media production learning experience. Given the many challenges of collaborative media production, which require so many decisions about the sequence of shots and editing, not to mention the content, actors, setting, action, conflict, resolution, and overall mood, tone and theme, it may be that remake videos scaffold the learning experience by simplifying the number of decisions required and helping learners to focus attention.

Critical Distance and Affinity

Remixes and mashups may celebrate or critique aspects of mass media, digital media, and popular culture. Because people have a complex love–hate relationship with popular culture, they may express themselves by creating media that helps build *critical distance* from the text – or they may create media that helps build *affinity* towards the text.[13]

Because we spend so much time using media, it's natural to develop a complex network of *taste preferences* that are linked to our social identity. For example, if you grow up with a parent who loves Old School rap, you are likely to know all about the South Bronx youth who created hip-hop culture during the mid-1970s, including the Sugarhill Gang, Kurtis Blow, and Grandmaster Flash and the Furious Five as well as those who brought hip-hop to the masses, including Run D.M.C, even if your own personal preference in music tends towards trance or electronica. If you grew up listening to Garth Brooks and Shania Twain, you may appreciate the mixture of honky-tonk and folk songwriting where the catchy chorus is blasted out at top volume – or you may avoid it like the plague. Your own current tastes in music may be different from your family's tastes, but the music you listened to when growing up helped to shape a complex love–hate relationship towards musical genres. Part of the motivation to create remixes and mashups comes from our impulse to both *celebrate and critique* the genres of media that are part of our families, communities and culture.

Celebrating Media Culture

Creating a remix is a very good way to understand the form and structure of media more deeply: by taking something apart, you can actually see how it works. To create and interpret a remix, a transparent awareness of the history and politics behind the object of art is necessary, according to remix theorist Eduardo Navas. Remix artists celebrate the works they transform and repurpose. He notes that all art "is defined by ideologies, and histories that are constantly revised." That's because "contemporary artwork, as well as any media product, is a conceptual and formal collage of previous ideologies, critical philosophies, and formal artistic investigations extended to new media."[14]

In his video, "Everything is a Remix," Kirby Ferguson argues that copying, transforming, and combining are practices at the heart of creative practice.[15] If you're into music, you may have already created your own remixes of your favorite tracks. The most popular and common music remixes consist of a pop or dance song that has been made into another style of music while keeping the theme and vocals. If you remix a song you really like, you may discover the many interesting elements of the song – the rhythm, instruments, voice, lyrics, and effects – that combine together to make it effective.

Digital tools for manipulating sound create an endless variety of ways to create transformational works. In the summer of 2016, Skrillex, a remix artist and record producer who collaborated with Justin Bieber on the mega-hit, "Sorry," was sued by indie artist Casey Dienel, who performs under the moniker White Hinterland. To counter this claim, Skrillex posted a fascinating video on social media to show how the song's unique vocal hook was created.[16] In the 30-second video, we see Skrillex using an a cappella demo of the song created by co-songwriter Julia Michaels. We watch as he digitally manipulates the pitch and contorts the semitones to form a vocal melody (see Figure 14.3).

 SKRILLEX @Skrillex · May 27

SORRY but we didnt steal this 🙏 @justinbieber @bloodpop

Figure 14.3 Tweet from Skrillex demonstrates audio editing.

Skrillex makes it look easy, of course, but learning to use a *digital audio workstation* (DAW) takes time. To create a music remix, you might build a new mix from scratch or simply replace the music with loops from an already established song. Audacity, a free software tool, is among the most well-known DAWs but there are a growing variety of online platforms for remixing sound. Some are challenging and others are easy to use. They all offer the ability to put separate sounds and music onto separate tracks as part of the manipulation process. It's actually quite fun to take music from one genre and mix it into a completely different one. For example, a country vocal part might fit superbly in a hip-hop song if you're clever enough to choose the right vocal phrases, timing and style.

Today, many remix artists are contributing and sharing using online platforms which enable anyone to create and share sounds privately with friends or publicly to blogs and social networks. Most remix artists learn techniques informally from others. Today much of that learning happens through YouTube, where audio professionals like Mike Russell demonstrate their craft in short video tutorials.[17] In one video, he demonstrates how to extract the vocal track to create a karaoke version of a song using the invert function. In another YouTube video, Russell demonstrates how he mixes the percussion from Ke$ha's "Die Young" and the vocals from Rihanna's "We Found Love." Learning to remix music consists of plenty of trial and experimentation, that's for certain. It is through this process of tinkering and manipulation that creative expression emerges.

Why Pop Culture is Popular

Some young creative artists have found that a sure-fire way to get attention is to imitate, remix, mashup, or comment on work that is already popular. What makes something popular? *Popular culture* is the term used for a variety of practices of sharing human expression that are as old as time. In traditional societies, people shared folk stories, songs, and poetry. Each generation retold, modified, and adapted traditional stories to meet the needs of their community. To attract and hold people's interest, ancient storytellers discovered how to include in their stories things that humans naturally are attracted to. Consider the emotional power of *Aesop's Fables* or the stories of the Brothers Grimm: they contain all five elements of *sensationalism:* sex, violence, children, animals, and the supernatural. When mass media developed in the nineteenth century with the rise of daily newspapers, editors discovered that news stories that included these elements sold more newspapers.

But during the Enlightenment, ideas about culture shifted to focus away from the people's ordinary sensational pleasures towards "the best that has been thought and read," a term used by Matthew Arnold in his book, *Culture and Anarchy*. He saw individual human refinement as the process of getting to know the finer things in life, including philosophy, literature, history, science, mathematics, and art.[18] Indeed, it is from this broad Enlightenment ideal that the academic subjects developed in higher education. In the twentieth century, people continued to make distinctions between high culture and low culture as a means to deal with how film, radio, advertising, and industrialization were reshaping cultural values. Serious (or high) culture was thought to enlighten, inspire, and challenge those who engaged with it, while popular (low) culture was thought to merely amuse, titillate, and pander to people's basest drives for sex and aggression.

In the twentieth century, critics like Theodor Adorno worried that the industrialization of popular culture by the mass media encouraged social passivity; by passively accepting what popular culture gives us, we grant more power to the corporations that control the culture industry. Adorno maintained that, in embracing popular culture, people may become obedient subjects who are psychically and economically coerced into cultural participation. In his view, the familiarity and sameness of popular culture may stunt and deaden the senses and discourage genuine individual identity formation.[19]

Today, the Internet has contributed to a blending and blurring of high and low culture, in ways that make both sides of the somewhat artificial binary richer. Some people feel guilty about the pleasures they take in consuming popular culture. Perhaps you have a guilty pleasure in playing certain video games or watching certain television programs, films, reading certain books, or listening to certain types of music. But what makes popular culture is the fact that it is common. It can be thrilling to find others who love the same media that you love. Reddit and other online communities are filled with people who are happy to talk endlessly about an online comic, a TV series, a video game character, a musician, or a celebrity.

Critiquing Media Culture

One important role of remix is as a means to critically analyze or comment about popular culture and mass media. People may do this as part of academic coursework, as independent media artists, as activists or as media professionals. One way to comment on media culture is to consider the relationship between *representation and reality*. Lauren Drinkard, an undergraduate student at the University of Pennsylvania, created a short film, *Outbreaks in Film*, to analyze the way that Hollywood films represent public health disasters like the spread of contagious disease.[20] She intercuts sequences from fiction films like *Contagion*, *I am Legend*, and *The Andromeda Strain* with CNN breaking news footage featuring Dr. Tom Frieden, Director of the Centers for Disease

Control and Prevention, announcing that the first US patient had tested positive for Ebola. There are some important similarities and many differences between how entertainment film and news media address the problem of contagious disease.

Some people comment on media culture by exploring the relationship between *authors and their audiences.* For example, in Anita Sarkeesian's video series, *Tropes vs. Women,* she addresses video game fans. Media representations can be understood through an analysis of the needs and interests of the users/audience and an identification of the goals of the producer or author. In this case, video game manufacturers seek to maximize profit by creating a highly popular game. Heterosexual male users may enjoy the sexual arousal that results from gazing upon a female body presented on screen. One episode, entitled "Body Language and the Male Gaze," uses clips of video games to show how movement of the bodies of video game characters is inflected with gender stereotypes. She uses clips from *Assassin's Creed Syndicate, Batman: Arkham City,* and *Bayonetta 2* to illustrate these ideas. For example, when a female video game character walks, there is a noticeable hip sway. When a character sits down, "she sits down like a delicate flower," notes Sarkeesian, even when she's supposed to be a highly trained fighter. The way women move in video games exudes a kind of sexuality that is presented for the presumed enjoyment of the game player.[21]

Another approach to critiquing culture focuses on the interpretation of media *messages and meaning.* John Oliver uses images from a variety of different media in constructing his comedy news show, *Last Week Tonight.* In one episode, entitled "Fashion," Oliver begins by making fun of men who wear plaid shirts before going on to offer a well-researched and highly critical analysis of fashion outlets like H&M and Forever 21. Reviewing news stories about child labor, factory safety, worker exploitation, and global supply chain management issues, Oliver uses images including print and television ads, still images of web pages, and news photographs and television news clips depicting fires in Asian clothing factories and sweatshops.[22] By remixing his commentary with relevant images, videos, and text, he observes that although the American public sporadically cares about the issue of the economics of fashion, we get blinded by low prices. As a result, the underlying structural, political and economic issues go unchanged.

But people aren't just creating media to critique mass media television shows and films. Some YouTubers specialize in creating *reaction videos,* where they critique and comment upon the YouTube videos produced by others, using bits of those videos and adding commentary to create new creative work. For example, Chris Rowe has a YouTube channel PrankInvasion. He creates "kissing videos" where he approaches a random woman and pranks them by kissing in public places.[23] These video feature beautiful young women, often dressed in sexually alluring clothes. In analyzing the reasons why this YouTuber's work is popular, another YouTuber, H3H3 Productions, created a reaction video where they used bits of PrankInvasion's work to critique it, noting that the models are paid to participate and comparing the videos to soft porn.[24]

Intertextuality

To understand why the reaction video has become so common and so popular on YouTube, it's worth reflecting on the concept of *intertextuality*, the way that meaning is shaped through texts referencing other texts. *The Simpsons* is famous for this: in many episodes, we see Homer and Marge, children Bart, Lisa, and Maggie watching television. In one episode, we see an ad for Duff Beer. In the ad, the delivery men encounter an angry mob of protesting feminists. By dousing them with beer, the men manage to "transform" the feminists into cavorting, bikini-clad women, whose protest signs no longer read, "We are NOT sex objects," but "I'm Easy" and "Get Me Drunk." As Jonathan Gray notes:

> Hence, the tired old advertising sub-genre of sexy women "summoned" by a product or service is lampooned, as are the industry's continued objectification and demeaning notions of women, the industry's inherent suspicion of progressive social movements, ads' use of sex to sell anything, and the frequently gendered nature of ads.[25]

Intertextuality is a key feature of many media messages. In each episode of *South Park*, we see examples of intertextuality that occur as the show quotes from, alludes to, borrows, or transforms a familiar current event, a literary work, or historical event. Many forms of media create meaning through intertextuality.

Russian theorist Mikhail Bakhtin has noted that intertextuality is a normal part of human communication: he argued that "nobody is the first speaker" because every utterance begins as a response to something else. Indeed, all communication is linked together in a complex chain of performances. Bakhtin recognized that a speaker may use intertextuality intentionally or unintentionally and that it may be exploited for a variety of purposes.[26] When you start paying attention to intertextuality, you will find it everywhere, especially in your ordinary conversation. Sometimes, the prevalence of *reference humor* is often more easy to spot in situations when it's unfamiliar, as when we watch an old film or television show and can't understand certain jokes because we're not familiar with the text, context or ideas being referenced.

Although researchers have found that intertextuality pervades classroom talk at all levels, from graduate school to preschool, they have also found that many educators ignore, dismiss, or marginalize the popular cultural connections learners make. When teachers demonstrate a lack of respect for popular culture, students may be discouraged from making explicit, formal, and well-reasoned connections between academic subjects they're studying and their familiarity with contemporary popular culture. For example, researcher Betsy Rymes explored an instance of intertextual conflict as she analyzed a teacher's non-recognition of her student's reference to Pokemon in a phonics lesson. In her view, the teachers' view of herself as an expert may have interfered with being able to learn about the Pokemon world from her student.[27]

But even when teachers do make space for popular culture connections in the classroom, students from different backgrounds or those not familiar with the specific cultural references may be left out of the meaning-making process. For example, new immigrants can be challenged by Americans' reliance on pop culture as a topic of conversation. As reported in an article in the *Columbia Spectator*, a Korean student at Columbia University described the challenge of transitioning from Korean K-pop culture to American pop culture and a Brazilian student described the challenge of keeping up with unfamiliar sports. Another student explained, "Every day there is this new acronym that's going on and this new hashtag and this new video, and this new very popular singer."[28] When we repeat a line from a popular film or pop song in a conversation, we may include or exclude listeners depending on their familiarity with the source material.

Copyright, Remix and Fair Use

Some remixes are derivative while others are transformative. For example, a shot-by-shot remake of a music video may simply exploit the popularity of the original source. Similarly, if you use the whole music track of a popular artist and add your own video images to it, your remix may serve as a substitute for the original, leading to a copyright violation. But perhaps your work adds new expression or meaning to the original content that you remixed. If so, it may be *transformative*, and that form of use is protected under copyright law. Borrowing small bits of material from an original work is more likely to be considered fair use than borrowing large portions. However, even a small amount may weigh against fair use in some situations if it constitutes the "heart" of the work.

When it comes to making money, even if you monetize a video, you may still be able to claim fair use. However, if your use of copyright content harms the copyright owner's ability to profit from his or her original work, then fair use may not apply, unless you are creating a critical analysis or a parody. The protection of intellectual freedom through guarding people's rights to "comment and criticism" is enabled by the doctrine of fair use.[29]

YouTube's Content ID Software

If you upload a video to YouTube that contains copyrighted content, you may get a takedown notice. YouTube's Content ID software analyzes samples of music provided by the recording industry and compares them with the videos uploaded to the web site. The software establishes a link between an existing work and an uploaded work such as a remix.

If the content matches, the video may be automatically blocked or the sound muted and the user is automatically informed by e-mail that the material has been disabled "as a result of a third-party notification claiming that this material is infringing." Scare tactics are used as the user is informed: "Repeat incidents of copyright infringement will result in the deletion of your account and all videos uploaded to that account."

But if you believe that your use of copyrighted material is a fair use, then you can file a counter notification, which is a legal request for YouTube to reinstate a video that has been removed. For these reasons, every digital author needs a good understanding of how copyright and fair use apply to their creative work.

The Ethics of Memes

On Facebook and Twitter, people post and share visual memes as a form of communication and expression. You have seen those somewhat familiar pictures with different words on them? The term *visual meme* is used to describe a form of media whereby a square or rectangular image is repurposed as a catchphrase that is easily understood and imitated. Some online communities form around the pleasure of memes. For example, on Instagram, "Gym Memes Official" collects memes that make fun of athletes and gym culture. One meme shows a sad panda image, including the phrase, "When You Kinda Want Abs." Below the image it reads: "But You Kinda Want to Eat 17 Donuts and 3 Large Pizzas." In another meme, an image of a gymnast balancing an elephant at the edge of the Grand Canyon is accompanied by the catchphrase, "Haters will say it's Photoshop." A meme can be described as "a group of digital items sharing common characteristics of content, form, and/or stance, which were created with awareness of each other, and were circulated, imitated, and/or transformed via the Internet by many users."[30] Figure 14.4 shows some memes about creativity and the Create to Learn approach to learning.

Meme culture is only ten years old. In 2007, as user-generated content was rising, Eric Nakagawa started icanhascheezburger.com. Teens loved the site for its funny visual gags. Over time, the company grew to develop over 50 online humor sites, reaching 10 million people each month, becoming the fourth

Figure 14.4 Memes about creativity.

most popular brand on Facebook. Working from their offices in Seattle, Ben Huh, CEO of The Cheeseburger Network, has been credited with bringing Internet memes to the mainstream.

Some people think that creative people who produce memes (and other types of remix creativity) are contributing to the Internet economy by adding products of value. Should they be paid? Companies like I Can Has Cheezeburger make money from the work of remix creators because the Internet economy depends on free labor. Those who create new content for web sites actually are the ones who keep the content fresh, meeting the expectations of the audience and thus sustaining or even increasing the value of Internet businesses over time.

Internet memes make it easy for people to express some of their darkest and most mean-spirited beliefs, opinions, and ideas. Each year, the staff of Know Your Meme offer some reflections on the themes they find in Internet meme culture. Know Your Meme staffers research the origins of the many widely circulating forms of remix creativity and they have found that people use memes to enact gender and culture wars by using inherently biased language and imagery. Increasingly extreme polarization of public opinions on the Internet is common. According to a review of controversies of 2015:

> In this online advertising economy, rage-inducing content is Internet gold, and those that fan its flames are rewarded with oh-so-precious shares, clicks and pageviews. In this new age of tribal warfare, social media platforms are the new battlefields and blogs are the new war profiteers.[31]

In 2015, people used memes to engage in vicious arguments over gender issues including Gamergate, weight loss ads, and video game characters. On university campuses, students shared memes to express their attitudes towards topics including cultural appropriation, microaggression, trigger warnings, and safe spaces.

Balancing the Familiar and Unfamiliar

Will people ever tire of remixes and mashups? Do remix genres have true staying power? Or are they a temporary phenomenon that resulted from the first decade of social media? Mashups have certainly become part of mainstream mass media culture: consider *Jimmy Kimmel Live*'s Mashup Mondays which feature performances of musical artists from different musical formats creating skillfully blended songs. In one episode, rapper Warren G performed with saxophonist Kenny G.[32]

According to Kirby Ferguson, all creative work can be balanced on *the continuum between familiar and novel.* When he examined the relationship between J.J. Abrams' *The Force Awakens* and the previous films from the Star Wars saga, including *A New Hope*, Ferguson discovered that the balance between novelty and familiarity is complex. For example many film critics celebrated or complained about the eerie intertextuality between the two films. Was this a good feature of the film or a sign that the remix method has gone stale? It's important to note that familiarity ensures solid performance at the box office. Abrams copies story elements from tried-and-true plot lines and genres; he specializes in rebooting familiar material, including the *Star Trek* series. In a remarkable critical analysis that compares and contrasts the two films, Ferguson identifies 14 similarities between *The Force Awakens* and *A New Hope*.[33] People may enjoy remixes and mashups because they combine the optimal blend of the novel and the familiar. If so, then these remix genres are likely to be part of our culture for a long time to come.

Activity: Create a Remix

Select a mentor text that is either audio, film, or video. Using excerpts from this work along with other choices, develop a remix audio or video approximately 2–5 minutes in length. You may use any form of media in your remix but most of the material you select should be copyrighted and repurposed moving images, still images, and music. Share your work with others and ask them to offer their interpretations of your remix. Then write a short essay that describes your creative process, beginning with your choice of mentor text. As you work, consider these questions:

- How did you find and select material to use in your remix?
- How did your ideas develop in the process of creating the remix?
- Which ideas from this chapter informed your strategy or message?
- How did your remix transform the original work's meaning and purpose?

15

Social Media

KEY IDEAS

People face a lot of decisions in sharing their creativity with the world. It takes effort and creativity to reach a large audience. Marketing and distribution are now the responsibility of the digital author. Shifting from personal use of social media to professional use can be challenging, as it requires re-orienting to the strategic goals of a communicator and understanding the economics of the Internet and mass media. Social data analytics provides digital authors with powerful evidence of effectiveness, and concepts like virality, tagging, and privacy help you use social media both for career development and social activism.

When Elan Morgan tried an unusual social experiment, she was surprised to see how it changed her life. On August 1, 2014, she decided to stop "liking" things on Facebook. It was hard, at first. "As I scrolled through updates," she wrote, "my finger instinctively gravitated towards the Like button on hundreds of posts and comments." She felt the pull of an automatic behavior as she tried to resist the instinct to hit the "Like" button. "I saw updates I liked or wanted others to know I liked, and I found myself almost unconsciously clicking my approval."

Within just a few days, she noticed that the content on her Facebook News Feed had changed. When she stopped liking pictures of animals, she got fewer pictures of animals. Since the algorithm that is used to display and sequence posts is based on what you "like," she no longer saw images of animal torture or "the influx of über-cuteness that liking kitten posters can bring on." To compensate for not "liking," she found herself commenting more, offering compliments and verbal support to her network of friends, colleagues, and family.[1] After the experiment was over, she never went back to "liking" because she had learned to prefer commenting instead.

Matt Honan tried the opposite experiment: he "liked" virtually everything that he saw on Facebook for 48 hours – literally everything – even those *sponsored content* ads, the ones that look like news, and are generally located at the bottom of the page.

Create to Learn: Introduction to Digital Literacy, First Edition. Renee Hobbs.
© 2017 John Wiley & Sons, Inc. Published 2017 by John Wiley & Sons, Inc.

What happened was fascinating: within hours, Matt's Facebook News Feed was 100 percent products and web sites. There were no human beings, no posts from his friends. When he "liked" a pro-Israel post about Gaza, the next day his Facebook account included more anti-immigrant, anti-gun control content. As he continued his "liking" experiment, the content delivered seemed to become more and more stupid. Soon he began seeing posts that asked, "Which Titanic Character Are You?" Other content explained, "Katy Perry's Backup Dancer is the Man Candy You Deserve."[2] Such is the power of "liking" as a key part of the economics of the Internet.

Who can be surprised that, as part of Matt's experiment in liking everything, his Facebook News Feed became inundated with advertising? After all, the economics of social media is built upon the practice of liking and sharing. It may be a surprise to you, but for every six minutes that people are on the Internet, they are using Facebook for one of those minutes. With 1.3 billion users, Facebook advertising enables companies to communicate with people who are interested in their products. In general, you'll see a Facebook ad once in every 20 items on your News Feed, but this will increase if you like or click on ads. Generally, these ads are for products or services that are associated with your online behavior. If you've used a dating service, you'll see Facebook ads for dating services, for example.

Social media like Facebook have distinctive qualities: *persistence* refers to the availability of content from anywhere on any device. Even when deleted, online content may have been spread and may be stored in a variety of digital locations maintained by other users. Online content is *scalable* in the sense that the audiences for it can expand far beyond a particular local interaction. Online content is *searchable*, making it available to anyone when the content matches with key terms typed in by another user.[3]

Facebook advertising works to sell products, there's no doubt about it. In analyzing an eight-week ad campaign on Facebook for fish oil which emphasized the emotional value of having a good heart, 18 million people saw the ads and the company sold more fish oil, earning twice as much money as was spent on the ad campaign itself, proving that the social marketing campaign was effective.[4] In considering the largest social networks, we understand that each one has a distinctive target audience and appeal and all depend upon sponsored content advertising as a primary revenue stream. Figure 15.1 shows six of the most popular social media networks.

Sharing as Relational Expression

Today, we share more information from more sources with more people, quickly and easily using the Internet and social media. Most people say that they get more value from information that has been shared by friends and

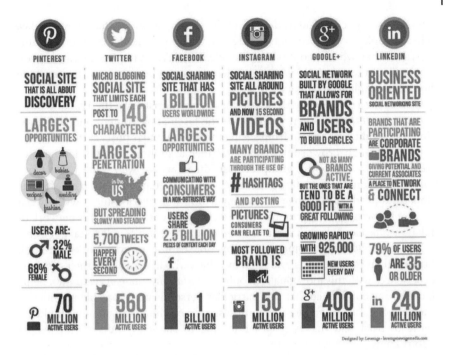

Figure 15.1 Some top social media networks.

family than from other sources. Moreover, people process information more deeply if they anticipate the possibility of sharing it with the people in their social networks. One of the most important reasons why we share information and entertainment using social media is to *define our identity* in relation to our peers. By sharing, you give others a sense of who you are and what you value. Online sharing also provides a sense of fulfillment and satisfaction.

Social media has also created new structures of social interaction by creating *networked publics*, where people construct a public or semi-public profile within a bounded system. We see a list of other users with whom we share a connection, and interact with others within the system.[5]

So decisions about sharing information and entertainment online are essentially decisions about your identity and your social relationships. You construct an online identity by deciding what to share and what not to share with others. These decisions are not truly independent because your identity has been influenced by the network of relationships you have with your family, peers, acquaintance and others.

The meaning of the word "sharing" is shifting as a result of social media's growing cultural importance. Of course, people have been sharing information, goods, and services throughout history: it's actually been key to our survival as a species. Today, the rise of the sharing economy has created eBay, where people recycle products; Craigslist, where people share job opportunities; and Uber, where people share car rides. If you're an inveterate traveler, you might like to use Airbnb, where people offer spare bedrooms or make whole houses available to strangers.

One of the reasons why these services have flourished is the rise of *crowdsourced evaluations*. When you explore the fascinating content and conversations on Reddit, you benefit from seeing the most popular posts at the top of the screen. Through crowdsourcing, digital media support the development of *weak social ties* among a group of individuals, where we establish trust not through personal face-to-face experience but through participation in informational and product exchanges stemming from these relationships. Weak social ties are surprisingly important if you're a change agent, because this network of relationships can help you spread new ideas or motive people to take action.[6]

When I decide to let someone into my house for a summer weekend rental, I review their reputation as evaluated by others who inform about their previous experiences with this individual. An online *reputation system of evaluation* helps increase my confidence that this particular person is a responsible member of the network. In a way, the information shared on the platform helps build my sense of trust and makes it easier for me to share my house with people I don't know.

The Facebook Emotional Contagion Study

How does Facebook affect your emotional life? In 2014, Facebook researchers worked with Cornell University scholars to experimentally modify the Facebook News Feed algorithm for 689,003 people. An *algorithm* is simply a set of computer instructions. To decide which posts to display, computer scientists at Facebook wrote an algorithm. When they adjusted it so that users see more negative posts on their News Feed, users' own posts tend to be more negative than when users see emotionally positive posts on their News Feed. This research showed that people experience *emotional contagion* when they use social media.[7] Developed by Professor Elaine Hatfield, the term conveys the idea that we can "catch" emotions from people we spend time with. If your roommate is depressed, you are more likely to become depressed yourself, for example. If everyone on your News Feed is having a bad (or a good) day, you may have one too.

When this research was published, people reacted strongly. Some were concerned that the nearly 700,000 people whose News Feeds were manipulated did not give consent to participate in this study. Others noted that the Facebook Terms of Service specifies that such algorithmic manipulations can and do occur as part of the continuous improvement of software services.

Human Behavior Adjusts to Technologies

Today, you probably experience most of your media on your smartphone. Each day, you interact with software on your mobile phone that packages and arranges data and relationships. For example, Waze helps you be aware of traffic problems. Yelp helps you decide where to have lunch when you are out of town. When you are waiting at the dentist office, you can play Scrabble with your online friends. These apps represent your geographical location as well as your visual and sonic experience. You might upload an image, text a friend, play a game, or look up a miscellaneous fact. Just using your phone involves you using, selecting, creating and sharing images, words and sounds with friends, acquaintances and strangers.

More than 185 million smartphone users check their cell phones an average of 47 times per day, with 18–24 year olds checking their phones an average of 74 times per day.[8] When we are using the tools on our smartphones, we are acting in concert with the software objects, adjusting ourselves to the requirements of the software. For example, if you are like me, you may have adjusted your life in relation to your Twitter community, checking in to see what people that you follow are talking about or sharing a 140-character post about what you are reading, viewing, watching or doing. Much of what we do involves manipulating and collecting digital objects, and fragments of data.

When Marshall McLuhan, a Canadian media philosopher, said, "We shape our tools and thereafter our tools shape us," he wasn't referring to the smartphone. But he was acknowledging *the power of communication tools to shape our behavior patterns*. He had observed how the newspaper, the radio, the telephone, and the television had influenced the lifestyles and values of people living in the twentieth century. When McLuhan died in 1980, a new generation of *media ecologists* arose to examine the new media that have emerged since then. They consider how media have changed the role of *place and space* as cellphones and the Internet enable us engage in social relationships from anywhere.[9] Metaphorically, you are in two places at the same time when you are conducting a business call at home. The GPS apps change your relationship with your encounters with new places, reducing your anxiety but also potentially decreasing your alertness to the objects in the physical environment. Joshua Meyrowitz, author of *No Sense of Place*, notes that unlike previous generations, who experienced a dependence on physical locations for certain kinds of social relationships, "our culture is becoming essentially placeless."[10]

To Share or Not to Share: Understanding Virality

The term *virality* is used to refer to the likelihood that a particular social media will be spread or shared. We share content online for many different reasons, but especially content that activates strong positive emotions. People also tend to share content that is funny, intense, or surprising. Jonah Berger and Katherine

Milkman say it's the power of awe that really distinguishes viral content from nonviral content. Awe is distinct from surprise in the sense that, "It involves the opening and broadening of the mind." In fact, content that inspires wonder is far more likely to be shared than other content.[11]

To discover the characteristics that are associated with online sharing, Jonah Berger and his colleagues analyzed 7,000 *New York Times* articles to identify which ones were most frequently shared. They found that, in addition to valuable information, the emotional tone of a news story matters: subjects that activate anxiety and anger are also important, as people seek to entertain others with surprising and interesting content. As the researchers note, "Such content does not clearly produce immediate economic value in the traditional sense or even necessarily reflect favorably on the self. This suggests that social transmission may be less about motivation and more about the transmitter's internal states."[12]

One of the easiest ways to create viral content is to exploit the rhetorical technique of *incongruency*, where a combination of unexpected and irrelevant content requires users, readers, or viewers to resolve the unexpected juxtaposition to find meaning. For example, a before-and-after image showing a Dalmatian dog with and without spots is incongruous until we understand it as an ad for Clearasil, an acne medication.

Interactive media is highly viral, which is one reason why social media users seem to love online quizzes, as Figure 15.2 shows. Buzzfeed's quiz, "Which City Should You Actually Live In?" attracted more than 20 million users in 2014. Buzzfeed identifies four different types of quizzes: *trivia* quizzes test your knowledge; *personality* quizzes offer you insight on your character by how you respond

Which Classy-Ass Cocktail Should You Learn How To Make?

Pick a merry old man and find out which cocktail will be your new *thing*.

👤 Hannah Jewell ⏱ 5 hours ago 💬 3 responses

How Well Do You Know British Landmarks?

But where IS Stonehenge?

👤 Sophie Gadd ⏱ 6 hours ago 💬 15 responses

What Delicious Food Should You Make On Your Next Camping Trip?

Mmmm so many types of s'mores.

👤 Sophie Gadd ⏱ 7 hours ago 💬 6 responses

Poll: So How Are You Really Feeling About "Harry Potter And The Cursed Child"?

Alrighty folks, let's hash this out. (MAJOR spoilers within.)

👤 Alanna Bennett ⏱ 20 hours ago 💬 71 responses

Figure 15.2 Buzzfeed quizzes go viral.

to questions; *polls* quizzes ask you to share an opinion; and *checklist* quizzes offer you statements and provide a response based on the number of items you check off. People seem to love quizzes because it's a light diversion from work or life and it provides an opportunity to reflect on personal identity. When you take a BuzzFeed quiz and received your results, you will see links on the right-hand side of the page to various topics, many of which will be Buzzfeed's sponsored content, which is a blend of information and persuasion. Marketers love quizzes because they are cheap to create and permit blatant references to their products: Disney, Time Warner, and Universal all create quizzes timed with their new movie releases.

Digital Learning Horoscope

As a way to increase people's digital and media literacy, the Media Education Lab created an online quiz for teachers to help them determine their Digital Learning Horoscope. After answering questions, teachers receive a customized profile that tells them about their values. Perhaps your teacher is a Demystifier, who likes helping students ask "how" and "why" questions about media, culture, and society. Or perhaps your teacher is a "Taste-maker," someone who widens your horizons by introducing you to ideas that you've not yet encountered.

YOU ARE A

TASTE-MAKER 🎩

You want students to be discriminating in their appreciation of a wide range of media messages, including those that address history, art, the sciences, culture and society.

read more >>

YOU ARE ALSO A

DEMYSTIFIER 🔍

You want your students to develop transferable critical thinking skills by pulling back the curtain on how all media messages are constructed.

WATCHDOG 📢

You're passionate about helping students appreciate the economic and political contexts of media and technology as complex systems that shape our everyday lives.

Figure 15.3 Digital Learning Horoscope results.

Measuring Impact

Social media platforms now enable people to measure the reach of their messages using *social data analytics*. While once this type of information was available only to a select few, today everyone can access data analytics associated with the social media accounts they control.

The ability to gather relevant information from social data is giving rise to new types of job opportunities. For example, as US retailers geared up for Black Friday, the day after Thanksgiving, they also monitored social media platforms, looking for evidence of public opinion about the upcoming sales holiday. Using a data analytics dashboard, retailers could see how people were using the term "Black Friday" on Twitter, Facebook, and other social media platforms. They could even see the use of related phrases like "boycott" and "staying home" to discover that some people consciously avoid buying things on this day.

Data visualizations show the rise in the topic over time and the positive and negative sentiment associated with people's posts. Dashboards even show geographical differences in the regions of the country. You can measure your influence on Facebook using the Insights data to see how many people saw your posts, and Facebook will inform you of their age, gender, and social class. They even provide information about their buying behavior, including the likelihood that they will buy a car in the next six months!

Privacy

There is plenty of joy in sharing pictures through social media, so much so that the average parent will post 1,000 pictures of their child online between birth and age five. Catherine Steiner-Adair, author of *The Big Disconnect*, explains that as children grow older, they come to have opinions and preferences about how they are represented online.[13] Sometimes our friends and family will post images of ourselves that just look terrible. On Snapchat, you decide on how long the receiver can view an image you send. But people can save or recover Snapchat images using data recovery software. On Facebook, you can untag a photo of yourself, of course, but the photo is still visible. If anyone has ever posted a photo of you that you dislike, you know how awkward it can be in asking them to remove it.

You have probably learned from experience how to manage your privacy online. Most teens and young adults learn from experience by disclosing information and then evaluating the consequences. Clearly, there are both benefits and risks to disclosing private information online. Researchers refer to this as the *privacy paradox*. While some may worry about the possibility that their Internet searches can be tracked, others may value the ability to gain access to sensitive material "without facing another human, without asking permission, and without being judged by the people around us."[14]

No two people will have the exact same concerns about privacy when it comes to the Internet and social media: privacy is a highly personal value. Some people will fear government surveillance while others will fear how corporations use information about our online behavior. We also consider privacy in relation to the people we work with or go to school with or live with every day. In general, people feel more concern about protecting their privacy from their immediate social circle than from more abstract privacy risks linked to corporations and government. This is why many forms of *digital citizenship* education fail so drastically: children and teens can easily parrot the "right" answer when asked about whether they should share information with strangers, for example. But research shows that most children begin withholding information about their online media use by age 10.[15]

Many people, both young and old, query search engines with questions about medical conditions that they might not want to reveal to their family physician. They buy products online because they prefer the privacy of online purchasing to the prospect of visiting a neighborhood store.

One especially sensitive privacy topic is, of course, sexuality. Library researchers have discovered that when public libraries install self-checkout devices, people check out more books on topics including LGBTQ issues.[16] Researchers have found that there is proportionally more use of online gay pornography in states which are less LGBTQ-friendly (generally in the southern United States), suggesting that "perhaps closeted individuals living in Bible Belt states are more concerned for their privacy from people in their immediate communities … than they are about protecting their privacy from remote online entities."[17]

Social Media for Civic Activism

One in three American adults claimed that they were active in supporting a social issue or cause in the past 12 months. Researchers who have examined the attitudes of Americans towards activism find that people's general stance can be triggered by personal experience, reading something in the news, having a family member affected by an issue, or even hearing about the issue from a religious leader.[18]

For these reasons, a powerful story can inspire others to take action on behalf of a cause or issue. Take, for example, the case of Carla Dauden, a 23-year-old Brazilian filmmaker who made a film in the summer of 2013 about the World Cup and Summer Olympics. Frustrated by public expenditures of $30 billion to build stadium for these glossy global sporting events, Dauden reflected on Brazil's stunning problems of illiteracy, sanitation, housing, unemployment, and crime in a country of more than 200 million people.

In documenting the promises made by Brazil in its bid for the Olympics, Dauden reveals the many social inequalities in Rio de Janeiro that are best characterized by the lives of the people living in the *favelas*, the informal settlement or slums surrounding the city. Despite the promises made by developers, over 75 percent of residents have toilets that are not connected to treated sewage systems, resulting in human waste from about 7.5 million people flowing untreated into the ocean. To promote her cause, she grew her Instagram account to more than 2,000 people and 4,000 followers on Twitter. Thanks to

---

Before I Die

Public art can be understood as a form of social media. When Candy Chang created an interactive wall on an abandoned building in her neighborhood in New Orleans, she wasn't sure what to expect. Using chalkboard paint, she stenciled the phrase, "Before I die I want to…" Passers-by could write their own endings to the sentences, sharing their hopes and dreams in a public space. When she shared the photos of the poignant messages left by people on the interactive wall, the concept went viral. More than 1,000 walls have been created in 70 countries, including Haiti, China, and Ukraine.[19]

Figure 15.4 Public art goes viral.

retweeting by some famous Brazilian football players, her YouTube video went viral, attracting 2.2 million viewers in just a few days.[20]

Managing Social Media: Personal and Professional Life

There's no one right way to handle social media as part of your personal and professional life. Researchers are finding that business leaders use a variety of different strategies to manage social media as part of daily life. Some people keep all their social networks open to both their personal friends and their professional colleagues and acquaintances. Others try to segment their social networks into distinct audiences, for example, by using LinkedIn for professional colleagues and Facebook for personal friendships.

One of the biggest shifts that many young people experience in college is the move from using social media as a form of entertainment to the use of social media as a form of career advancement and professional development. For example, media literacy educator Julie Smith explains the power of using Twitter as a form of personal and professional development. She explains that Facebook is for the people she knows, while Twitter is for the people she wishes she knew.[21] By following thought leaders and other writers, journalists, activists and artists whose work she admires, Twitter becomes a very personal tool for learning. By using social media to create a *personal learning network*, informal learning is activated through the strategic selection of people to follow. Figure 15.5 shows an infographic created by LinkedIn to depict some of the differences between personal and professional use of social networking.

Context Collapse

To participate in social media, we manage invisible audiences and the blurring of private and public life. For most of human history, we have shared meaning within particular relational contexts, adjusting our speech and behavior to the particular audience and situation we find ourselves in. But mass media and social media have altered how we experience *situation and context* as part of the communicative process.

In 1980, George Trow wrote a lyrical essay that tried to capture how television was shaping the texture of American life by reshaping the context of people's lived experience. Television was simultaneously speaking to millions but with a "grid of intimacy."[22] Today the concept of *context collapse* captures the idea that to speak online is to be aware that you are speaking to someone and everyone (and no one), all at the same time. As Michael Wesch puts it, when you're participating in social media, there are "an infinite number of contexts collapsing upon one another."[23] Your online words, images, and actions can be

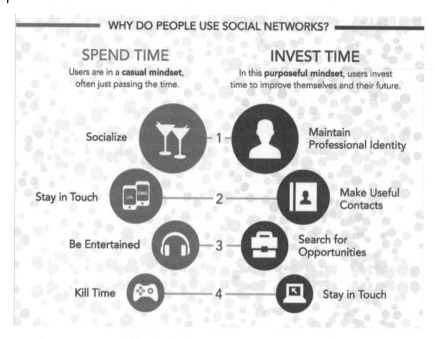

Figure 15.5 Infographic: Personal vs. professional use of social networks. *Source*: LinkedIn.

interpreted differently by your mother, your girlfriend, or your boss. Ultimately, you can never know how your images and language will be interpreted. As you participate in social media, you may experience intense social pressure, the need to fulfill others' expectations, or even a genuine freedom from social constraints where, as Jan Fernback notes, you have "convenient togetherness without real responsibility."[24] For these reasons, social media offers a fascinating set of paradoxes for the professional communicator.

Activity: Develop a Social Media Campaign

Select a social media platform and using your Scope of Work, develop at least 15 messages designed to reach your target audiences. Be sure your social media includes entertaining, persuasive and informative content, a relevant hashtag, an image, and a reference to an influential person. After you launch your campaign, review the social data analytics to examine which of the 15 messages was most influential. Based on this evidence, compose an essay to reflect on your strategy and consider how you might modify your campaign in the future.

Notes

Chapter 1

1 Accenture Strategy (2014) *Digital Disruption*, https://www.accenture.com/t20160113T204412__w__/us-en/_acnmedia/PDF-4/Accenture-Strategy-Digital-Workforce-Future-of-Work.pdf

2 Ibid.

3 Weinberger, David (2011) *Too Big to Know*. New York: Basic Books.

4 Hobbs, Renee and Moore, David Cooper (2013) *Discovering Media Literacy*. Thousand Oaks, CA: Corwin/Sage.

5 National Council of Teachers of English (2005) *Position Statement on Multimodal Literacies*, http://www.ncte.org/positions/statements/multimodalliteracies

6 Gerbner, George (1992) The cultural environment movement, 1992. *Access! Manhattan*, **1**(2), 4–5.

7 Ito, Mizuko *et al.* (2015) *Connected Learning: An Agenda for Research and Design*, The Digital Media and Learning Research Hub Reports on Connected Learning, John D. and Catherine T. MacArthur Foundation, Chicago.

8 Pennell, Michael (2010) The H1N1 virus and video production: New media composing in first-year composition. *Pedagogy*, **10**(3), 568–573.

9 Taylor, Michael *et al.* (2013) Student video projects: Examples of freshman multimedia research in the geosciences with an eye towards community engagement. Geological Society of America conference, 49th Annual Meeting, https://gsa.confex.com/gsa/2014NE/webprogram/Paper236412.html

10 Dartmouth College (2014) *Media Projects at Dartmouth*, http://sites.dartmouth.edu/mediaprojects/

11 Jenkins, Henry, Katie Clinton, Ravi Purushotma, Alice J. Robison, and Margaret Weigel. 2006. *Confronting the Challenges of Participatory Culture: Media Education for the 21st Century*. Chicago: The MacArthur Foundation.

12 Barron, Brigid, Kimberly Gomez, Nicole Pinkard and Caitlin Martin (2014) *The Digital Youth Network: Cultivating Digital Media Citizenship in Urban Communities*. Cambridge: MIT Press.

Create to Learn: Introduction to Digital Literacy, First Edition. Renee Hobbs.
© 2017 John Wiley & Sons, Inc. Published 2017 by John Wiley & Sons, Inc.

13 Ito, Mizuko *et al.* (2008) *Living and Learning with New Media: Summary of Findings from the Digital Youth Project,* John D. and Catherine T. MacArthur Foundation, Chicago.

14 Lenhart, Amanda and Madden, Mary (2005) *Teens as Content Creators.* Pew ResearchCenter,http://www.pewinternet.org/2005/11/02/part-1-teens-as-content-creators/

15 Dewey, Caitlin (2016, June 16). 6 in 10 of You will Share this Post Without Reading It, a New Depressing Study Says. *Washington Post.* http://wapo.st/2lpu4Zk

16 Rogers, Katie and Bronwich, Jonah Engel (2016, November 8). The Hoaxes, Fake News and Misinformation We Saw on Election Day. *New York Times.* http://nyti.ms/2lpvDqi

17 Borchers, Callum (2017, February 9). Fake News has Now Lost all Meaning. *Washington Post.* http://wapo.st/2lpxafV

18 Fabian, Jordan (2017, January 21). Trump Attacks Time Reporter for Mistake about MLK Bust. *The Hill.* http://bit.ly/2mQvRUl

Chapter 2

1 Maul, Ginae (2014) *First Semester Freshman College Experience!* [Video], https://www.youtube.com/watch?v=I-ixyZnHm4w

2 Science with Tom (2009) *Regulatin' Genes.* [Video], https://www.youtube.com/watch?v=9k_oKK4Teco

3 Weiss, Robert Alan (1971) *A Protein Primer.* [Video], https://www.youtube.com/watch?v=u9dhO0iCLww

4 YouArentBenjamin (2011) *Pivot Tables Make Everything Just Right* [Video], https://www.youtube.com/watch?v=GwbSJFtRmDw

5 Jacksfilms (2009) *Trailer: The Very Hungry Caterpillar.* [Video], https://www.youtube.com/watch?v=cph-eko-f-s

6 Hobbs, Renee (2010) *Digital and Media Literacy: A Plan of Action,* Aspen Institute and the John S. and James L. Knight Foundation.

7 Finke, Ronald, Ward, Thomas, and Smith, Steven (1999). *Creative Cognition: Theory, Research and Applications.* Cambridge: MIT Press.

8 Ibid.

9 Griffin, W. Glenn and Morrison, Deborah (2010) *The Creative Process Illustrated.* Cincinnati, OH: F+W Media.

10 Bourdieu, Pierre (1986) The forms of capital. In J.G. Richardson (ed.), *Handbook for Theory and Research for the Sociology of Education* (pp. 241–258). New York: Greenwood Press.

11 Quoted in Griffin and Morrison, ibid.

12 Ibid.

13 Hobbs, Renee and Moore, David Cooper (2013) *Discovering Media Literacy.* Thousands Oaks, CA: Corwin/Sage.

14 Quoted in Griffin and Morrison, ibid.

15 Ibid.

16 Ibid.

17 Huffington, Arianna (1988) *Picasso: Creator and Destroyer*, http://www.theatlantic.com/magazine/archive/1988/06/picasso-creator-and-destroyer/305715/

18 Kleon, Austin (2016) *Newspaper Blackout*, http://newspaperblackout.com/

19 Quoted in Griffin and Morrison, ibid.

20 Stokes, Patricia (2006) *Creativity from Constraints*. New York: Springer.

21 Csíkszentmihályi, Mihaly (1990). *Flow: The Psychology of Optimal Experience*. New York: Harper Collins.

22 Wallas, Graham (2014/1926) *The Art of Thought*. Kent, England: Solis Press.

23 Quoted in Griffin and Morrison, ibid.

24 Weksler, Marc and Babbette Weksler (2012) The epidemic of distraction. *Gerontology*, **58**(5), 385–390.

Chapter 3

1 Dove Campaign for Real Beauty (n.d.) *Onslaught*. [Video], Mind Over Media, http://propaganda.mediaeducationlab.com/rate/789

2 Greenpeace (2013) *Onslaught(er)*. [Video], Mind Over Media, http://propaganda.mediaeducationlab.com/rate/722

3 Neff, Jeff (2008, October 2) Unilever unleashes "Onslaught" on beauty industry. *AdvertisingAge*, http://adage.com/article/news/unilever-unleashes-onslaught-beauty-industry/120886/

4 Greenpeace (2009) *Public Pressure for Indonesia's Forests, Ask Unilever*, http://www.greenpeace.org/international/en/campaigns/forests/asia-pacific/dove-palmoil-action/

5 IDEA (n.d.) *What is Strategic Communication?* http://www.idea.org/blog/2011/03/16/what-is-strategic-communications/

6 Chaffee, Steve and Roser, Connie (1986) Involvement and the consistency of knowledge, attitudes and behaviors. *Communication Research*, **13**(3), 373–399.

7 Fishbein, Martin and Ajzen, Icek (2010) *Predicting and Changing Behavior: The Reasoned Action Approach*. New York: Taylor & Francis.

8 Packtor, Jordanna (2014) *Fantasy in the Classroom*. [Video], https://www.youtube.com/watch?v=FY42bZmo7uc

9 Atkins, Larry (2010, September 7) Go web, young dude: College students should create their own web sites. *Huffington Post*, http://www.huffingtonpost.com/larry-atkins/go-web-young-dude-college_b_706831.html

10 Kauffmann, Leah (2016) About, http://www.leahkauffman.com/about/

11 Hobbs, Renee (2013) Math Goes Pop. *Journal of Media Literacy Education*, **2**(2), http://digitalcommons.uri.edu/jmle/vol2/iss2/7/

12 Koblin, John (2016, January 12). Serial podcast, needing more, time, goes bi-weekly. *New York Times*, http://www.nytimes.com/2016/01/13/business/media/serial-podcast-needing-more-reporting-time-goes-biweekly.html

13 Pulitzer Center on Crisis Reporting (2016) *Hurricane Katrina and the Wars in Afghanistan and Iraq*, http://pulitzercenter.org/projects/hurricane-katrina-afghanistan-iraq

14 Robertson, Campbell and Richard Fausset (2015) 10 Years After Katrina. New York Times [multimedia]. URL: https://www.nytimes.com/interactive/2015/08/26/us/ten-years-after-katrina.html

15 Campbell, Gardner (2006) There's something in the air: Podcasting in education. *Educause Review*, http://er.educause.edu/articles/2005/1/theres-something-in-the-air-podcasting-in-education

16 Penn State University (n.d.) *One Button Studio*, http://onebutton.psu.edu/

17 Spitalnik, Ilya (2013) *The Power of Cartoon Marketing*, https://s3.amazonaws.com/powtoon/books/PowerOfCartoonMarketing_Book.pdf

18 Metro Australia (2013) *Dumb Ways to Die*, https://www.youtube.com/watch?v=IJNR2EpSOjw

19 Barthes, Roland (1977) The death of the author. *Image Music Text* (pp. 142–148). London: Fontana.

20 Rushkoff, Douglas (2011) *Program or Be Programmed*. New York: Or Books.

Chapter 4

1 Krents, Tatyana (2015) *Marketing and YouTube: 12 Most Popular Beauty Bloggers on Earth*, http://popsop.com/2015/11/marketing-and-youtube-12-most-popular-beauty-bloggers-on-planet-earth/

2 Lange, Patricia (2014) *Kids on YouTube*. Walnut Creek, CA: Left Coast.

3 Dewey, John (1938) *Logic: The Theory of Inquiry*. New York: Henry Holt and Company.

4 Head, Alison J. (2016) *How Today's Graduates Continue to Learn Once They Complete College*, http://projectinfolit.org/images/pdfs/2016_lifelonglearning_full%20report.pdf

5 Head, Alison J. and Eisenberg, Michael B. (2009) *Finding Context: What Today's College Student Say about Conducting Research in the Digital Age*, Project Information Literacy Progress Report, University of Washington's Information School.

6 Grossman, Martin (2007) The emerging academic discipline of knowledge management. Management Faculty Publications, Paper 11, http://vc.bridgew.edu/management_fac/11

7 Ibotson, Paul and Michael Tomoasello (2016, September 10). What's universal grammar? Evidence rebuts Chomsky's theory of language. Slate Magazine. http://www.salon.com/2016/09/10/what-will-universal-grammar-evidence-rebuts-chomskys-theory-of-language-learning_partner/

8 Kuh, George D. (2008) *High-Impact Educational Practices: What They Are, Who Has Access to Them, and Why They Matter*. Washington, DC: Association of American Colleges and Universities.

9 Friesem, Elizaveta (2016) Question-based dialogue on media representations of social problems: Enhancing civic engagement by uncovering implicit knowledge accumulated from the media. *Journal of Communication Inquiry*, **40**(1), 46–66.

10 Seelig, Tina. 2012. *InGenius: A Crash Course on Creativity*. New York: Harper Collins.

11 Weinberger, David (2011) *Too Big to Know*. New York: Basic Books.

12 Association of College and Research Libraries (2015) *Framework for Information Literacy in Higher Education*, http://www.ala.org/acrl/sites/ala.org.acrl/files/content/issues/infolit/Framework_ILHE.pdf

13 Kurtyleben, Danielle (2017, February 17) With 'fake news,' Trump moves from alternative facts to alternative language. National Public Radio. http://www.npr.org/2017/02/17/515630467/with-fake-news-trump-moves-from-alternative-facts-to-alternative-language?sc=tw

14 Baudrillard, Jean (1988) *Selected Writings*. Cambridge: Polity.

15 Bushack, Licia (2015) *E-books are Damaging Your Health*. Medical Daily, http://www.medicaldaily.com/e-books-are-damaging-your-health-why-we-should-all-start-reading-paper-books-again-317212

16 Fish, Stanley (1980) *Is there a Text in this Class? The Authority of Interpretive Communities*. Cambridge, MA: Harvard University Press.

17 Masterman, Len (1983) Media education in the 80s. *Journal of the University Film and Video Association*, **35**(3), 44–58.

Chapter 5

1 Berger, John (1972) *Ways of Seeing*. London: Penguin.

2 Prakash, Neha (2015, February 23). Stay weird, stay different. Graham Moore 's Oscar speech inspires, Mashable, http://mashable.com/2015/02/23/graham-moore-oscars-speech/#4VOpqgV1qkqm

3 Burstein, Julie (2011) *Spark: How Creativity Works*. New York: Harper Collins.

4 Piaget, Jean (1962) *Play, Dreams and Imitation in Childhood*. New York: W.W. Norton.

5 Shenk, Joshua Wolf (2014) *Powers of Two: Finding the Essence of Innovation in Creative Pairs*. New York: Houghton Mifflin Harcourt.

6 Shlain, Tiffany (2011) *Declaration of Interdependence*. [Video], https://www.youtube.com/watch?v=fzZ1Gl5UfE0

7 Johnson, Steven (2011) *Where Good Ideas Come From*. New York: Penguin.

8 Jenkins, Henry *et al.* (2007) *Confronting the Challenges of Participatory Culture: Media Education in the 21st Century*. Chicago: John D. and Catherine T. MacArthur Foundation.

9 Reilly, Erin Jenkins, Henry, Felt, Laurel, and Vartabedian, Vanessa (2012) Shall we play? http://www.slideshare.net/ebreilly1/play-doc-01-15613677

10 Bruner, Jerome (1962) *The Process of Education*. Cambridge: Harvard University Press.

11 Ferguson, Kirby (2016) Everything is a remix, http://everythingisaremix.info/

12 Powers, Ann (2012) *On Bob Dylan and Jonah Lehrer, Two Fabulists*, http://www.npr.org/sections/therecord/2012/08/01/157736941/on-bob-dylan-and-jonah-lehrer-two-fabulists

13 Hobbs, Renee (2011) *Copyright Clarity: How Fair Use Supports Digital Learning*. Thousand Oaks, CA: Corwin/Sage.

14 Ibid.

15 Leval, Pierre N. (1990) Toward a fair use standard. *Harvard Law Review*, **103**(5), 1105–1136.

16 Parkinson, Hannah (2015) Instagram, an artist and the $100,000 selfies – Appropriation in the digital age. *The Guardian*, https://www.theguardian.com/technology/2015/jul/18/instagram-artist-richard-prince-selfies

17 Rosensteil, Tom and Mitchell, Andrea (2012) *YouTube and News: A New Kind of Visual Journalism*. Pew Research Center, http://www.journalism.org/2012/07/16/youtube-news/

18 Strunk, William (2011/1918) *The Elements of Style*. Project Gutenberg, http://www.gutenberg.org/files/37134/37134-h/37134-h.htm

19 Pitaru, Diana (n.d.) *Keys to Creativity: Taking Risks*, http://blogs.psychcentral.com/unleash-creativity/2015/01/taking-risks/

20 Potchekailov, Valeri (2015) *One Project a Day Challenge*, http://oneprojectadaychallenge-blog.tumblr.com/

21 Bloomberg News (2012) *Calvin Coolidge Persisted in Deed if Not in Word*, https://www.bloomberg.com/view/articles/2012-06-11/calvin-coolidge-persisted-in-deed-if-not-in-word

Chapter 6

1 Glass, Jake (2012) *en Plein Air*. [Video], https://vimeo.com/46852120

2 Bennett, Amanda (2015, November 19) How does it feel to be a problem? *Huffington Post*, http://www.huffingtonpost.com/amanda-bennett/how-does-it-feel-to-be-a-_2_b_8499258.html

3 POPPYN (2014) *Episode 16: Youth and Housing Insecurity*. University Community Collaborative, Temple University. [Video], https://www.youtube.com/watch?v=Cp-9wj1wgSg

4 Jenkins, Henry, Shresthova, Sangita, Gamber-Thompson, Liana, Kligler-Vilenchik, Neta, and Zimmerman, Arely M. (2016) *By Any Media Necessary: The New Youth Activism*. New York: New York University Press.

5 Dewey, John (1933) *How We Think*. Boston: D.C. Heath.

6 Bransford, John D., Brown, Ann L., and Cocking, Rodney R. (2000) *How People Learn: Brain, Mind, Experience, and School*. Washington, DC: National Academy Press.

7 McLuhan, Marshall (1967/2010) *Understanding Me: Lectures and Interviews: Herbert Marshall McLuhan* (eds. Stephanie McLuhan and David Staines). Toronto: McClelland and Stewart.

8 Rundle, Margaret, Weinstein, Emily, Gardner, Howard, and James, Carrie (2015) *Doing Civics in the Digital Age: Casual, Purposeful and Strategic Approaches to Participatory Politics*, Youth and Participatory Politics Research Network, Working Papers #2, http://ypp.dmlcentral.net/sites/default/files/publications/YPP_WorkinPaper_02.pdf

9 Bowyer, Benjamin and Kahne, Joseph (2015) Youth comprehension of political messages on YouTube, *New Media and Society*, doi: 10.1177/1461444815611593

10 Russell, Jason (2013) *Do You Like it Thick or Thin?* Civic Commons Idea Stream, http://theciviccommons.com/blog/do-you-like-it-thick-or-thin

11 Gordon, Eric and Mihailidis, Paul (Eds.) (2016) *Civic Media: Design, Technology, Practice*. Cambridge, MA: MIT Press.

12 Jaffe, Morgan (2015) Social justice and LGBTQ communities in the digital age: Creating virtual and social affinity spaces through media literacy. In Julie Frechette and Rob Williams (eds.), *Media Education for Digital Generations* (pp. 103–118). New York: Routledge.

13 Jenkins, *et al.*, ibid., p. 29.

14 Rheingold, Howard (2012) *Net Smart: How to Thrive Online*. Cambridge, MA: MIT Press.

15 Wingfield, Nick (2014, October 14) Feminist critics of video games facing threats in "GamerGate" campaign. *New York Times,* http://www.nytimes.com/2014/10/16/technology/gamergate-women-video-game-threats-anita-sarkeesian.html

16 Kavoori, Anandam (2008). *Thinking Television*. New York: Peter Lang.

17 Cabral, Nuala (2013, November 15) Community talk back: *Orange is the New Black*. FAAN Mail, https://faanmail.wordpress.com/tag/orange-is-the-new-black/

18 Hutcheon, Linda (2000) *A Theory of Parody*. Urbana: University of Illinois Press.

19 Ibid.

20 Duncum, Paul (2009) Towards a playful pedagogy: Popular culture and the pleasures of transgression, *Studies in Art Education*, **50**(3), 232–244.

21 Gramsci, A. (2009) Hegemony, intellectuals, and the state. In J. Storey (ed.), *Cultural Theory and Popular Culture: A Reader* (pp. 75–80). Harlow, England: Pearson.

22 Independent Lens (2015) Test your implicit bias with science. [Video], http://www.pbs.org/independentlens/blog/implicit-test/

23 Groom, Dean (2013, September 10). Using the Disney method in teaching, https://deangroom.wordpress.com/2013/09/10/using-the-disney-method-inclassroom-gaming/

Chapter 7

1 Kellner, Jessamyn (2016) *Girls' Feminist Blogging in a Postfeminist Age*. New York: Routledge.

2 Winer, Dave (2003) *What Makes a Weblog a Weblog?*, http://blogs.harvard.edu/whatmakesaweblogaweblog.html

3 O'Sullivan, Catherine (2005) Diaries, on-line diaries and the future loss to archives; or blogs and the blogging bloggers who blog them, *The American Archivist*, **68**, 53–73.

4 Ibid.

5 Swain, Sherry Seale, Graves, Richard, and Morse, David (2015) The emerging shape of voice, *English Journal*, **104**(5), 30–36.

6 Olson, Ann (2013, August 13) The Theory of Self-Actualization. *Psychology Today* https://www.psychologytoday.com/blog/theory-and-psychopathology/201308/the-theory-self-actualization

7 Hyland, K. and Guinda, C.S. (eds.) (2012) *Stance and Voice in Written Academic Genres*. Basingstoke: Palgrave Macmillan.

8 *Rookie Magazine* (2015). http://www.rookiemag.com/submit/

9 Carr, Nicholas (2010) *The Shallows*. New York: W.W. Norton.

10 Edidin, Rachel (2015) *Five Reasons Why Listicles are Here to Stay and Why That's OK*, http://www.wired.com/2014/01/defense-listicle-list-article/

11 Auerbach, David (2015) *The Death of Outrage*, http://www.slate.com/articles/technology/bitwise/2015/03/outrage_clickbait_its_internet_dominance_is_about_to_fade.html

12 Paul, Richard (1984) Teaching critical thinking in the "strong" sense: A focus on self-deception, world views, and a dialectical mode of analysis, *Informal Logic* **4**(2), 2–7.

13 Rand-Hendricksen, Morten (2014) *Code of Ethics for Bloggers, Social Media andContentCreators*,https://mor10.com/code-of-ethics-for-bloggers-social-media-and-content-creators/

14 Shirky, Clay (2010) *Cognitive Surplus: How Technology Makes Consumers into Collaborators*. New York: Penguin.

15 Mihailidis, Paul (2014) *Media Literacy and the Emerging Citizen*. New York: Peter Lang.

16 Freire, Paulo (1970) *Pedagogy of the Oppressed*. New York: Penguin.

Chapter 8

1 Love + Radio (2011) *The Wisdom of Jay Thunderbolt* [audio recording], http://loveandradio.org/2011/04/the-wisdom-of-jay-thunderbolt/

2 Huizinga, Johan (1955) *Homo Ludens: A Study of the Play-Element in Culture*. Boston, MA: Beacon Press.

3 Wang, Harvey (2010) *StoryCorps Shorts: Dave Isay Interview*, http://www.pbs.org/pov/storycorps/interview-dave-isay/

4 Stephens, Autumn (n.d.) *Digital Art and Soul*, http://themonthly.com/up-front-08-08.html

5 Salmon, Christian (2010) *Storytelling*. New York: Verso.

6 White, Emily (2015, March 15). *Where is the Instagram for Audio?*, https://medium.com/cuepoint/radio-cures-technical-barriers-in-audio-cf98440ee5c4#.l54g3kpvt

7 Londono, Ernesto (2015) Hooked on the freewheeling podcast, Serial, *New York Times*, http://www.nytimes.com/2015/02/13/opinion/hooked-on-the-freewheeling-podcast-serial.html?_r=0

8 Crowley, Sharon and Hawhee, Debra (2012) *Ancient Rhetoric for Contemporary Students*, 5th edition. New York: Pearson.

9 Tomalin, Claire (2012) *Charles Dickens: A Life*. New York: Penguin.

10 Wells Fargo (2016) *Password*, https://www.ispot.tv/ad/AgHU/wells-fargo-password

11 Amnesty International (2016, May 24) *Look Refugees in the Eye*, https://www.amnesty.org/en/latest/news/2016/05/look-refugees-in-the-eye/

12 Njeru, J.W., Patten, C., Hanza, M. *et al.* (2015) Stories for change: Development of a diabetes digital storytelling intervention for refugees and immigrants to Minnesota using qualitative methods, *BMC Public Health*, **15**, 1311.

13 Freire, Paulo (1999) *Pedagogy of the Oppressed*. New York: Bloomsbury.

14 Digital Storytelling Project (2014) *Silence Speaks: Using Narrative and Participatory Media to Explore the Links between Gender, Violence, and HIV and AIDs in South Africa*, http://www.genderjustice.org.za/publication/silence-speaks/

15 Glass, Ira (2012) *Ira Glass on Storytelling* [video], https://www.youtube.com/watch?v=f6ezU57J8YI

16 DeLay, Logan (2012) *Why Prosody Matters: The Importance of Reading Aloud with Expression*, http://www.scilearn.com/blog/prosody-matters-reading-aloud-with-expression

17 Miller, Geoffrey, Beaber, Rex, and Valone, Keith (1976) Speech of speed and persuasion, *Journal of Personality and Social Behavior*, **34**(4), 615–624.

18 Ebeling, Martha B. (1999, March). *Ten Commandments for Effective Extemporaneous Delivery*. The Rostrum (National Forensic League), https://debate.uvm.edu/NFL/rostrumlibextimp.html

19 Kauffman, Johnny (2013) *Don't be Afraid of Silence: Tips from NPR Interview Host Rachel Martin*, http://www.npr.org/sections/npr-extra/2013/11/20/246336891/it-s-not-about-you-listening-tips-from-weekend-edition-sunday-host-rachel-martin

20 Olsen, Hanna (2014, August 28). *Radiolab's Jad Abumrad on the "Radical Uncertainty" of Creating Something New*. Creative Live Blog, http://blog.creativelive.com/radiolab-jad-abumrad/

21 Stocco, Diego (2013) *Explorer of Sounds*, http://www.diegostocco.com/

22 *Listen to Wikipedia* (2015) http://listen.hatnote.com/

23 Kitchen Sisters (2014) *Fugitive Waves: Horses, Unicorns, and Dolphins*, http://www.kitchensisters.org/2015/07/29/fugitive-waves-horses-unicorns-dolphins/

24 Aitchison, Jean (1996) *The Seeds of Speech: Language Origin and Evolution.* Cambridge: Cambridge University Press.

25 Hall, Cougar, West, Joshua, and Hill, Shane (2011). Sexualization in lyrics of popular music from 1959 to 2009: Implications for sexuality educators. *Sexuality & Culture.* DOI:10.1007/s12119-011-9103-4

26 Groce, Nancy (n.d.) *History of the American Folklife Center.* Library of Congress, American Folklife Center, http://www.loc.gov/folklife/AFChist/

27 Kimmel, Jimmy (2013, October 1). *Six of One: Obamacare vs. The Affordable Care Act,* https://www.youtube.com/watch?v=sx2scvIFGjE

Chapter 9

1 Saltz, Jerry (2014) Art at arm's length: A history of the selfie. *New York Magazine,* **47**(2), 71–75.

2 Senft, Theresa and Baym, Nancy (2015) What does the selfie say? Investigating a global phenomenon: Introduction. *International Journal of Communication,* **9**, 1588–1606.

3 Culkin, J.M. (1967, March 18) A schoolman's guide to Marshall McLuhan. *Saturday Review,* pp. 51–53, 71–72.

4 Ashkenaz, Jeremy, Buchanan, Larry, DeSantis, Alicia, Park, Haeyoun, and Derek Watkins (2015, May 3) A portrait of the Sandtown neighborhood in Baltimore. *New York Times,* http://www.nytimes.com/interactive/2015/05/03/us/a-portrait-of-the-sandtown-neighborhood-in-baltimore.html

5 Grunberg, Andy (1981, August 23). *Death in the Photograph* [Review of Camera Lucida by Roland Barthes], http://www.nytimes.com/1981/08/23/books/death-in-the-photograph.html

6 Baker, Alan (2013) Simplicity. *The Stanford Encyclopedia of Philosophy,* https://plato.stanford.edu/archives/fall2013/entries/simplicity/

7 Ravi, Nikhil (2012, June 18) *Truth and Beauty.* Common Ground, the Blog, http://www.commongroundgroup.net/2012/06/18/truth-and-beauty/

8 Sontag, Susan (2003) *Regarding the Pain of Others.* New York: Farrar Strauss and Giroux.

9 Thein, Ming (2015, November 11) *Ambiguity,* https://blog.mingthein.com/2015/11/11/ambiguity/

10 Postman, Neil and Powers, Steve (1992) *How to Watch TV News.* New York: Penguin.

11 Ecker, Ullrich, Lewandowsky, Stephan, Chang, Ee Pin, and Pillai, Rekha (2014) The effects of subtle misinformation in news headlines. *Journal of Experimental Psychology: Applied,* **20**(4), 323–335.

12 Konnikova, Maria (2014, December 17) How headlines change the way we think. *The New Yorker.*

13 *New York Times* (2015, October 16) Staging, manipulation and truth in photography. *New York Times*, http://nyti.ms/28RW5CT

14 Hadland, Adrian, Campbell, David, and Lambert, Paul (2015) *The State of News Photography: The Lives and Livelihoods of Photojournalists in a Digital Age*, Reuters Institute for the Study of Journalism in Association with World Press Photo, http://bit.ly/28RXmKd

15 Ibid.

16 Shroff, H. and Thompson, J.K. (2006) The tripartite influence model of body image and eating disturbance: A replication with adolescent girls. *Body Image*, **3**, 17–23

17 Alpert, Meryl (2013) *War on Instagram: Framing Conflict Photojournalism with Mobile Photography Apps*, http://www.academia.edu/4529765/War_on_Instagram_Framing_mobile_photography_apps_in_embedded_photojournalism

18 Przybylski, A.K., Murayama, K., DeHaan, C.R., and Gladwell, V. (2013) Motivational, emotional, and behavioral correlates of fear of missing out. *Computers in Human Behavior*, **29**(4), 1814–1848.

19 Araújo, Camila Souza, Corrêa, Luiz Paulo, Couto da Silva, Damilton, Ana Paula, Prates, Raquel Oliveira, and Wagner, Meira (2014) It is not just a picture: Revealing some user practices in Instagram, in *Web Congress (LA-WEB)*, 2014, 9th Latin American, IEEE, pp. 19–23.

Chapter 10

1 Rosling Rönnlund, Anna (2015) *Using Photos as Data to Understand How People Live*, TEDx Stockholm, https://www.youtube.com/watch?v=vvsAvvKeGhc

2 Tufte, Edward (1983) *The Visual Display of Quantitative Information*. Cheshire, CT: Graphics Press.

3 Paivio, Allan (2006) Dual coding theory and education, in *The Conference on Pathways to Literacy Achievement for High Poverty Children*, pp. 1–20, http://www.csuchico.edu/~nschwartz/paivio.pdf

4 Konnikova, Maria (2014, July 16) Being a better online reader. *The New Yorker.*

5 Praetor, Sandra (2013, March 6) *Big Data Analysis Interview with Hjalmar Gislason*, Big Data Public Private Forum, http://big-project.eu/blog/big-data-analysis-interview-hjalmar-gislason

6 Faces of Fracking (2014) *California's Getting Fracked*, http://www.facesoffracking.org/data-visualization/

7 Yau, Nathan (2014, May 29) *Where Bars Outnumber Grocery Stores*, https://flowingdata.com/2014/05/29/bars-versus-grocery-stores-around-the-world/

8 Kennedy, H., Hill, R., Allen, W. and Kirk, A. (2016) Engaging with (big) data visualisations: factors that effect engagement and resulting new definitions of effectiveness, *First Monday*. http://firstmonday.org/ojs/index.php/fm/article/view/6389

9 Kahnemann, Daniel (2013) *Thinking Fast and Slow*. New York: Farrar, Straus and Giroux.

10 Hill, Rosemary Lucy (2015) *Data Visualizations and You*, http://seeingdata.org/understanding-data-visualisations/data-visualisation-and-you/

11 Kuropatwa, Darren (2012) *60,000 Times Faster than Text: Really? A Difference Blog*, http://adifference.blogspot.com/2012/07/60-000-times-faster-than-text-really.html

12 Vigen, Tyler (2016) *Spurious Correlations*, http://www.tylervigen.com/spurious-correlations

13 Marr, Bernard (2016) *Big Data: 33 Brilliant and Free Data Sources for 2016*, http://www.forbes.com/sites/bernardmarr/2016/02/12/big-data-35-brilliant-and-free-data-sources-for-2016/#7c0dc8b66796

14 Eagle, Nathan (2014) *What's the Value of Your Personal Data?* World Economic Forum, https://www.weforum.org/agenda/2014/09/whats-value-personal-data/

Chapter 11

1 Newman, Michael (2008) Ze Frank and the poetics of web video. *First Monday*, **13**(5), 5, http://firstmonday.org/article/view/2102/1962

2 Couldry, Nick (2009) Does "the media" have a future? *European Journal of Communication*, **24**(4), 437–449.

3 PewDiePie (2016) *About PewDiePie* [Video], https://youtube.com/user/PewDiePie/about

4 Vlogbrothers (2016) *What's Wrong with Monopoly?* [Video], https://youtube.com/watch?v=L99xD5lBuV4

5 Van Dijck, Jose (2013) *The Culture of Connectivity*. New York: Oxford University Press.

6 Hong, Y. Euny (2014) *The Birth of Korean Cool*. New York: Picador.

7 Hobbs, Renee (2013) The blurring of art, journalism, and advocacy: Confronting 21st century propaganda in a world of online journalism. *I/S: A Journal of Law and Policy for the Information Society*, **8**(3), 625–638.

8 Gordon, Eric and Mihailidis, Paul (2016) *Civic Media: Technology, Design, Practice*. Cambridge, MA: MIT Press.

9 Bordwell, David and Thompson, Kristin (2003) *Film Art: An Introduction*, 7th edn. New York: McGraw-Hill.

10 Goffman, Erving (1967) *Interaction Ritual: Essays on Face-to-Face Behavior*. Chicago: Aldine.

11 Talvitie-Lamberg, Karoliina (2014) *Confessions in Social Media: Performative, Constrained, Authentic and Participatory Self Representations in Blogs*. Ph.D. dissertation, University of Helsinki.

12 Schiappa, Edward, Gregg, Peter and Hewes, Dean (2005) The parasocial contact hypothesis. *Communication Monographs*, **72**(1), 92–115.

13 Cova, Bernard, Kozinets, Robert and Shankar, Avi (2007) *Consumer Tribes.* New York: Routledge.

14 ERB (2016) *Austin Powers vs. James Bond – Epic Rap Battles of History* – Season 5, https://www.youtube.com/watch?v=Iy7xDGi5lp4

15 MissFenderr (2014) *How I Make My Videos (Step-by-Step Tutorial)* [Video], https://www.youtube.com/watch?v=gr2PAzk1Qvo

16 Turner, Kimberly (2012) *Vlog Virgins* [Video], https://www.youtube.com/user/KimberlyTurnerOnline/videos

17 Ahmad, T., Doheny, F., Faherty, S., and Harding, N. (2013) How instructor-developed screencasts benefit college students' learning of maths: Insights from an Irish case study. *Malaysian Online Journal of Educational Technology*, **1**(4).

18 Kadkhoda, Tiana (2013) *Student View: How Making Math Videos Prepared Me for College*, Center for Digital Education, http://www.centerdigitaled.com/news/Student-View-How-Making-Math-Videos-Prepared-Me-for-College.html

19 Ibid.

20 Lange, Patricia (2007) *The Vulnerable Video Blogger: Promoting Social Change Through Intimacy*, Scholar and Feminist Online, http://sfonline.barnard.edu/blogs/lange_01.htm

21 Lange, Patricia (2007) *Searching for the You in YouTube: An Analysis of Online Response Ability*, EPIC Conference, http://www.patriciaglange.org/page3/assets/Lange%20EPIC07%20Paper.pdf

22 Thompsen, P. (1994) An episode of flaming: A creative narrative. *ETC: A Review of General Semantics*, **51**, 51–72.

23 Blaque, Kat (2015) *Stop Supporting Media Trolls* [Video], https://www.youtube.com/watch?v=mA6ZhlrlyZs

Chapter 12

1 Larsh, Daniel (2013) *Ocean Tales: The Ever-Changing Coast* [Video], https://www.youtube.com/watch?v=69oTFVR8-Vw

2 Ibid.

3 Strombery, Joseph (2012, October 29) *Can We Link Hurricane Sandy to Climate Change?* http://www.smithsonianmag.com/science-nature/can-we-link-hurricane-sandy-to-climate-change-98794096/?no-ist

4 Wang, Yue (2013, March 25), *More People Have Cell Phones Than Toilets, UN Study Shows*, http://newsfeed.time.com/2013/03/25/more-people-have-cell-phones-than-toilets-u-n-study-shows/

5 Hobbs, Renee (1994) *Tuning in to Media: Literacy for the Information Age* [Video], http://mediaeducationlab.com/tuning-media-literacy-information-age

6 Torchin, Leshu (2013) *Creating the Witness: Documenting Genocide on Film, Video and the Internet*. Minneapolis: University of Minnesota Press.

7 Berger, John (1972) *Ways of Seeing*. London: Penguin.

8 Buckingham, David, Pini, Maria, and Willett, Rebekah (2007) "Take Back the Tube!": The discursive construction of amateur film and video making. *Journal of Media Practice*, **8**(2), 183–201.

9 The Frame (2016, August 29) *Don't Breathe Director Fede Alvarez*, http://www.scpr.org/programs/the-frame/2016/08/29/51684/don-t-breathe-director-fede-alvarez-i-want-to-be-t/

10 Buckingham, David, Pini, Maria, and Willett, Rebekah (2007) "Take Back the Tube!": The discursive construction of amateur film and video making. *Journal of Media Practice*, **8**(2), 183–201.

11 Rodriguez, Robert (1995) *Rebel without a Crew*. New York: Dutton Books.

12 Windolf, Jim (2004) *Raiders of the Lost Backyard*, http://www.vanityfair.com/news/2004/03/raiders200403

13 Kent, Abby (2013) *Spectacles*, https://vimeo.com/84315133

14 Marshall, Kelli (2012) *Video Essays in the Cinema History Classroom*, http://framescinemajournal.com/article/video-essays-in-the-cinema-history-classroom/

15 Bresland, John (2010) *On the Origin of the Video Essay*, http://www.blackbird.vcu.edu/v9n1/gallery/ve-bresland_j/ve-origin_page.shtml

16 Tastemade (2016) *Potato Pizza*, https://www.youtube.com/watch?v=MXCMMpAY6YQ

17 Mogenson, David (2015) *"I Want-to-Do" Moments: From Home to Beauty*, https://www.thinkwithgoogle.com/articles/i-want-to-do-micro-moments.html

18 Muller, Derek (2013, March 25) *World's Roundest Object! Veritasium* [Video], https://www.youtube.com/watch?v=ZMByI4s-D-Y

19 Mathalicious (2014) *Xbox Xponential*, http://www.mathalicious.com/lessons/xbox-xponential

20 Tepperman, Charles (2011) Mechanical craftsmanship: Amateurs making practical films. In Charles Acland and Haidee Wasson (eds.), *Useful Cinema* (pp. 289–314). Durham, NC: Duke University Press.

21 Ibid.

22 Canadian International Documentary Association (n.d.) *Looking at Documentaries*, http://resources.hotdocs.ca/docs/edu_modules/looking_at_documentaries_3.pdf

23 Godmilow, Jane and Shapiro, Ann-Louise (n.d.) *How Real is the Reality in Documentary Film?* http://www3.nd.edu/~jgodmilo/reality.html

24 Haynes, Melissa (2013) Regulating abjection: Disgust, tolerance, and the politics of *The Cove*. *English Studies in Canada*, **39**(1), 27–50.

25 Poniewozik, James (2016, July 7) *A Killing. A Pointed Gun. And Two Black Lives, Witnessing*, http://www.nytimes.com/2016/07/08/us/philando-castile-facebook-police-shooting-minnesota.html?login=email&ref=todayspaper&_r=0

26 Rosenstiel, Tom and Mitchell, Andrea (2013, July 16) *YouTube and News*, Pew Research Center, Project for Excellence in Journalism, http://www.journalism.org/2012/07/16/youtube-video-creationa-shared-process/

27 Andén-Papadopoulos, Kari and Pantti, Mervi (2013) Re-imagining crisis reporting: Professional ideology of journalists and citizen eyewitness images. *Journalism*, **14**(7), 960–977.

28 PBS (2005, March 29) *Wave that Shook the World* [video], http://www.pbs.org/wgbh/nova/transcripts/3208_tsunami.html

29 Andén-Papadopoulos, Kari (2013) Media witnessing and the crowd-sourced video revolution. *Visual Communication*, **12**(3), 341–357.

30 Ibid.

31 WITNESS (2009) *Video Advocacy Training Guide*, https://witnesstraining.wordpress.com/

32 Truth Initiative (2016, March 18) *Effort to Get Teens to Left-Swipe Earns 2 Top Awards from PR Week*, http://truthinitiative.org/news/effort-get-teens-%E2%80%9Cleft-swipe%E2%80%9D-tobacco-earns-2-top-awards-pr-week

33 Casey, R. (1944) *What is Propaganda?* https://www.historians.org/about-aha-and-membership/aha-history-and-archives/gi-roundtable-series/pamphlets/what-is-propaganda/the-story-of-propaganda

34 CNN (2015, November 24) *ISIS Releases New Propaganda Videos*, http://www.cnn.com/videos/us/2015/11/24/isis-releases-new-propaganda-video-todd-tsr.cnn

35 Ellul, Jacques (1965) *Propaganda: The Formation of Men's Attitudes*. New York: Vintage.

36 Cunningham, Walter (2002) *The Idea of Propaganda: A Reconstruction*. New York: Praeger.

37 Orwell, George (1949) *Nineteen Eighty-Four*. London: Secker and Warburg.

38 United States Memorial Holocaust Museum (2014) *The State of Deception* [Interactive], https://www.ushmm.org/propaganda/

39 Hobbs, Renee and McGee, Sandra (2014) Teaching about propaganda: An examination of the historical roots of media literacy. *Journal of Media Literacy Education*, **6**(2), 56–67.

40 Rheingold, Howard (2012) *Net Smart: How to Thrive Online*. New York: Basic Books.

41 Craven, J. (2015, September 30) *Black Lives Matter Co-Founder Reflects on the Origins of the Movement*, http://www.huffingtonpost.com/entry/black-lives-matter-opal-tometi_us_560c1c59e4b0768127003227

42 It Gets Better (2016) *It Gets Better Project*, http://www.itgetsbetter.org/

Chapter 13

1 Safire, William (2007) *Suspension of Disbelief*, http://www.nytimes.com/2007/10/07/magazine/07wwln-safire-t.html

2 Gomes, Paulo, Paiva, Ana, Matinho, Carlos, and Jhala, Arnav (2013) *Metrics for Character Believability in Interactive Narrative*, http://bit.ly/29kZSFh

3 Booker, Christopher (2005) *The Seven Basic Plots: Why We Tell Stories*. New York: Continuum.

4 New York Magazine (2014, March 11) *Ballad of a Wi-Fi Hero (McSweeney's and VultureExclusive)* [Video], https://www.youtube.com/watch?v=21OwTUEiGGM

5 Game Designing (2015) *The 50 Best Animation Studios in the World*, http://www.gamedesigning.org/animation-companies/

6 Bazzini, Doris, Curtin, Lisa, Joslin, Serena, Regan, Shilpa, and Martz, Denise (2010) Do animated Disney characters portray and promote the beauty–goodness stereotype? *Journal of Applied Social Psychology*, **40**, 2687–2709.

7 Carr, Nicholas (2014) *The Glass Cage*. New York: Norton.

8 McCloud, Scott (1993) *Understanding Comics*. Northampton: Kitchen Sink Press.

9 Ibid.

10 Eisner, Elliot W. (1985) *The Educational Imagination*. New York: Macmillan.

11 Huang, Jasmine (2010, June 4) *The Imagination Animation* [Video], https://www.youtube.com/watch?v=OV4imswCc0E

12 Sartre, Jean-Paul (1940/2001) *The Psychology of the Imagination*. New York: Routledge.

13 Phillips, Cheryl (n.d.) *Exploring History through Animation*, http://bit.ly/29n6YwI

14 Tram, Trisha Nhu-y (2015) *Draw My Life: An Exercise to Help Students Connect with Counselors and Peers*, http://bit.ly/29kGDPP

15 Booker, ibid.

16 Animoto (n.d.) *The Power of Video for Small Businesses*, https://animoto.com/blog/business/small-business-video-infographic/

17 Cauchi, Stephen (2013, February 14) *No Dumb Luck: Metro Claims Safety Success*, http://bit.ly/29kD505

18 The School of Life (2016, May 2) *Being a Good Listener* [Video], https://www.youtube.com/watch?v=-BdbiZcNBXg

19 Garcia, Alejandro (2012) *Principles of Animation Physics: Course Notes*, http://www.algarcia.org/Pubs/PoAP_Siggraph.pdf

20 Burn, Andrew (2016) Making machinima: Animation, games, and multimodal participation in the media arts. *Learning, Media and Technology*, **41**(2), 310–329.

21 Premo, Mac (2016) *The Function of Music with Jam Abumrad* [Video], https://vimeo.com/172016440

Chapter 14

1 McIntosh, Jonathan (2011) *The HMTL 5 Gendered Ad Remixer* [Interactive], http://www.genderremixer.com/html5/

2 Ibid.

3 Duggan, Maeve (2015, August 19) *The Demographics of Social Media Users*, Pew Research Center, http://www.pewinternet.org/2015/08/19/the-demographics-of-social-media-users/

4 Livingstone, Sonia (2000) Television and the active audience. In D. Fleming (ed.), *Formations: 21st Century Media Studies* (pp. 175–195). Manchester: Manchester University Press.

5 Ibid, p. 177.

6 Lessig, Lawrence (2008) *Remix: Making Art and Commerce Thrive in the Hybrid Economy*. New York: Penguin.

7 Navas, Eduardo (2016) *Remix Theory*, http://remixtheory.net

8 Murphy, James (2014) *Remixes Made With Tennis Data*, https://soundcloud.com/ibm/sets/remixes-made-with-tennis-data

9 HitRecord (2016) *About Us* [Video], http://hitrecord.com

10 Kim, Yeran (2011) Idol republic: The global emergence of girl industries and the commercialisation of girl bodies. *Journal of Gender Studies*, **20**(4), 333–345.

11 Duncum, Paul (1998) To copy or not to copy: A review. *Studies in Art Education*, **29**(4), 203–210.

12 Jubilee Project (2010, November 2) *Love Language, Original Jubilee Project Short Film* [Video], https://www.youtube.com/watch?v=QyB_U9vn6Wk

13 Hobbs, Renee and Moore, David Cooper (2013) *Discovering Media Literacy: Digital Media and Popular Culture in Elementary School*. Thousand Oaks, CA: Corwin/Sage.

14 Navas, Eduardo (2012) *Remix Theory: The Aesthetics of Sampling*. New York: Springer.

15 Ferguson, Kirby (2015). *Everything is a Remix* [Video], https://vimeo.com/139094998

16 Skrillex (2016, May 28) *Skrillex Proof That He Did Not Steal "Sorry" by Justin Bieber* [Video], https://www.youtube.com/watch?v=RLeYsy9g4r0

17 Russell, Mike (2016) *Music Radio Creative Videos*, https://www.youtube.com/user/musicradiocreative/videos

18 Arnold, Matthew (1932) *Culture and Anarchy*. Cambridge: Cambridge University Press. Project Gutenberg, http://www.gutenberg.org/ebooks/4212

19 Adorno, Theodor (1996) *Aesthetic Theory*. Minneapolis: University of Minnesota Press.

20 Drinkard, Lauren (2015) *Outbreaks in Film* [Video], http://repository.upenn.edu/showcase_videos/55/

21 Sarkeesian, Anita (2015) *Body Language and the Male Gaze. Tropes vs. Women* [Video], https://www.youtube.com/watch?v=QPOla9SEdXQ

22 Last Week Tonight with John Oliver (2015, April 26) *Fashion* [Video], https://www.youtube.com/watch?v=VdLf4fihP78

23 PrankInvasion (2015, March 18) *PrankInvasion – Kissing Prank – Magic Trick* [Video], https://www.youtube.com/watch?v=6AIJvtocvP8

24 H3H3 Productions (2014, December 3) *Kissing Pranks – H3H3 Reaction Video* [Video], https://www.youtube.com/watch?v=4-Btkke8O6Q

25 Gray, Jonathan (2005) Television teaching: Parody, *The Simpsons*, and media literacy education. *Critical Studies In Media Communication*, **22**(3), 223–238.

26 Bakhtin, Mikhail (1984) *The Dialogic Imagination: Four Essays*. Austin: University of Texas Press.

27 Rymes, Betsy (2008) The relationship between mass media and classroom discourse. *Working Papers in Linguistics*, **23**(1), 65–88.

28 Chhabra, Parth (2016, January 27) *Pop Culture: Both a Bridge and A Barrier,* http://columbiaspectator.com/eye/2016/01/27/pop-culture-both-bridge-and-barrier

29 Hobbs, Renee (2010) *Copyright Clarity: How Fair Use Supports Digital Learning.* Thousand Oaks, CA: Corwin/Sage.

30 Shifman, Limor (2013) *Memes in Digital Culture.* Cambridge, MA: MIT Press.

31 Know Your Meme (2015) *KYM Review: Internet Outrages of 2015,* http://know yourmeme.com/blog/meme-review/kym-review-internet-outrages-of-2015

32 Regan, Helen (2015, February 24) *Watch Kenny G and Warren G Mashup on Jimmy Kimmel Live,* http://time.com/3720047/jimmy-kimmel-mashup-warren-g-kenny-g/

33 Ferguson, Kirby (2016) *Everything is a Remix: The Force Awakens* [Video], https://vimeo.com/167069783

Chapter 15

1 Morgan, Elan (2014, August 13) *I Quit Liking Things on Facebook for Two Weeks. Here's How it Changed My View of Humanity,* https://medium.com/swlh/i-quit-liking-things-on-facebook-for-two-weeks-heres-how-it-changed-my-view-of-humanity-29b5102abace#.pgct2ih0n

2 Honan, Matt (2014, August 11) *I Liked Everything I Saw on Facebook for Two Days. Here's What it Did to Me,* http://www.wired.com/2014/08/i-liked-everything-i-saw-on-facebook-for-two-days-heres-what-it-did-to-me/

3 boyd, danah (2008) Why youth heart social network sites: The role of networked publics in teenage social life. In D. Buckingham (ed.), *Youth, Identity, and Digital Media* (pp. 119–142). Cambridge, MA: MIT Press.

4 Goel, Vindu (2014, August 2) *How Facebook Sold You Krill Oil,* http://www.nytimes.com/2014/08/03/technology/how-facebook-sold-you-krill-oil.html?_Facebookr = 0

5 boyd, ibid.

6 Granovetter, Mark (1983) The strength of weak ties: A network theory revisited. *Sociological Theory,* **1**, 201–233.

7 Meyer, Robinson (2014, June 28) *Everything We Know About Facebook's Secret Mood Manipulation Experiment,* http://www.theatlantic.com/technology/archive/2014/06/everything-we-know-about-facebooks-secret-mood-manipulation-experiment/373648/

8 Eadiccio, Lisa (2015, December 15) *Americans Check Their Phones 8 Billion Times a Day,* http://time.com/4147614/smartphone-usage-us-2015/

9 Meyrowitz, Joshua (1985) *No Sense of Place.* New York: Oxford University Press.

10 Ibid.

11 Berger, Jonah and Milkman, Katherine (2011) What makes online content viral? *Journal of Marketing Research,* **49**(2), 192–205.

12 Ibid.

13 Steiner-Adair, Catherine (2013) *The Big Disconnect*. New York: Harper Collins.

14 Wittes, Benjamin and Liu, Jodie (2015) *The Privacy Paradox: The Privacy Benefits of Privacy Threats*, http://brook.gs/2apHMG5

15 Hobbs, Renee and Moore, David Cooper (2013) *Discovering Media Literacy: Digital Media and Popular Culture in Elementary School*. Thousand Oaks, CA: Corwin/Sage.

16 Mathson, Stephanie and Hancks, Jeffrey (2007) Privacy please? A comparison between self-checkout and book checkout desk circulation for LGBT and other books. *Journal of Access Services*, **4**, 27–37.

17 Wittes and Liu, ibid.

18 McKinsey Consulting (2015) *Activists, Pundits and Quiet Followers: Engaging the Public on Social Issues*, http://mckinseyonsociety.com/downloads/reports/Social-Innovation/Public_Engagement_final_2010%2008%2013.pdf

19 Ted (2012) *Candy Chang: Before I Die I Want To ...* [Video], https://www.ted.com/talks/candy_chang_before_i_die_i_want_to

20 Dauden, Carla (2013, June 17) *No I am not going to the World Cup* [Video], https://www.youtube.com/watch?v=ZApBgNQgKPU

21 Smith, Julie (2016, April 18). *Twitter Chat Tutorial* [Video], https://www.youtube.com/watch?v=WD4QZP_pUVU

22 Trow, George W.S. (1989). *Within the Context of No Context*. New York: Atlantic Monthly Press.

23 Wesch, Michael (2009) YouTube and you: Experiences of self-awareness in the context collapse of the recording webcam. *Explorations in Media Ecology*, **99**, 19–34.

24 Fernback, Jan (2007) Beyond the diluted community concept: A symbolic interactionist perspective on online social relations. *New Media and Society*, **9**, 49.

Index

Create to Learn: Introduction to Digital Literacy, First Edition. Renee Hobbs.
© 2017 John Wiley & Sons, Inc. Published 2017 by John Wiley & Sons, Inc.